IMAGES
of America

SPRING GROVE

MINNESOTA'S FIRST NORWEGIAN SETTLEMENT

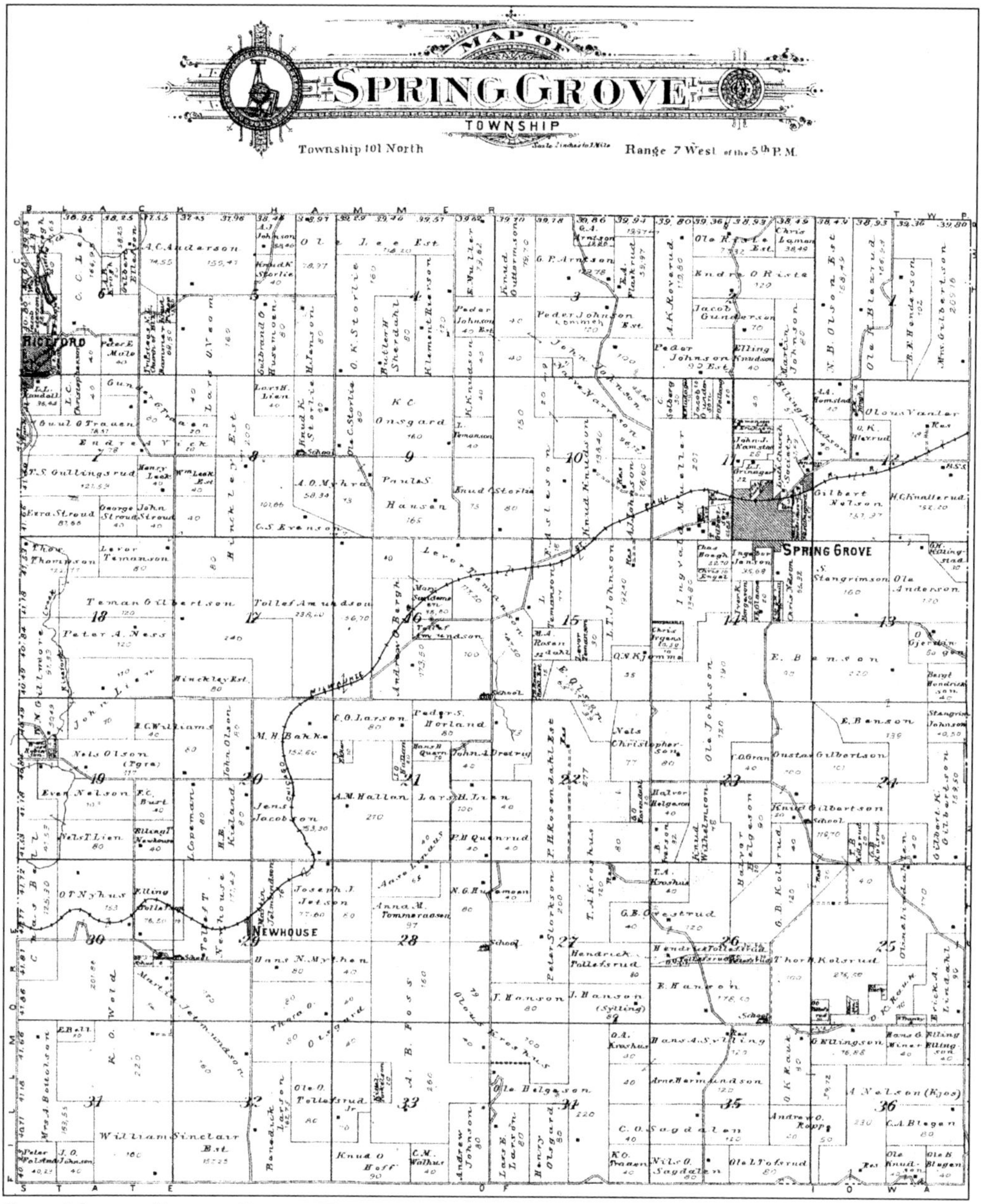

PLAT-MAP OF SPRING GROVE TOWNSHIP, 1896.

IMAGES
of America

SPRING GROVE

MINNESOTA'S FIRST NORWEGIAN SETTLEMENT

Chad Muller

ARCADIA
PUBLISHING

ISBN 978-0-7385-1949-4

Published by Arcadia Publishing
Charleston, South Carolina

Printed in the United States of America

Library of Congress Catalog Card Number: 2001098839

For all general information contact Arcadia Publishing at:
Telephone 843-853-2070
Fax 843-853-0044
E-mail sales@arcadiapublishing.com
For customer service and orders:
Toll-Free 1-888-313-2665

Visit us on the Internet at www.arcadiapublishing.com

CONTENTS

ACKNOWLEDGMENTS

Many individuals and organizations contributed to this book.

I would like to thank Georgia Rosendahl for her dedication to this project. Her passion for Spring Grove history made my apprenticeship a wonderful experience and her interest in genealogy is inspiring.

Karen Gray, Lee Grippen, and Paul Wiste also gave invaluable time and advice. My appreciation is also due to Shirley Johnson and the staff of the Houston County Historical Society in Caledonia, Minnesota, for allowing me access to archival materials. The majority of the images collected here are housed by this organization.

Spring Grove residents who provided photos and useful information include: Lee and Louise Sundet, Neva Bunge, Olga Ellingson, Howard Burtness, Patricia Ashman Foss, Lori Foss, Phyllis Elmquist, Ted Tweito, Harriet Trehus Kvingedal, Reuben Kolsrud, John and Leva Haugland, Lynn Reichel Haugland, Carl Muller, Margaret Morken, Doris Kjome, Howard and Arlene Van Minsell, Robert Solum, Ellsworth Ulven, Joan Wiste, Sharon Auna, Orestes Qualey, Ragnild St. Mary, Helen and Caroline Storlie, Orpha Weymiller, Dolly Onstad. I would also like to thank Fred Onsgard of the *Spring Grove Herald* for helping to spread interest in this project.

The following organizations and institutions also provided valuable material: Carol Hasvold and Charlie Langton of Vesterheim Norwegian-American Museum in Decorah, Iowa; Harry Cleven of Nordmanns-Forbunet in Oslo, Norway; Kari Fuglesang of the Norwegian Emigrant Museum; the Norwegian-American Historical Association in Northfield, Minnesota; the Minnesota Historical Society in St. Paul, Minnesota; the Spring Grove Area Past, Present, and Future organization.

Heartfelt appreciation and thanks to Jenny Wagner for encouraging me to undertake this project and for keeping me on track throughout the process. Her advice enhanced this publication in many ways. Thanks also to Don, Kris, and Linnea Wagner.

Thanks to Chris Mashak for editorial work.

This history is dedicated to my family: Dennis, Sandra, and Brian Muller.

INTRODUCTION

Thousands of years ago, the area that is now Houston County in southeastern Minnesota escaped the awesome leveling power of glacial drift. As a result, the landscape is made up of deep valleys, fjord-like bluffs, and winding streams. It was here, not long after the glaciers receded, that prehistoric nomads hunted mammoth and mastodon, and later, people of the Woodland tradition built burial mounds and made pottery. By 1000 A.D., the people of the Mississippian tradition brought agriculture to this area with the cultivation of maize. Before the first Norwegian immigrants arrived in Spring Grove, many people had called this land home.

The year is 1848. The federal government forcibly removes most of the Winnebago Indians from Wabashaw County in the Territory of Minnesota. They are taken West in a caravan of over 150 wagons. By 1852, settlers begin to arrive. One of the pioneers is James Smith. In the spring he builds a cabin along the Territorial Road and opens a post-office. Surrounding Smith and his cabin, there is vast wilderness. Inspired by the landscape, he names this place Spring Grove.

Later that same year, Torger Tendeland, an inquisitive Norwegian intrigued by newspaper accounts of a new territory, walks over 30 miles to Spring Grove from his home in Iowa. He finds a section of land near Smith's place that reminds him of Stavanger, Norway, where he was born. After staking the four corners of his claim, Tendeland begins the long walk back to Iowa. One month later, when he returns with his family in an ox-drawn covered wagon, he is surprised to find three other Norwegians who have started farming in the area. They are Fingal Flatin, Knut Kieland, and Haaken Narveson. They had purchased acreage from a speculator named John Vale, who claimed he had paid preemption rights but in fact had no legal claim to the land.

Opportunists like Vale and Arthur Bow, another notorious speculator, swindle countless naive emigrants. But some newcomers—like Ole Gulbransgutton—are not intimidated. Big Ole, as he is called, is an imposing giant of a man who hews logs with the greatest of ease. Big Ole builds his cabin single-handedly, but before it is complete he leaves the area for several months. When he returns, he finds Arthur Bow with a large revolver at his side. Bow claims that the property is his and demands that Big Ole pay him for the land *and* the cabin. This so enrages Big Ole that he grabs Bow like a log and slams the swindler to the ground. The wind knocked out of him, Bow gasps for air. But Big Ole is not through. He takes three bullets from the chamber of Bow's revolver and force-feeds them down Bow's throat. "Now you get the hell out of here," the giant yells. "Come back, and I'll feed you the revolver too!" Big Ole succeeds in ridding Spring Grove of Arthur Bow, who conveniently relocates to Fillmore County.

Government land is being sold at $1.25 per acre, and a land office is erected in nearby Brownsville. On September 11, 1854, Embrick Opheim becomes the first Norwegian to officially file a land-claim in Spring Grove. Towns with land offices are dangerous places. There are constant disputes among settlers who are seeking land. Greedy claimants push their way into the land-officer's cabin and trick other settlers into drinking so much that by morning they are too hung-over to make their declaration of intent. But Opheim successfully claims his land along the Territorial Road, just west of James Smith's original homestead.

Many Norwegian immigrants settle in Spring Grove, and it becomes the first Norwegian settlement in Minnesota. Word continues to spread and soon the town becomes a way-station for recent immigrants who are welcomed with shelter and advice in the new world. Spring Grove becomes their *vesterheim*.

* * * *

Spring Grove has changed dramatically over the last 150 years. Driving through town, it's hard to imagine how it must have looked in earlier times. There were pioneer cabins where there are now open fields, and a luxurious brick hotel once stood on what is now the school playground. People and structures come and go, but photography and written and oral history preserve them. Through images and stories we have an opportunity to re-observe and understand the past. Even though this is not a complete history of Spring Grove, we can still see some of the early pioneers and imagine what it was like to live in their time.

Christian Engell came to town in 1872, with his heavy photography equipment, and set up a studio on Main Street. He knew the importance of preserving the past. His photos, many of which are included in this book, capture the nuances of Spring Grove life. "Photography is a modern necessity," Engell once wrote. "We know this from past experience. It is unwise to delay in having your photograph taken. In years to come your collection of photographs will form the most important part of the family history." The contributions of amateur photographers such as Edmund Ovestrud and Peter J. Rosendahl should also be recognized.

O.S. Johnson was the first Spring Grove historian. He emigrated from Ringerike, Norway, in 1870, and his interest in the stories of the early pioneers led to the publication of *Nybyggerhistorie fra Spring Grove og omegn*. His foresight has provided future generations with firsthand accounts of early pioneer life. Also, the diary entries of Paul H. Rosendahl and the historical sketches of Percival Narveson offer insightful personal narratives, as well as important historical information. Finally, we must not forget the oral historians among us. They have many stories to tell if we are only willing to listen.

One

Descendants of Norwegian Ridge

Spring Grove is recognized as the first Norwegian settlement in Minnesota. Because of the large number of Norwegian immigrants who settled in this area after 1852, it was also known as Norwegian Ridge. The land, with its deep valleys and winding streams, reminded these newcomers of the old country. The first Norwegian immigrants to settle in Spring Grove were Torger Tendeland, Haaken Narveson, Fingal Flatin, and Knut Kieland. They made their journeys in ox-drawn covered wagons, traveling across miles of prairie from Iowa and Wisconsin. They were soon joined by other Norwegians who had learned of new land being opened in the Territory of Minnesota.

As in many other immigrant communities, the drive to assimilate was strong. The merging of the old with the new was part of every day life, as evidenced by the development of an "immigrant" language that combined Norsk and English words. This amalgamation was the humorous center of many of the *Han Ola og Han Per* comic-strips by Peter J. Rosendahl. The merging of Norwegian and American styles in furniture and fashion was also common. In the photograph of early Spring Grove pioneers that begins this chapter, there are Norwegian textiles on the floor in the foreground. Their inclusion in this rare photo seems to indicate a respect for old-world objects, despite the desire to "buy new." Ultimately, the pressure to speak English and to become "American" caused the language and many Norwegian objects and traditions to be forgotten by the second and third generations.

Nevertheless, several current residents of Spring Grove have managed to hold on to their Norwegian heritage. Heirlooms such as trunks and textiles have remained in families for generations, and many of the descendants of Norwegian Ridge still live in Spring Grove, on land purchased 150 years ago by their immigrant relatives.

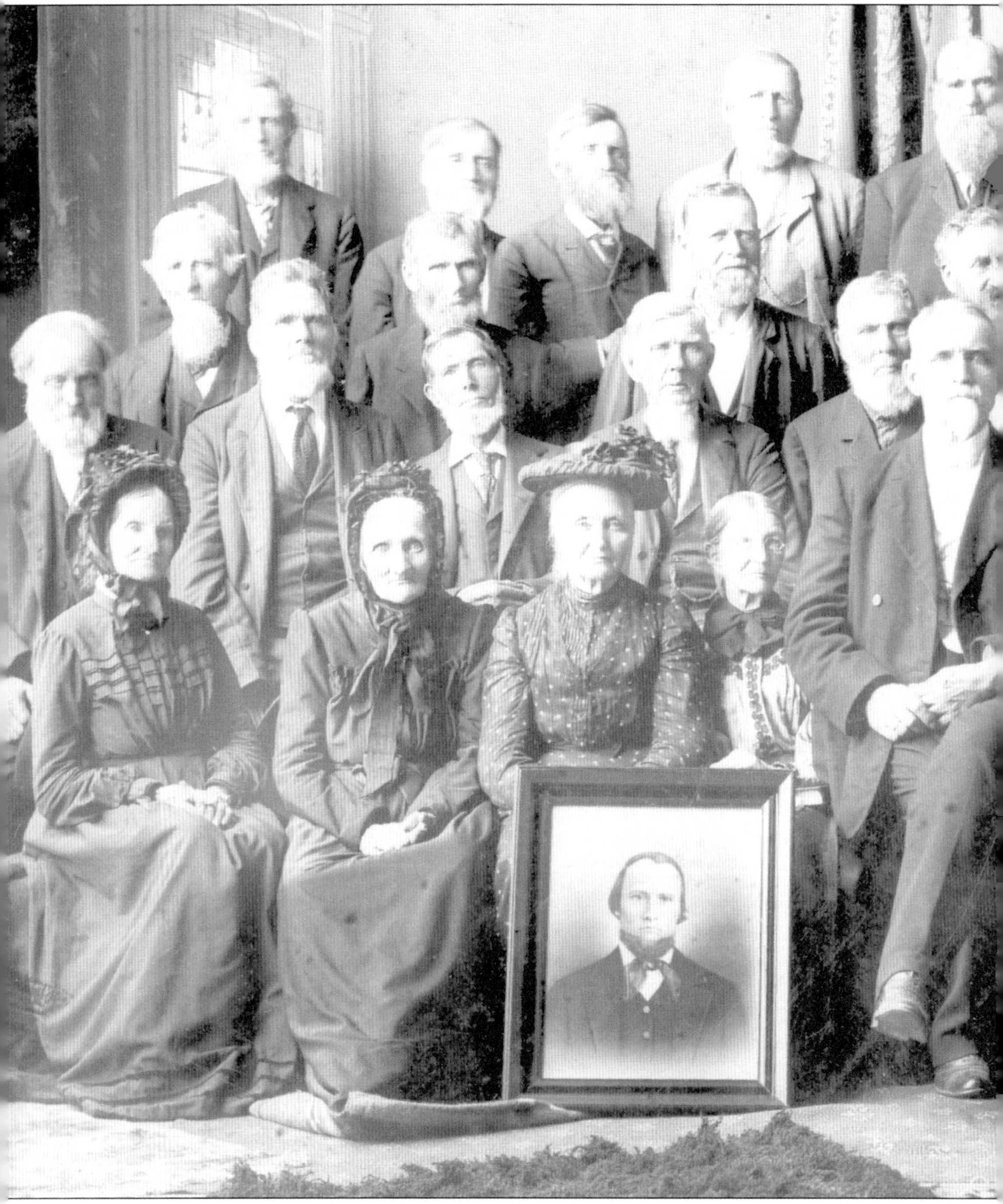

EARLY SETTLERS. This is the oldest known group photo of early settlers to Spring Grove. Seen here, from left to right, are the following: (front row) Martha Vinjum, Mari Blexrud, Kari Solberg, Helga Svartebraaten, Reverend Styrk Reque, Beret Burtness, Mari Tyrebakken, Gunhild Berg, Anna Myhro, and Johanna Dusterud; (second row) Knut Kieland, Tosten Lommen, John Lommen, Ole Wolden, Amund Lunde, Jorend Kolsrud, Gunhild Tyrebakken, Beret Steneroden, Marit Bergsrud, and Anna Gilbertson; (third row) Jens Vinjum, Knut

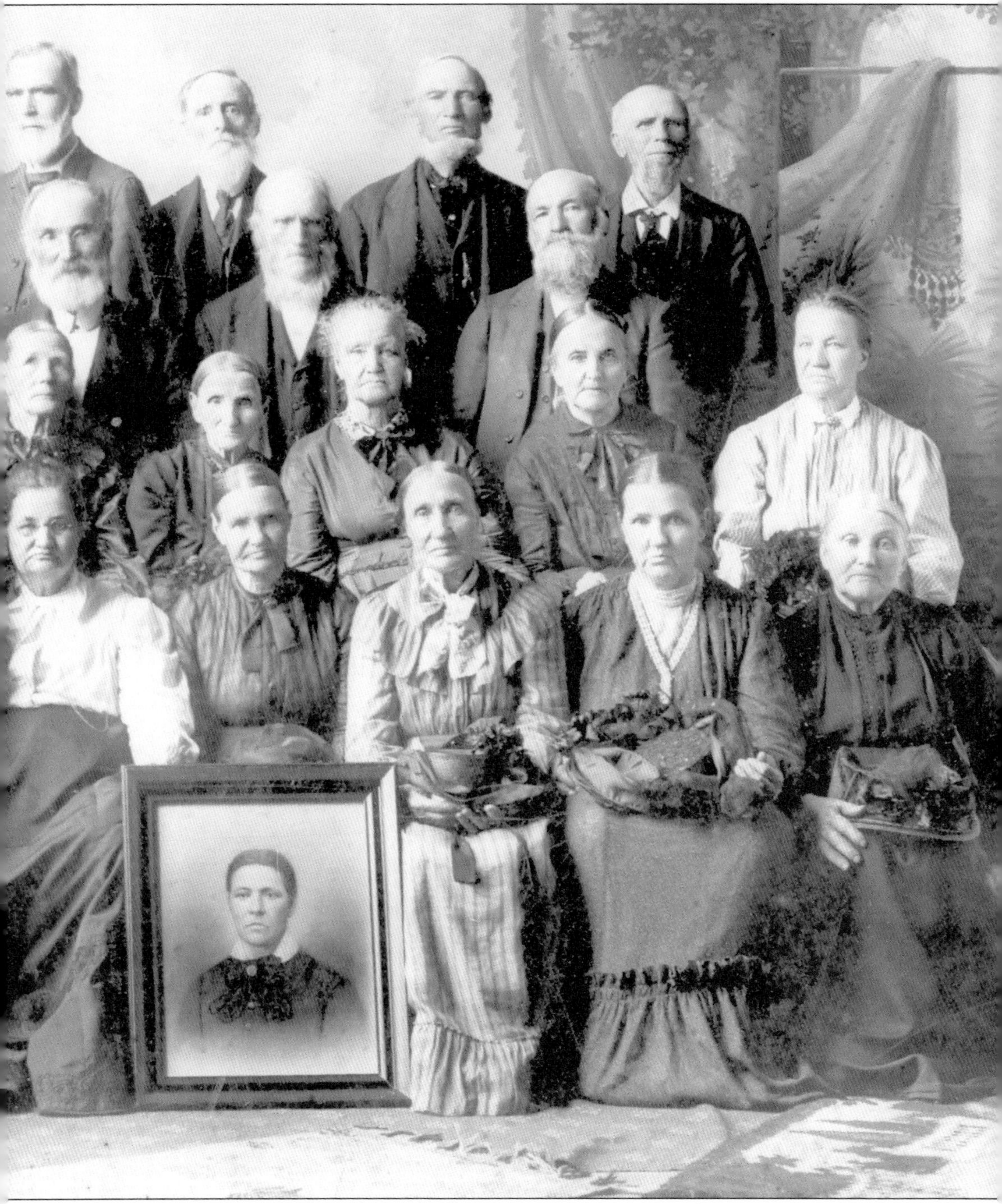

Gilbertson, Mikkel Walhus, Gunder Traaen, Christen Lamen, Helge Bergsrud, and Nias Glasoe; (back row) Embrick Melbraaten, Johannes Hallan, Stengrim Bergrud, Teman Gilbertson, Andreas Hallan, Ove Johnson Hallan, Martin Jetmundson, Embrick Benson, and Levor Quarve. The framed portraits on either side of Reverend Styrk Reque, sitting front row center, are of Haaken and Astrid Narveson.

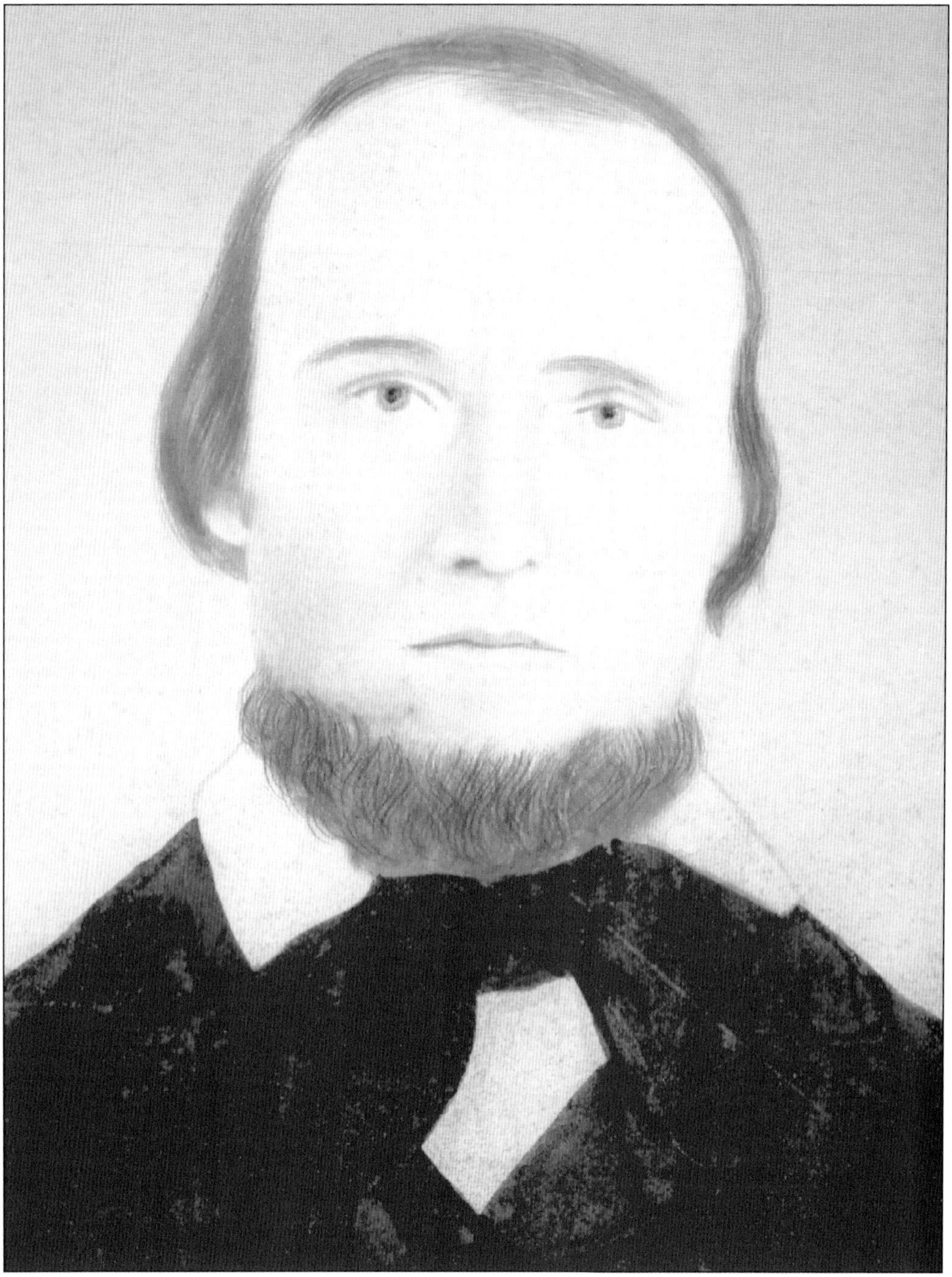

HAAKEN NARVESON. Narveson was one of the first four Norwegian settlers in this area. He was born in 1824, on the Grøhovd farm in Sigdal, Norway, and immigrated to America in 1848. Along with Fingal Flatin and Knut Kieland he came from Wisconsin to Spring Grove in 1852, and was manipulated into purchasing a section of land from a speculator named John Vale, who led them to believe that he owned the land. One year later, Narveson married Astrid Olsdatter and they had six children: Gunhild, Narve, Randi, Ingeborg, Marie, and Olaf. Haaken Narveson died in 1880.

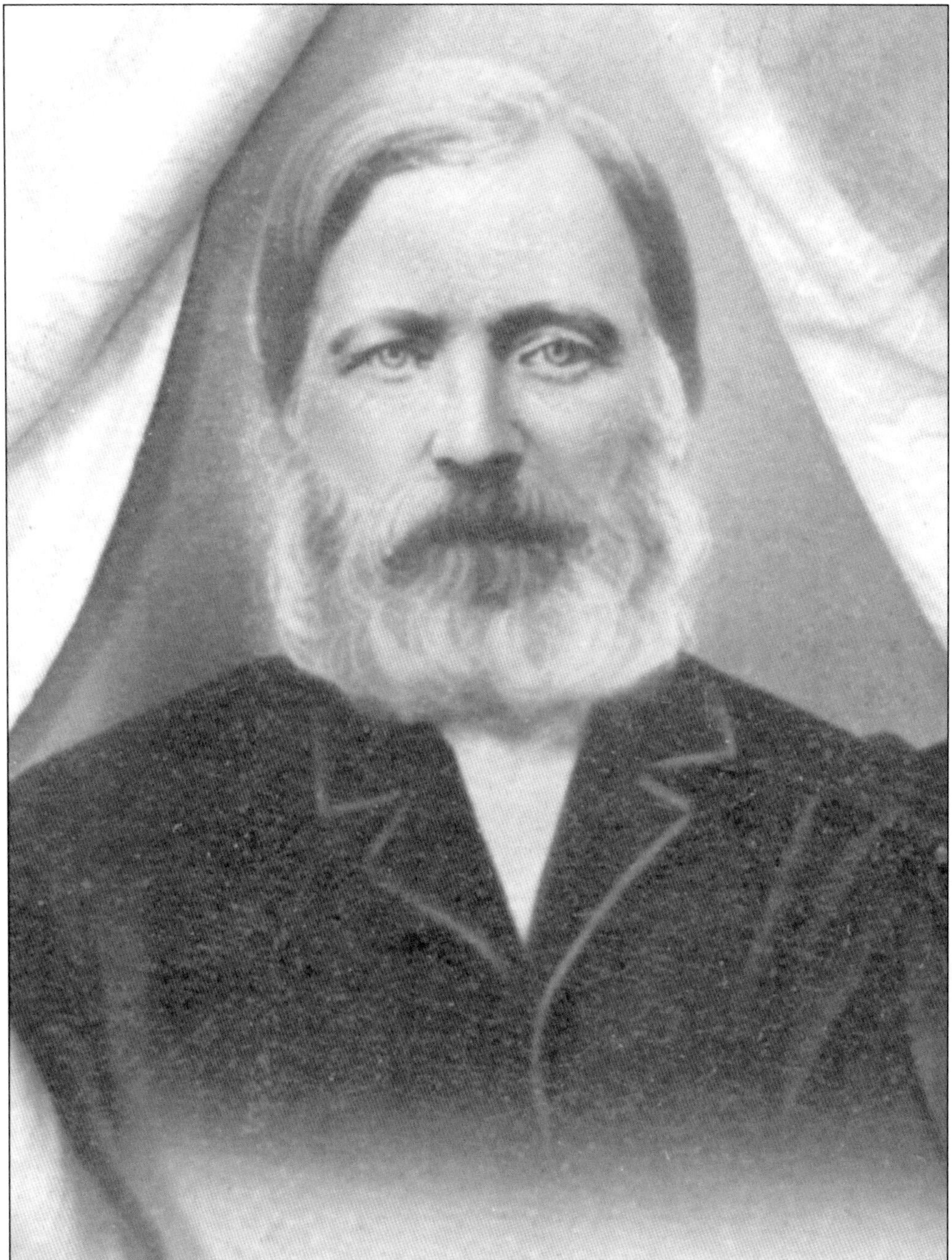

KNUT KIELAND. Kieland was one of the first four Norwegian settlers in this area. He was born in 1827, in Sigdal, Norway, and immigrated to America in 1848. He settled in Wisconsin for a few years and then came to Spring Grove with Haaken Narveson and Fingal Flatin. In 1855, the Norwegian Evangelical Lutheran Congregation of Norwegian Ridge was officially organized at a church meeting held in Kieland's log cabin. In 1858, he married Anna Olsdatter and they had nine children: Christian, Berit, Knut, Olaus, Anton, Karoline, Antonette, Olaf, and Louisa. Knut Kieland died in 1907. (Courtesy of Patricia Ashman Foss.)

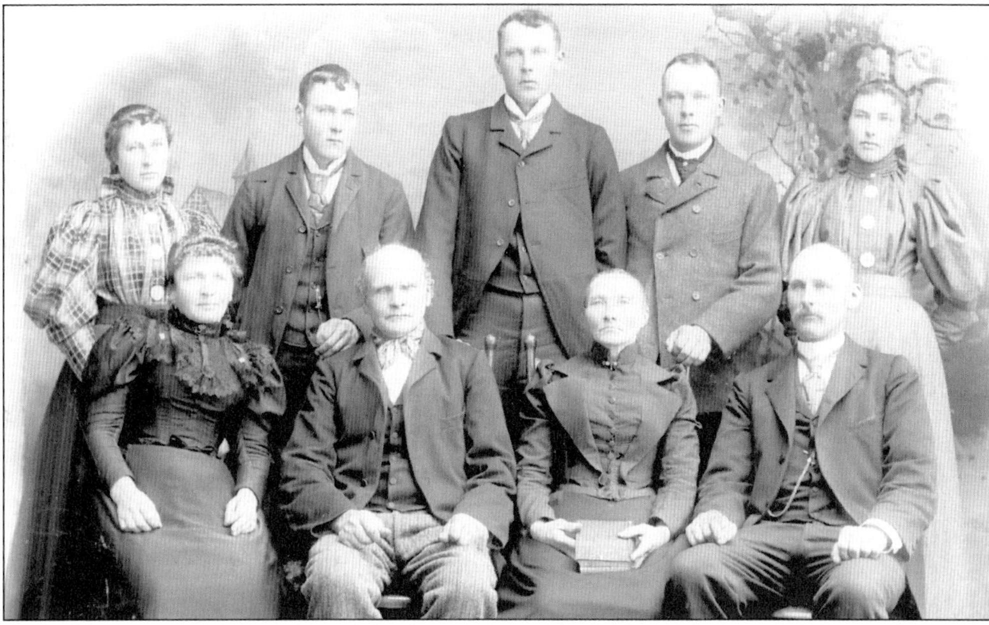

FINGAL FLATIN. Flatin was one of the first four Norwegian settlers in this area. He was born in Sigdal, Norway, in 1826, and immigrated to America when he was 23. As was common with many new emigrants, he first settled in Wisconsin. He worked as a hired man on a farm for a few years and then, along with Haaken Narveson and Knut Kieland, ventured into the newly opened Territory of Minnesota. He was married first to Randi Støen and they one child, Asle. He remarried in 1866 to Guri Slenta and they had six children: Gustav, Ole, Anton, Marie, Minnie, and Randina. Fingal Flatin died in 1902.

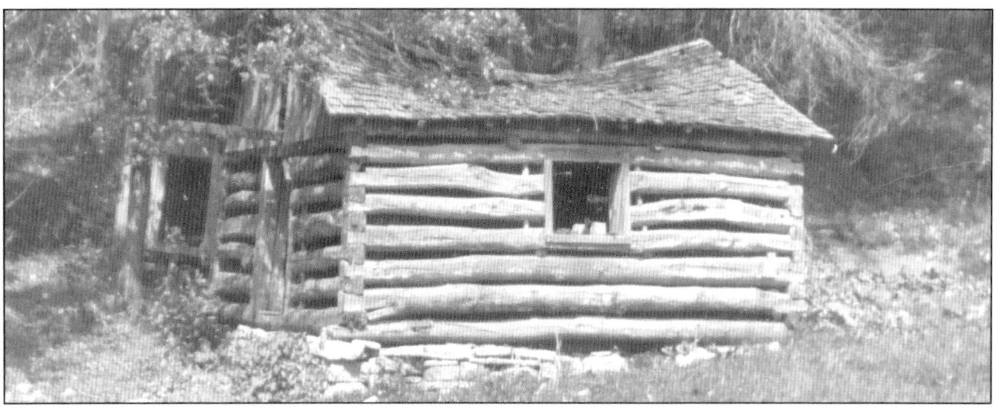

PIONEER CABIN. The remains of a typical pioneer cabin built by Hans Rosendahl, who emigrated from Hadeland, Norway, in 1852. Cabins such as this usually consisted of one room, where the family cooked, ate, and slept. Logs were hewed with a broadaxe, or *adze*, and notches were cut into both ends so as to fasten the corners of the frame. It was difficult to flush these logs against one another, so the space between was plugged with moss, clay, or mud. The roof was made of wooden shakes, brush-thatch, or straw. If available, glass was used for windows, but usually pioneers resorted to oiled paper or cotton cloth. Leather or thin strips of wood were used as hinges for the door. The floor was nothing more than hard-packed earth until puncheons could be laid. Furniture was not extravagant; emigrant trunks usually doubled as tables and places for storage. With leftover wood the pioneer might have made a *kubbestole*, which is a chair carved out of a tree stump.

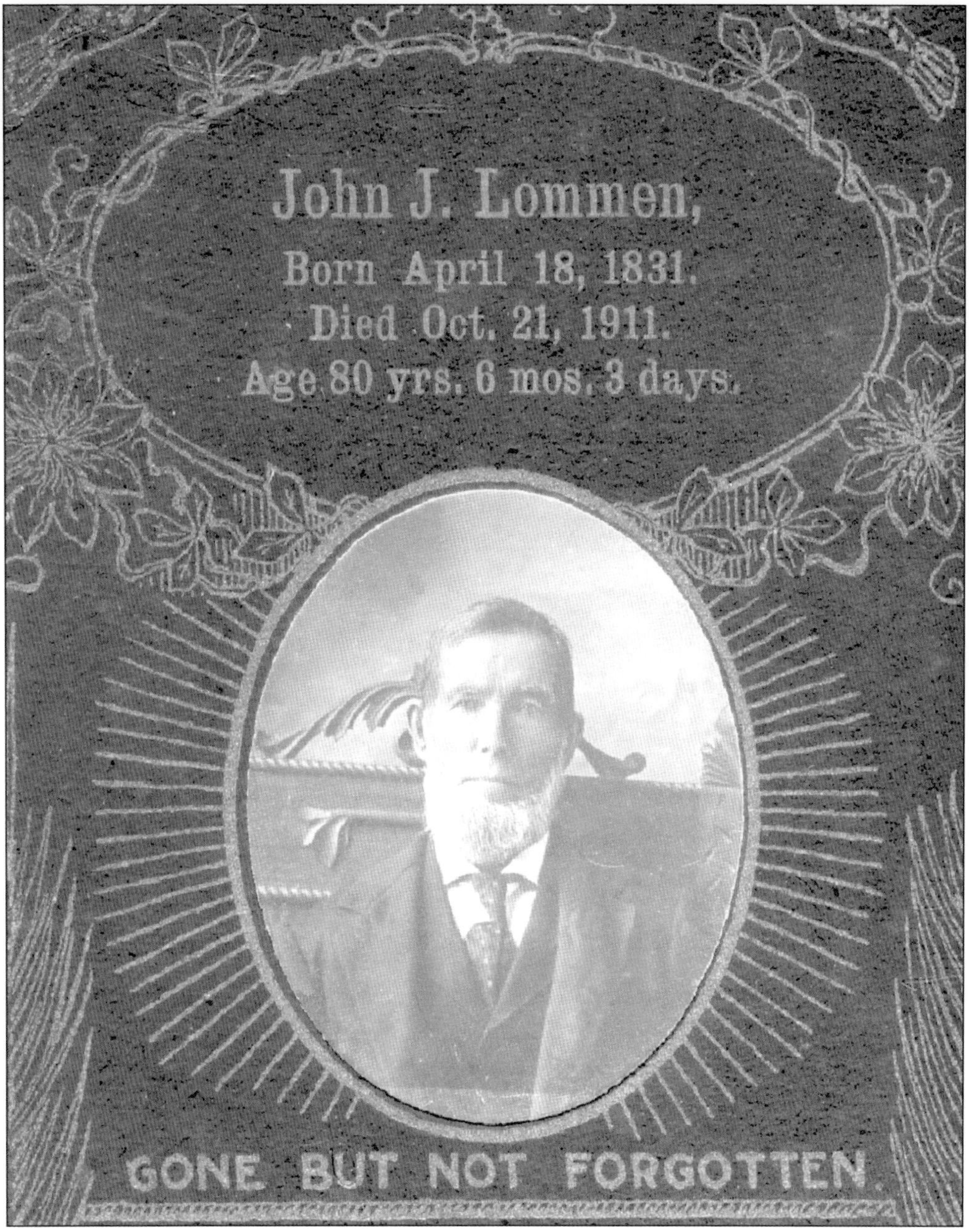

FUNERAL CARD. From a 1911 issue of the *Spring Grove Herald*:

> *John Lommen died at his home in this village at the age of 80 years, 6 months, 3 days. Deceased was born in Valdres, Norway on April 18, 1831 and at the age of 13 years was parentless. On June 20, 1855 he was united in wedlock to Marit Riste in Knut Kieland's first log hut, by Reverend Koren, the event being the first of its kind here. The men of the axe, the breaker, the cradle and the hoe who transformed the roaming places of the savages and the wild animals into fertile clearings and fields, the men and women who in those strenuous days of old, pillared our churches and schools at great sacrifices are fast departing. Great blessings have come to us through these rugged pioneers, and our respect and gratitude should be theirs.*

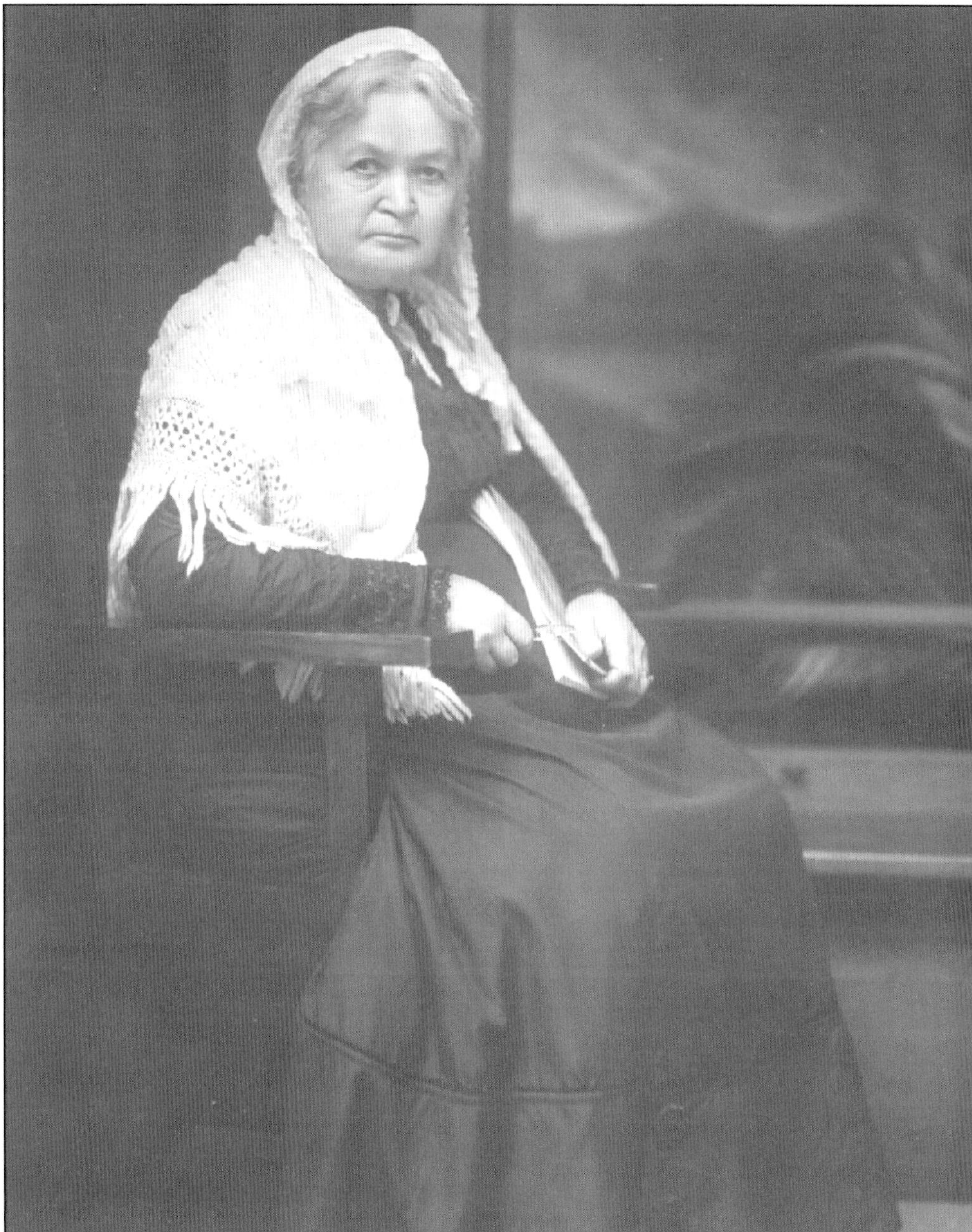

Joran Lommen. In his 1927 *Memoir of My Mother, Mrs. M. Fladager*, Arnold Fladager writes:

> *In the year 1852, Peter Johnsen Lommen, and his wife, Joran, with two little girls, Joran, and her sister Marit, came from Wisconsin in a cumbersome and lumbering emigrant wagon drawn by two oxen, Dick and Bride. They were bent on finding a home in the Territory of Minnesota, where wilderness was still king, where the foot of the white man, with but few exceptions, had never trod. They came with an undaunted courage to face the hazards which hitherto had put fear into many a heart." Early on "the family lived in the wagon using a newcomer's chest for a table and had no other light than furnished by the sun, moon and stars when they went to bed in this strange and tranquil country.* (Courtesy of Lee and Louise Sundet.)

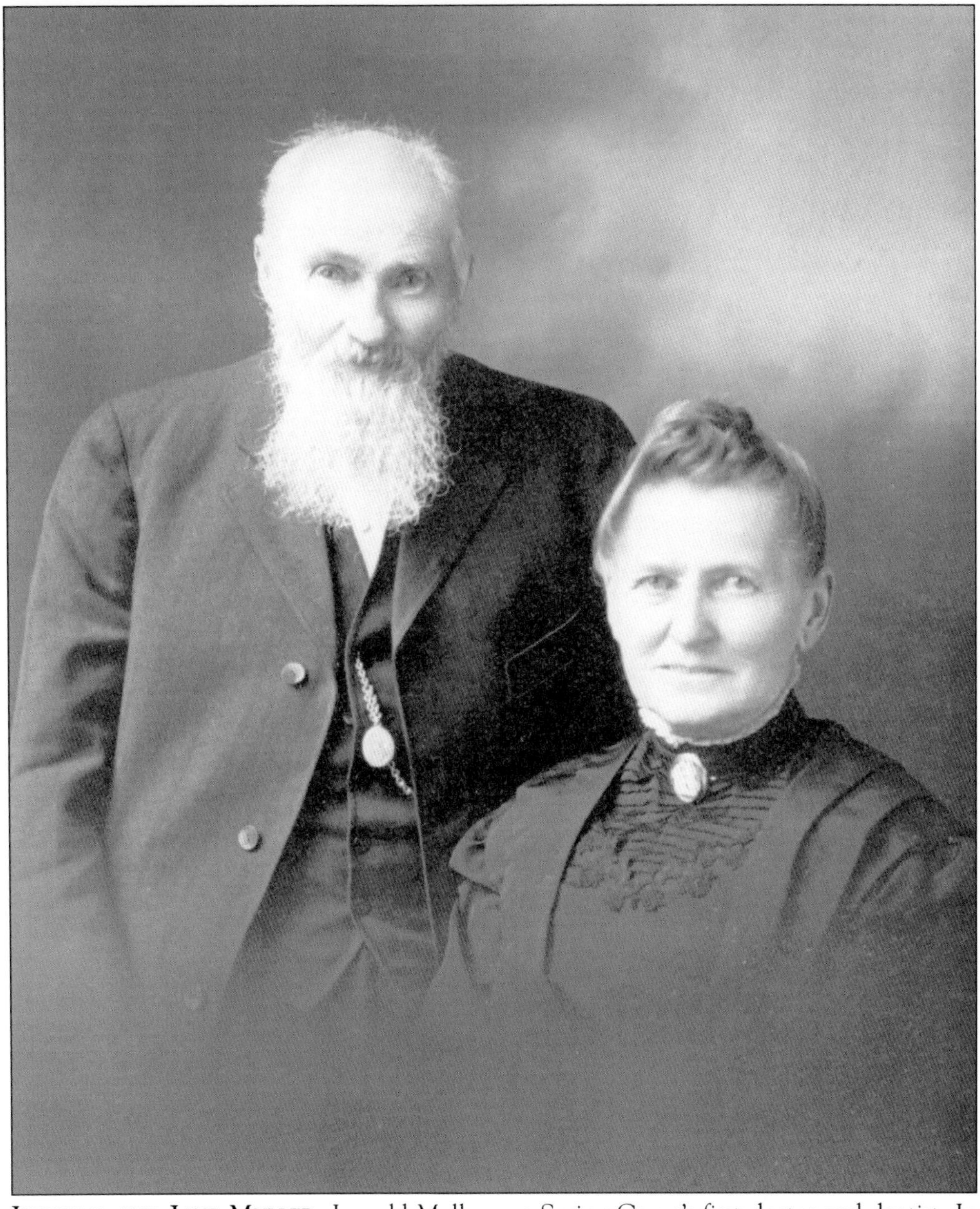

INGVALD AND LIVE MULLER. Ingvald Muller was Spring Grove's first doctor and dentist. In 1864, he emigrated from Trondheim, Norway, in order to further his training at Rush Medical College in Chicago. Because of the language barrier, he left the college after only a few months and moved to Spring Grove to become a farmer. After he was married, he purchased a farm from his father-in-law, Ole Stensrud. One of the rooms in their house was used as a drug store and doctor's office. Live Muller was in great demand as a midwife, but would often help her husband care for patients. Many times, when a tooth needed pulling, she would hold the patient's head while Ingvald extracted the tooth with a rough-looking implement. This was before Novocain had been introduced, and as one story goes, a frightened patient hopped out of the extracting chair—with his tooth hanging by the root—and ran off into the woods. The Mullers held many *gjestebud* (social gatherings) at their home. They also gave shelter to many new emigrants.

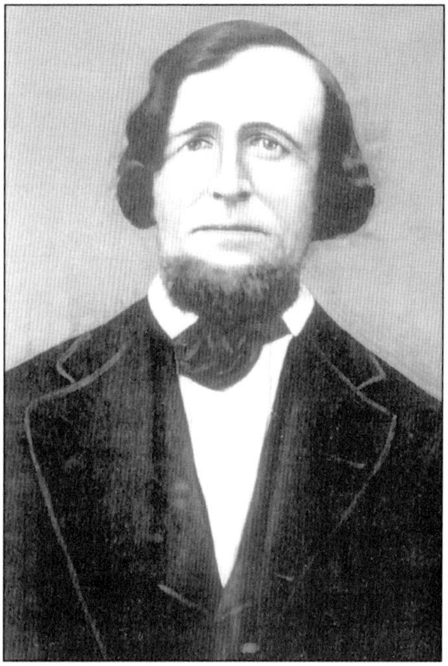

ØSTEN HELGESEN BØRTNESS. Before Børtness came to America, a letter from the Børtness farm in Hallingdal, Norway, dated May 16, 1848, was sent to relatives who had already emigrated:

> *By this occasion I am going to write you a few words more, and let you know how we are doing here at home, and I thank God for the good health, and I wish to hear the same from you, too. I really wanted to follow after you this spring, but our father has been so weak and did not feel very well and did not want me to leave him. But my intention is to follow you as soon as there will be a transport available. I also want to ask you from our father that you will be so kind with our brother Østen who now intends to come over to you and has far too little money. So you, my son Tideman, be so kind and give greetings.*

The letter was addressed to Tideman and John Helgesen Børtness, "now living in Wisconsin in the North America." (Courtesy of Howard Burtness.)

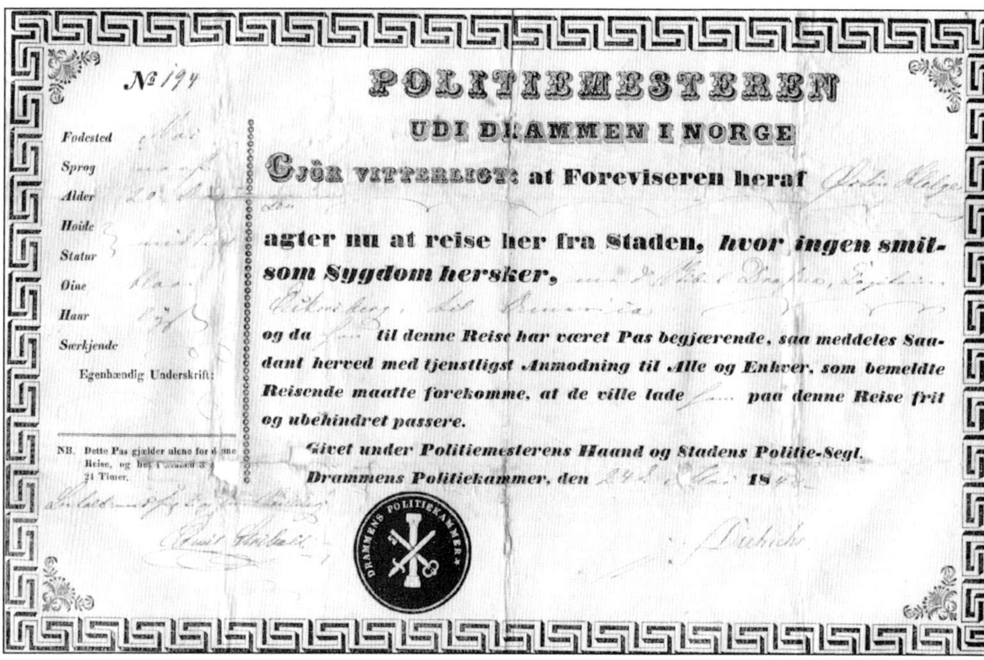

№ 194

POLITIEMESTEREN
UDI DRAMMEN I NORGE

Fødested
Sprog
Alder
Hoide
Statur
Øine
Haar
Særkjendte
Egenhændig Underskrift:

NB. Dette Pas gjælder alene for denne Reise, og ... 24 Timer.

Gjør vitterligt: at Foreviseren heraf ... agter nu at reise her fra Staden, *hvor ingen smitsom Sygdom hersker,* ...

og da ... til denne Reise har været Pas begjærende, saa meddeles Saadant herved med tjenstligst Anmodning til Alle og Enhver, som bemeldte Reisende maatte forekomme, at de ville lade ... paa denne Reise frit og ubehindret passere.

Givet under Politiemesterens Haand og Stadens Politie-Segl.

Drammens Politiekammer, den ... 18..

DRAMMENS POLITIEKAMMER

EMIGRANT PASSPORT. This is the passport of Østen Helgesen Børtness, who immigrated to America in 1848. Emigrant documents such as this are extremely rare. The first two lines read, "The Police Chief of Drammen in Norway," followed by, "Be it known that the person, Østen Helgesen, who at this time wishes to travel from this place where no infectious diseases reign. He is traveling aboard the ship Drafna under Captain Eikenberg to America." The document lists his birthplace *(fødested)* as Hallingdal, Norway. His age *(sprøg)* is 20 years old. His height and stature *(hoide og statur)* are medium. His eyes *(øine)* are blue, and his hair *(saerkjende)* is blond. (Courtesy of Howard Burtness)

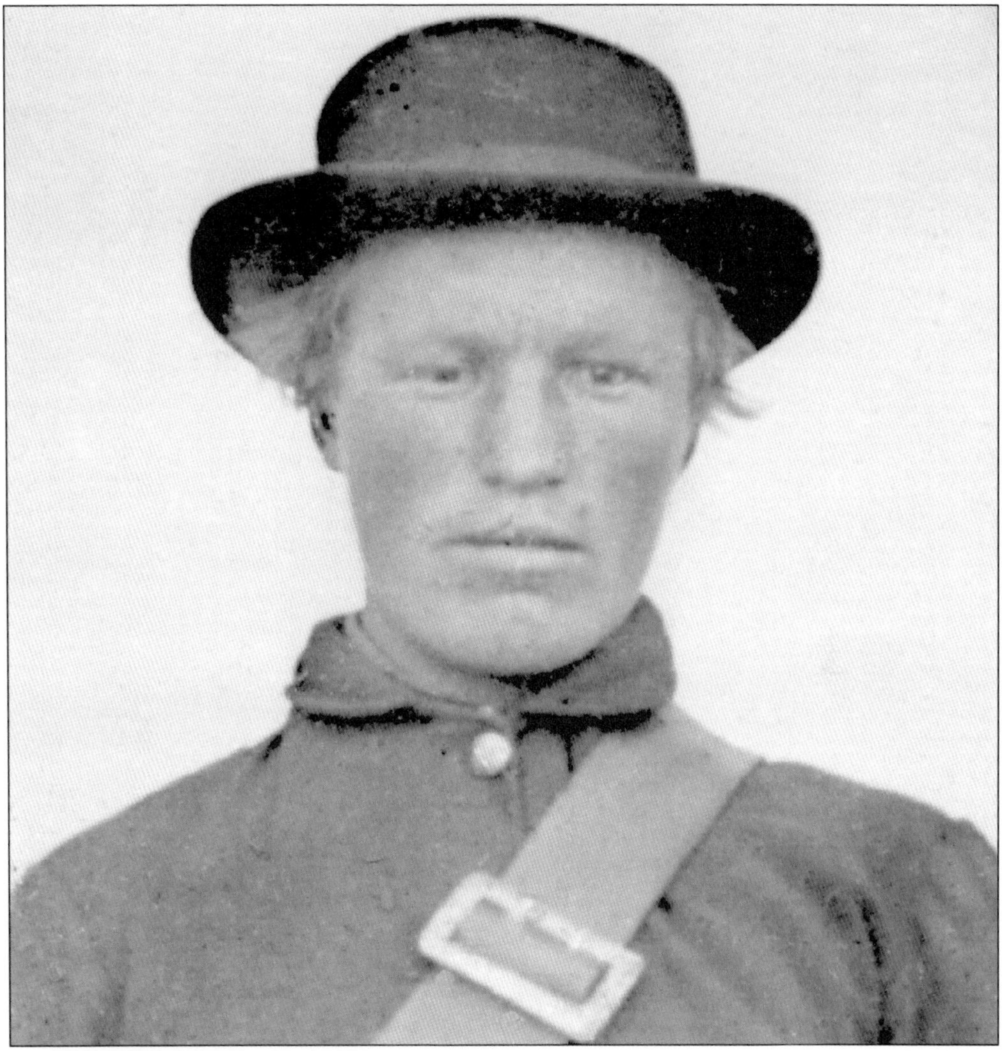

Paul H. Rosendahl. Rosendahl served from 1862 to 1863 in Henry Sibley's expedition against the Sioux after the Dakota Conflict of 1862. Here are extracts from his diary (the spelling of which has been left unchanged):

> July 24—*Battle of Big Hill. . . the most event full day of our campaign. Came into Camp at 2 p.m. the Indian Camp 3 miles Distant. Indians on every hill. . . a parley proposed. Indien killed Doc Wiser at 4 p.m. and Batle Camince imidiately cleared then from the hills and chased them about 10 miles. . . killed about 20, lost 5. . .* ; July 26—*Battle of Buffalo Lake. . . traveled about 12 miles and had another scrimage with the Indians. . . they lost 10 or 12 killed and we got one wounded it being a runing Cavalery fight. . . the Indians led on good Ponyes. . .* ; August 29—*Traveled through tamerock Swamps and over Pine openings. . . passed many Beutiful Norway Pines. . .* ; September 3—*Fort Ripley...Made Buffalo rings. . .* ; September 4–9—*Made Buffalo rings for Gods sake. . . the same as yesterday.*

Two years later Rosendahl enlisted in the Civil War. In 1869, he married Gunhild Brubraaten and they had seven children: Julia, Olaus, Hannah, Oliver, Hans, Carl, and Peter. In 1873, he became a representative in the Minnesota State Legislature, and in 1875 was named Registrar of Deeds for Houston County. He was born in Hadeland, Norway, in 1838, and died in Spring Grove in 1880.

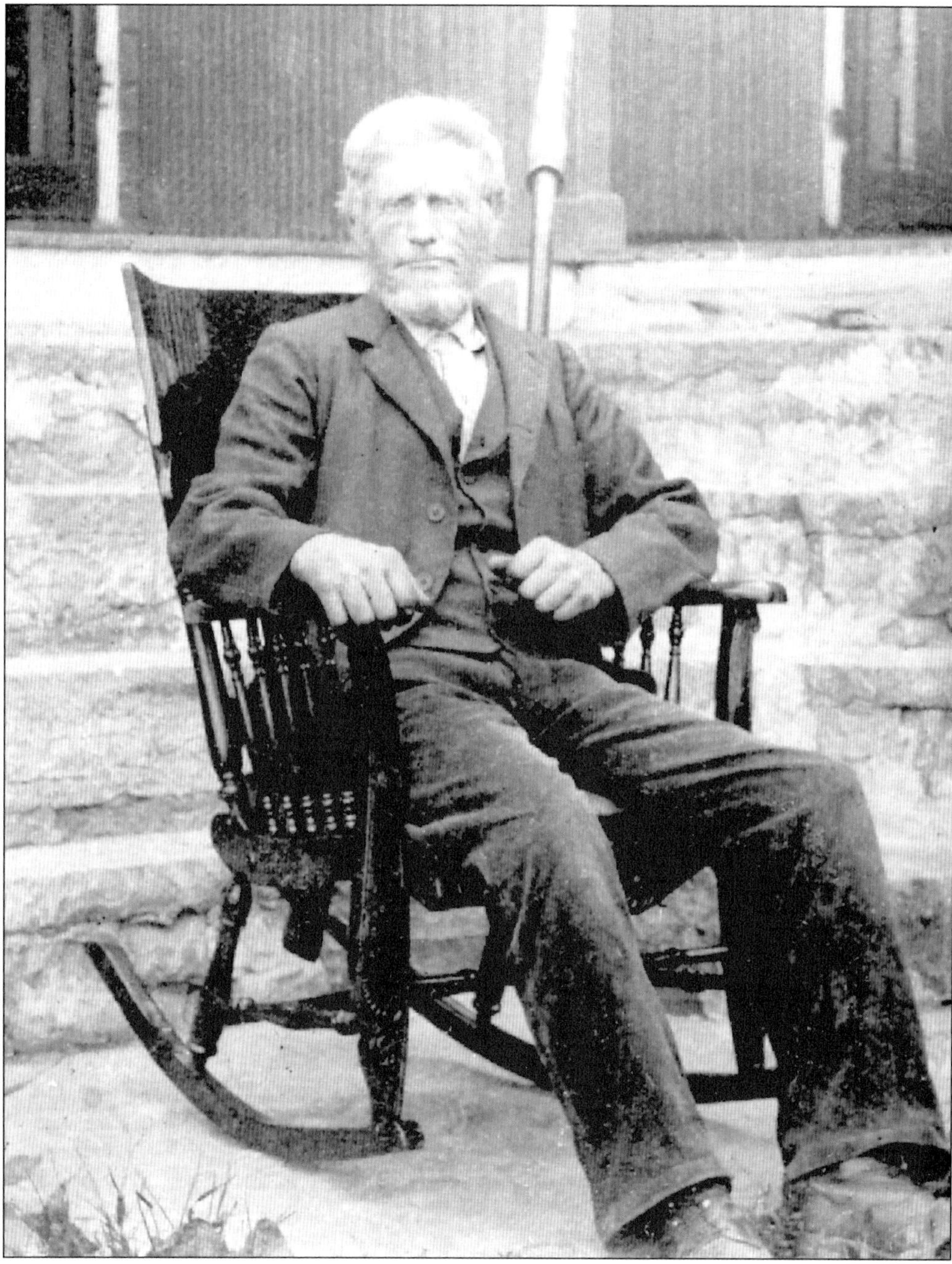

EMBRICK MELBRAATEN. Melbraaten was born in Hallingdal, Norway, in 1834, and immigrated to America in 1852 with his parents. During the winter of 1856-57, the snow was so deep in and around Spring Grove that reaching a mill or market for provisions had become impossible. People were forced to live off corn ground in coffee mills and the wheat that was available. Melbraaten had the brilliant idea of constructing snowshoes specifically designed for his horse. He was thus able to pass over the deep snow and high drifts to bring provisions to the community. In future years, his snow-shoed horse was in great demand, especially for wintertime funerals.

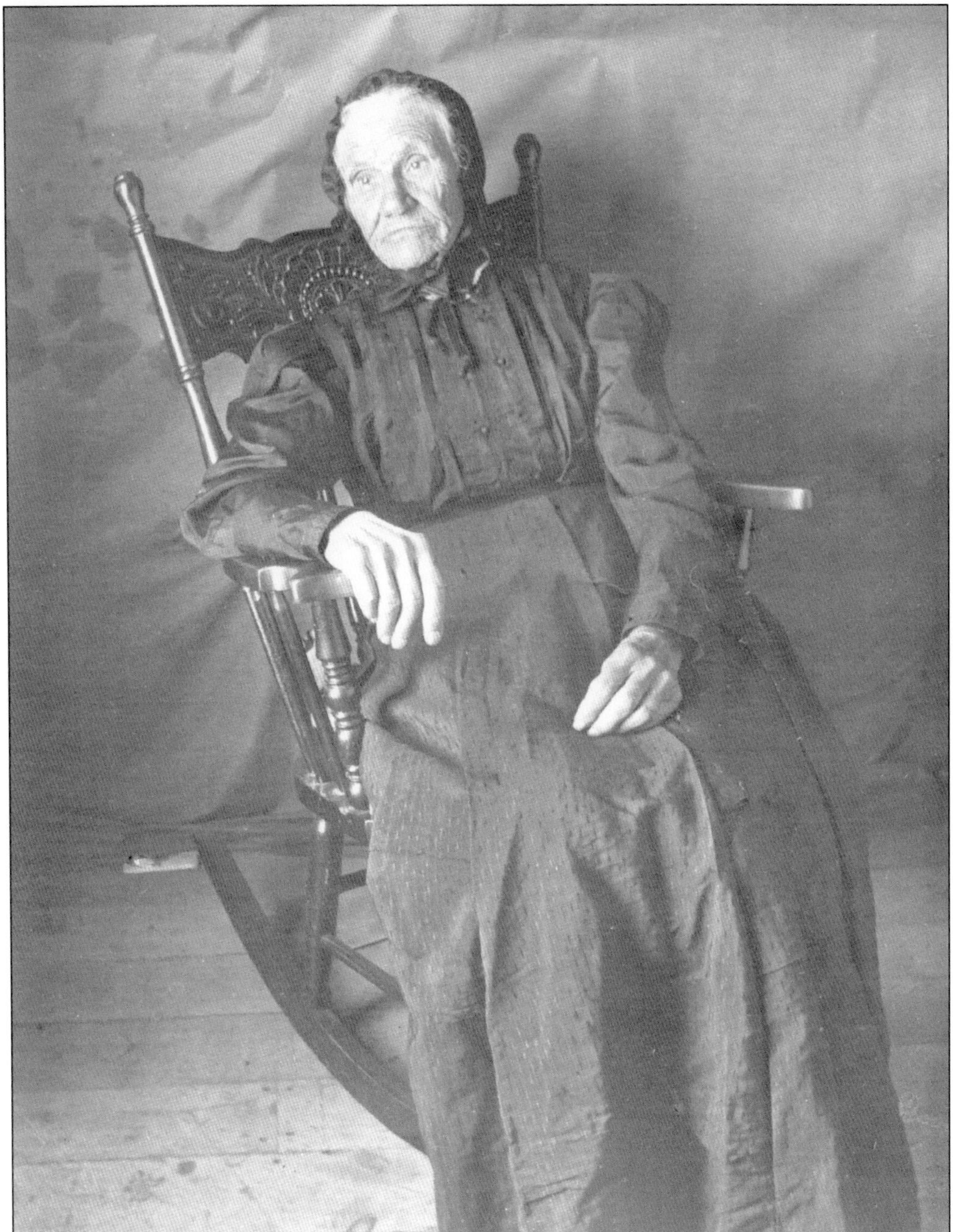

RAGNILD MOLLERSTUEN. Ragnild Augedahl was born in Hadeland, Norway, in 1831, and immigrated to America in 1861. Her husband, Engebret Mollerstuen, purchased a section of land in Spring Grove owned by Han Rosendahl. In keeping with the common Norwegian practice of using the farm name as surname, Engebret dropped Mollerstuen and took Rosendahl. This practice has caused plenty of genealogical confusion over the years. Ragnild Mollerstuen was known to smoke a pipe in her old age, which was a surprisingly common vice among women. This sight inspired Peter J. Rosendahl, the creator of the famous *Han Ola og Han Per* cartoon strip, to sketch a humorous cartoon of Ragnild walking the countryside amidst an ominous cloud of pipe-smoke.

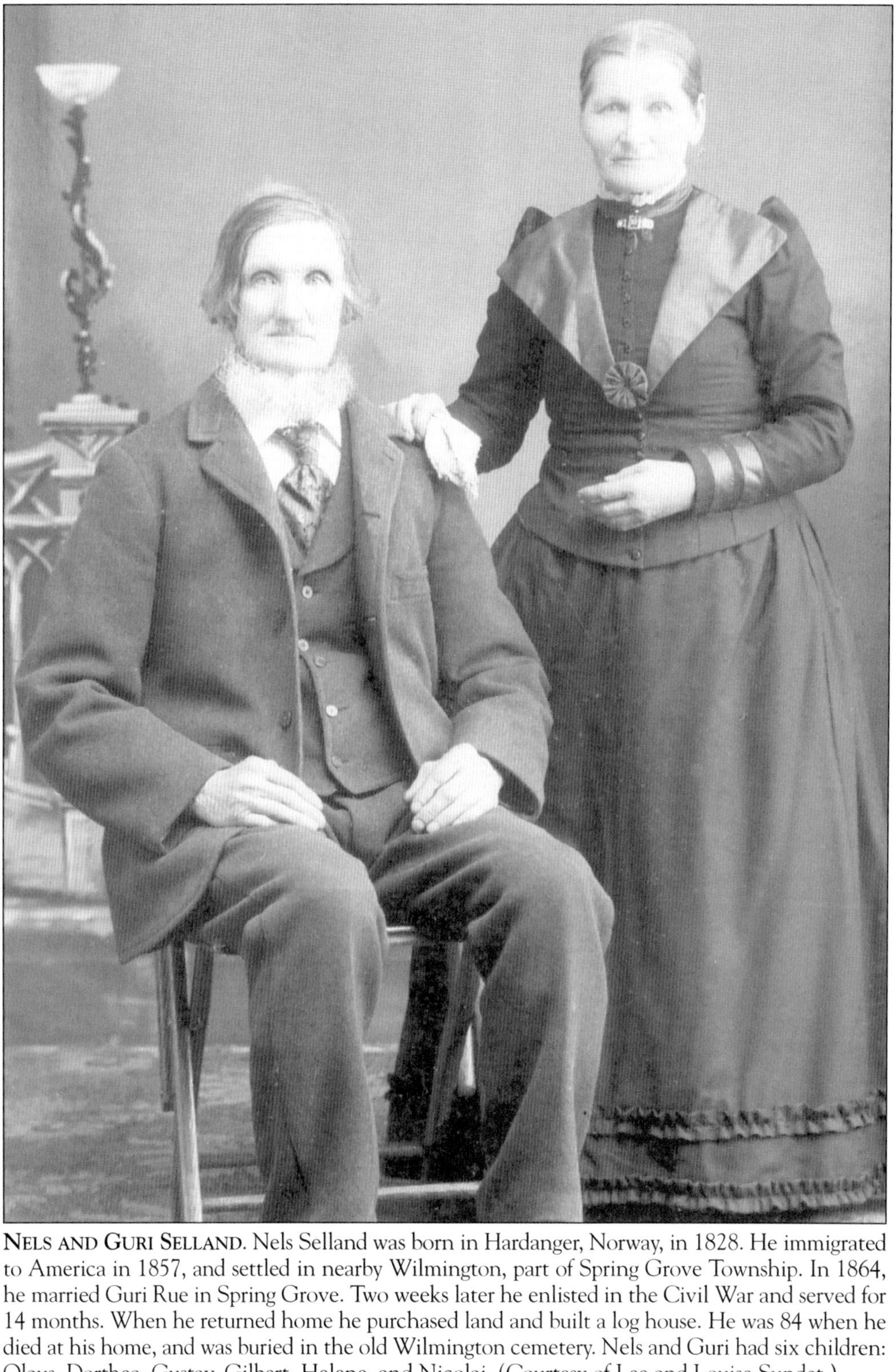

NELS AND GURI SELLAND. Nels Selland was born in Hardanger, Norway, in 1828. He immigrated to America in 1857, and settled in nearby Wilmington, part of Spring Grove Township. In 1864, he married Guri Rue in Spring Grove. Two weeks later he enlisted in the Civil War and served for 14 months. When he returned home he purchased land and built a log house. He was 84 when he died at his home, and was buried in the old Wilmington cemetery. Nels and Guri had six children: Olaus, Dorthea, Gustav, Gilbert, Helene, and Nicolai. (Courtesy of Lee and Louise Sundet.)

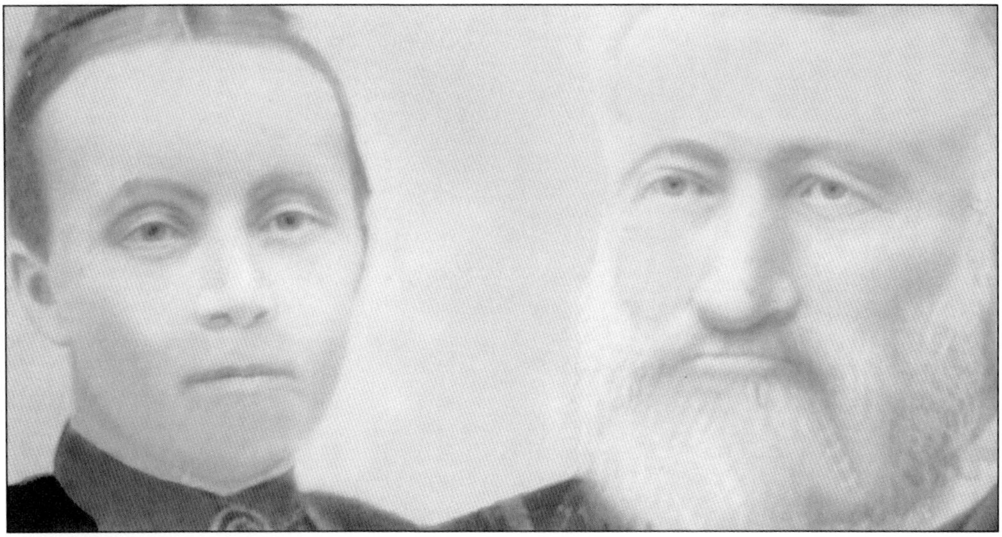

Ole and Kari Stensrud. Ole Stensrud immigrated to America in 1852 with his wife Kari and their two daughters. They stayed in Wisconsin for about a year and then moved to Spring Grove, where Ole bought Embrick Opheim's homestead and started farming and blacksmithing. Horseshoes were his specialty. In O.S. Johnson's *Nybyggerhistorie fra Spring Grove og omegn*, Stensrud "was very interested in the church and anxious to get it built. In his old age, weak and stiff, he still made it to his seat in church with the help of a cane."

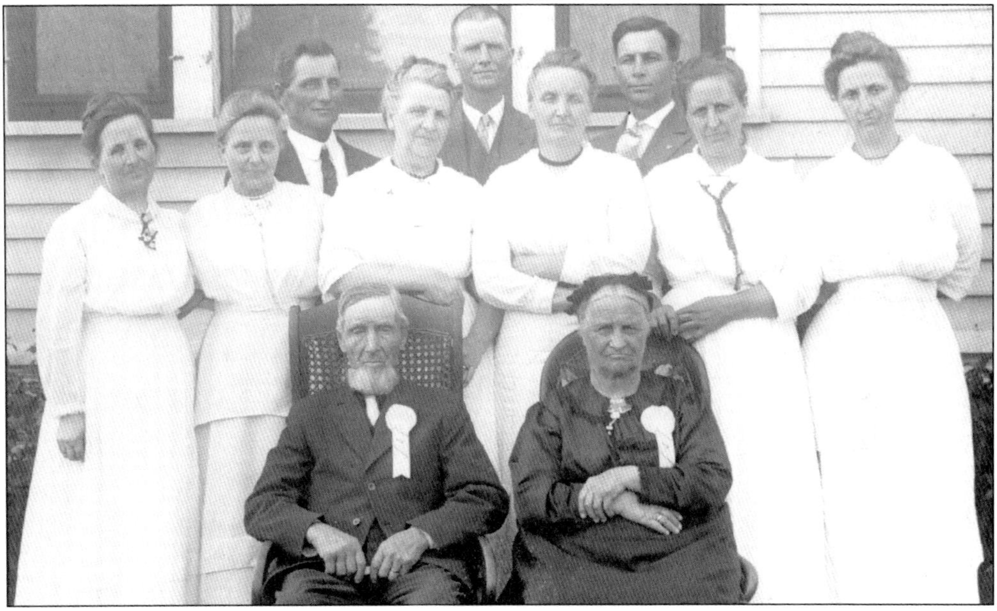

Golden Anniversary. Anders Foss and Anna Solberg celebrated their golden wedding anniversary on June 20, 1905, with their children: (from left to right) Albert, Peter, Eddie, Johanna, Gjertina, Marie, Martha, Julia, and Anna. Anders Foss led a very adventurous life. He immigrated to America in 1848, where he was soon seduced by the California Gold Rush. Anders and six other men formed a partnership and headed west in five covered wagons. After months of travel, the group had many unforgettable experiences, but little luck finding gold. Anders made his way back on a mule and eventually settled in Spring Grove. (Courtesy of Patricia Ashman Foss.)

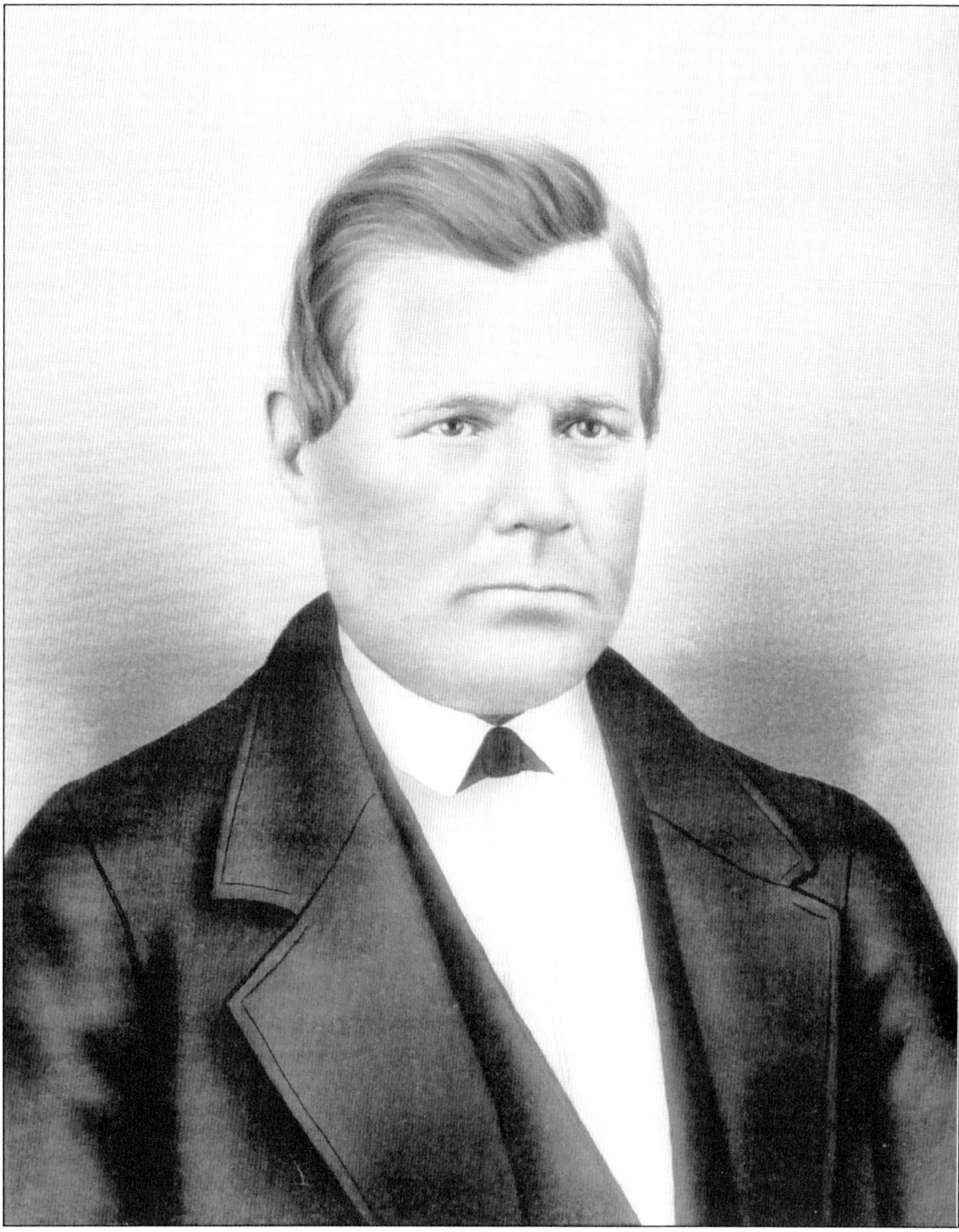

Christopher Vaaler. Vaaler was born Eidsvold, Norway, in 1824. He immigrated to America in 1853 and settled in Spring Grove. He was a timber-hewer by trade. From the 1919 *History of Houston County*:

> *There were many Indians in the neighborhood in those days, and on one occasion when Mr. Vaaler was engaged in hewing logs for a building, using a large old-fashioned broad-axe, and finding the axe dull, he paused in his work and went into the cabin to grind it. It happened that an Indian had just previously gone into the cabin to warm himself, and on seeing the axe took it for a monstrous tomahawk and thinking himself in danger made a rapid exit.* (Courtesy of Patricia Ashman Foss.)

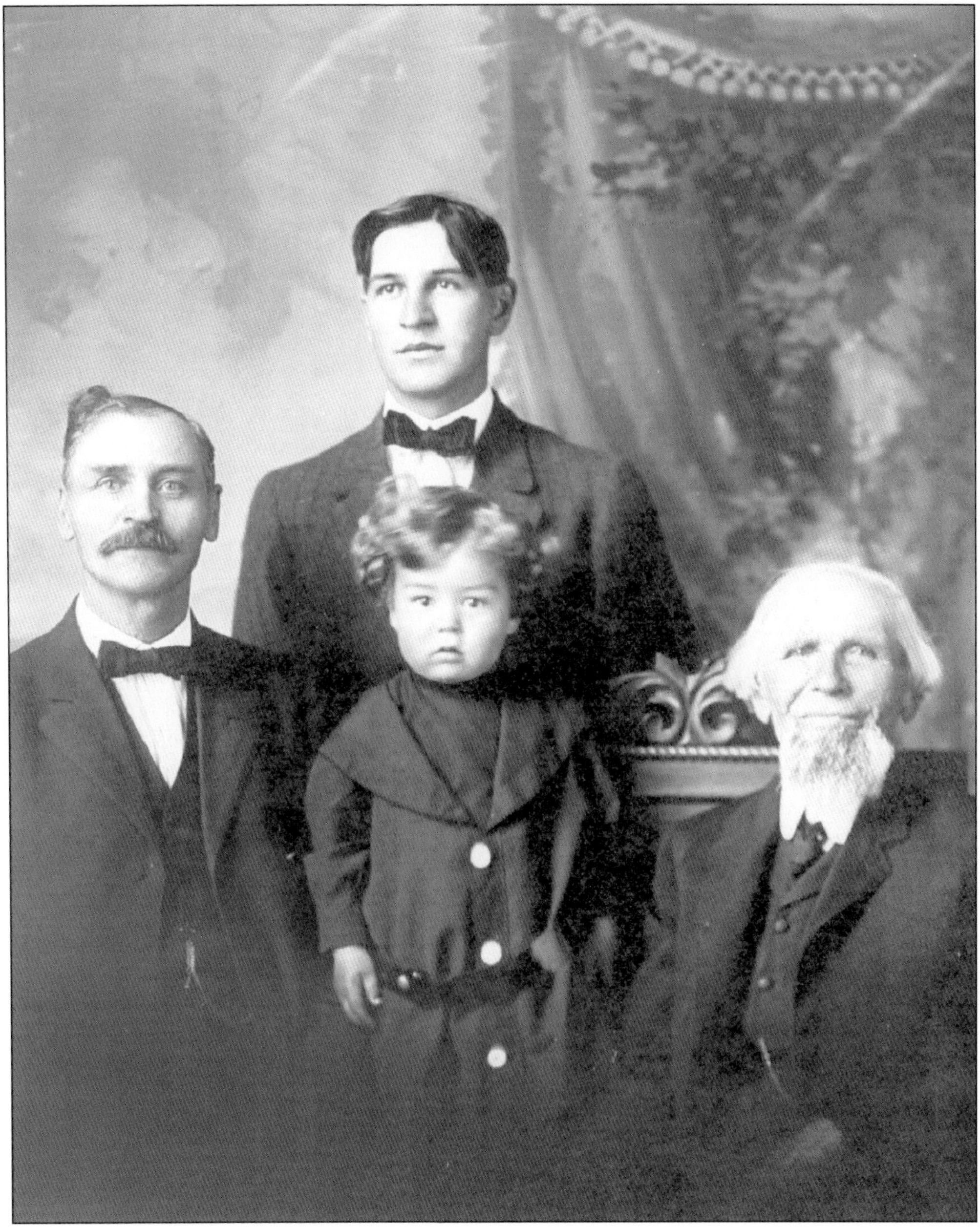

FOUR GENERATIONS. Members of the Quarve family, shown here from left to right, are Timan, Arnold, Kermit, and Levor. Levor Quarve was one of the earliest pioneers in Spring Grove. He was born in Hallingdal, Norway, in 1830, and immigrated to America with his parents in 1846. His father, Timan Olsen, died in New York after their voyage. His mother, Kjersti Garnaas, continued on with the family and settled in Wisconsin. Levor eventually ventured on his own and bought land in Spring Grove. In 1856, he married Kristi Berg and they had 11 children. His son Timan, to quote from O.S. Johnson's *Nybyggerhistorie fra Spring Grove og omegn*, "is an eager defender of everything Norwegian, down to herring and cod." And concerning Levor, "He has suffered a lot on his road through life, setbacks and personal sorrow, but he took it all quietly and left his life in God's hands."

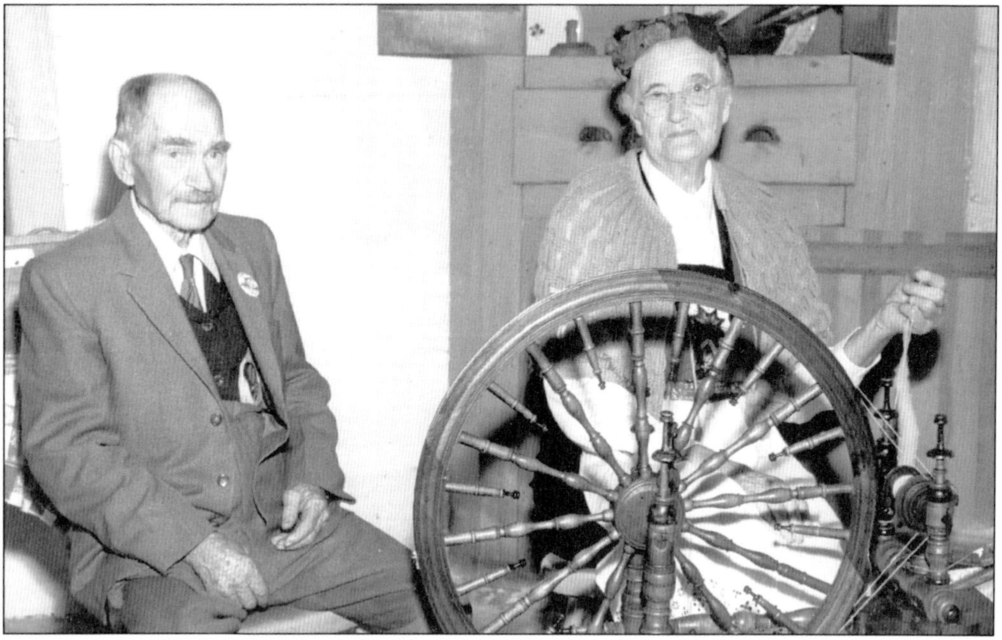

JOHN AND ANNA HAUGLAND. The Haugland's were both from Haugesund, Norway. John immigrated to America in 1885, after working on a Norwegian ship for nearly three years. According to the 1919 *History of Houston County*, the ship, on one of its return voyages, hit an iceberg off the coast of Iceland. Most of the crew was saved and brought to Ellis Island. John then decided to abandon a life at sea and worked as a hired man until he earned enough money to bring his fiancé, Anna, to America. In 1901, they were married in Caledonia, Minnesota. They walked—carrying all their luggage—15 miles to Black Hammer, where John had purchased a farm.

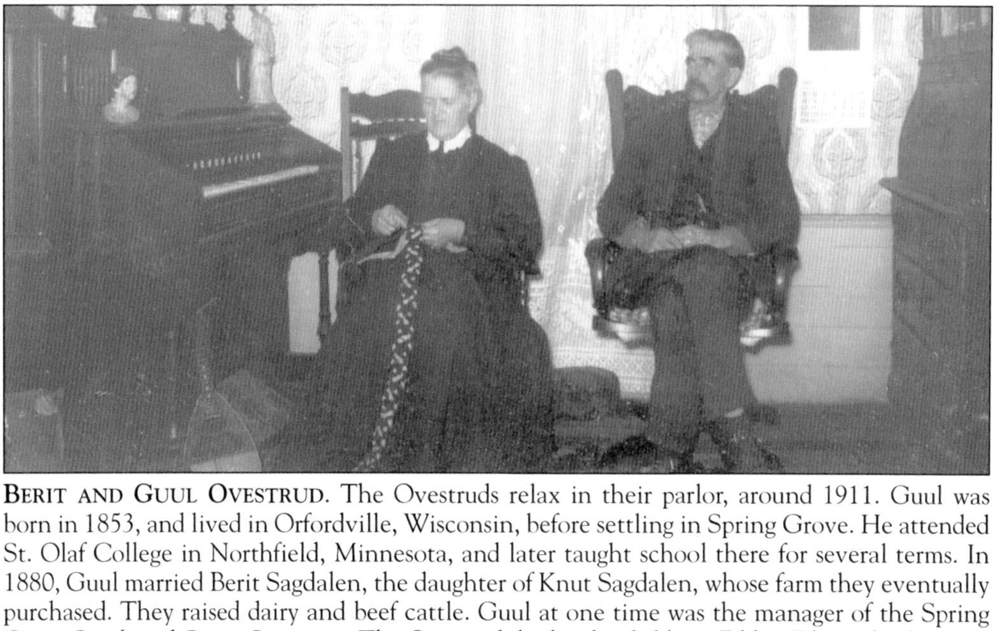

BERIT AND GUUL OVESTRUD. The Ovestruds relax in their parlor, around 1911. Guul was born in 1853, and lived in Orfordville, Wisconsin, before settling in Spring Grove. He attended St. Olaf College in Northfield, Minnesota, and later taught school there for several terms. In 1880, Guul married Berit Sagdalen, the daughter of Knut Sagdalen, whose farm they eventually purchased. They raised dairy and beef cattle. Guul at one time was the manager of the Spring Grove Stock and Grain Company. The Ovestruds had eight children: Eddie, Edmond, Clarence, Melvin, Matilda, Millie, Geneva, and Ernest.

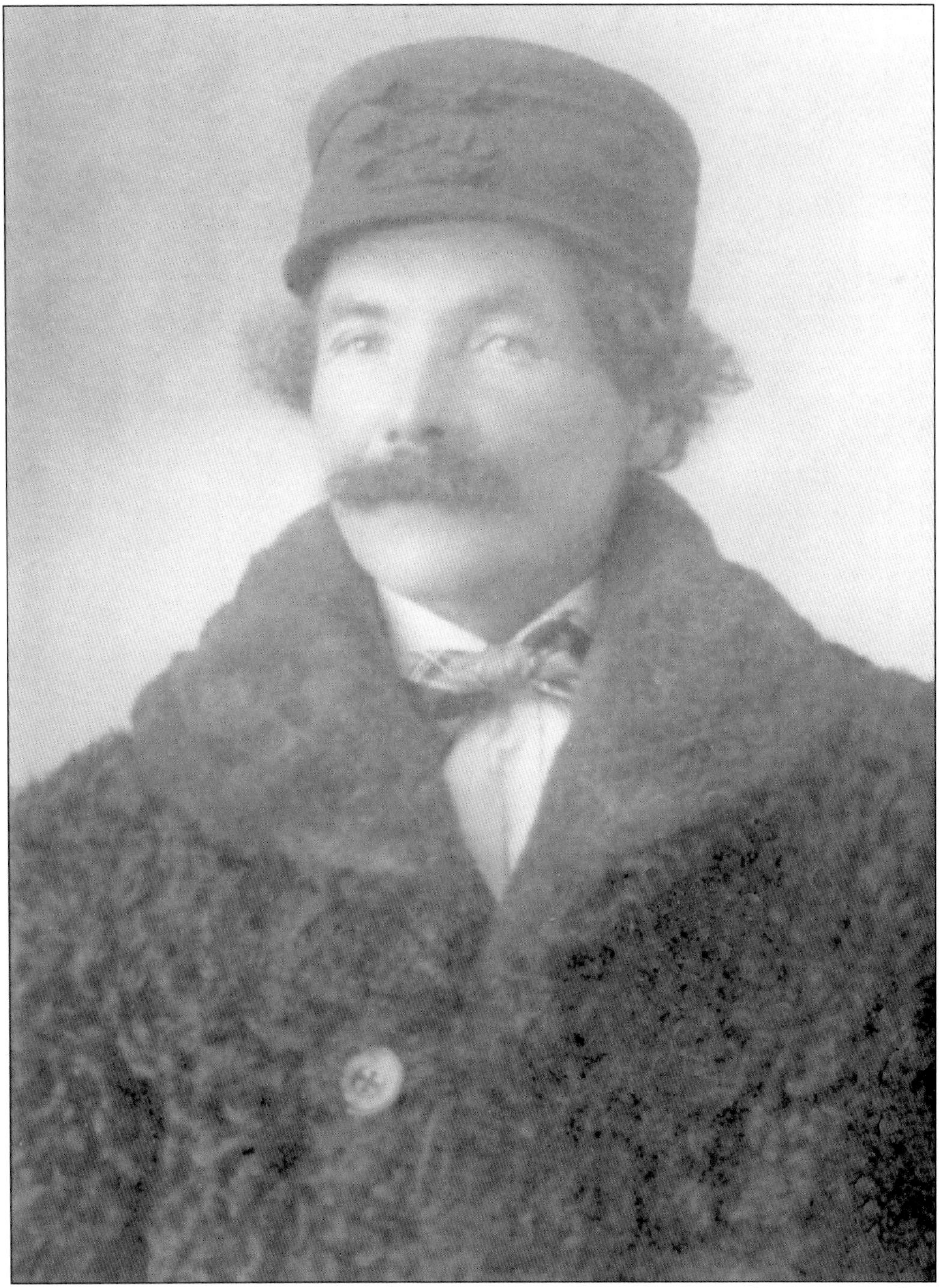

KNUT OPSAHL. Opsahl was born in Fogn, Norway, in 1850. He immigrated to America when he was 18 years old and first settled in Highland Prairie. In 1872, he married Rachel Erickson and they moved just north of Spring Grove, near Riceford, where they farmed. They had fourteen children: Tina, Rasmus, Isabella, Alma, Thomas, Edward, Clara, Bina, Selmer, Elda, Roy, Clarence, Rudolph and Fortinius. Knud Opsahl died in 1919. Notice the buffalo coat. This was a common garment for many pioneers. (Courtesy of Paul Wiste.)

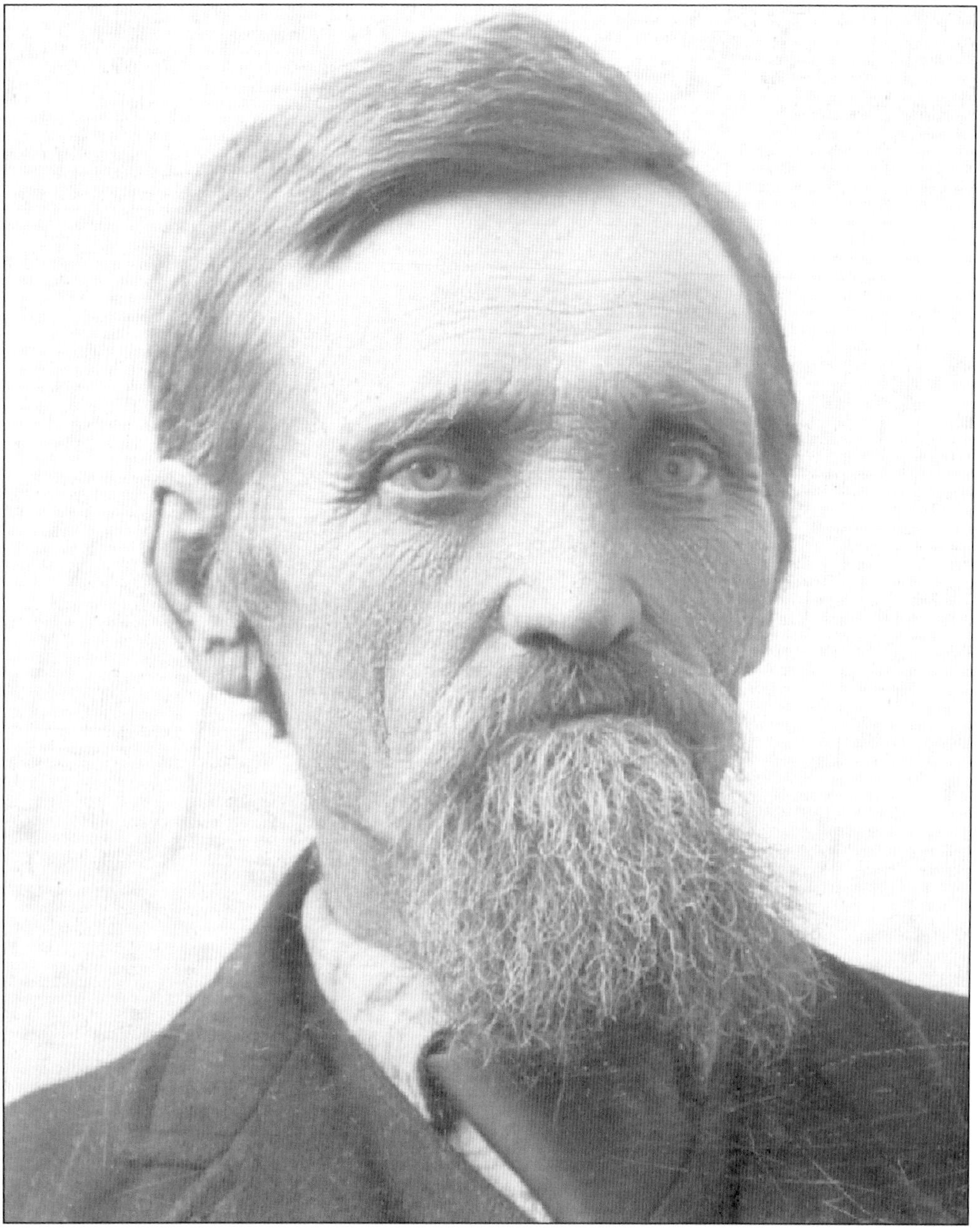

Stengrim Bergrud. Born in Sigdal, Norway, in 1836, Bergrud was orphaned when he was 8 years old. When he turned 18, he immigrated to America with an inheritance of $800. He made his way on foot to Mineral Point, Wisconsin, where he worked in the lead mines. After saving enough money to bring his fiancée to America, she refused his offer of marriage because he had become ill with lead poisoning. Bergrud bought a farm in Spring Grove, and in 1855 Reverend Ulrik Koren held services under one of his oak trees, where eighteen children were baptized. In 1860, he met and married Marthe Ruen. During the Indian scare of 1862, the Bergruds, along with other townspeople, took refuge in the old stone church until it was learned that there was no threat in Spring Grove. Stengrim and Marthe had seven children: Annette, Louise, Maria, Helene, Sophia, Amanda, and Peter.

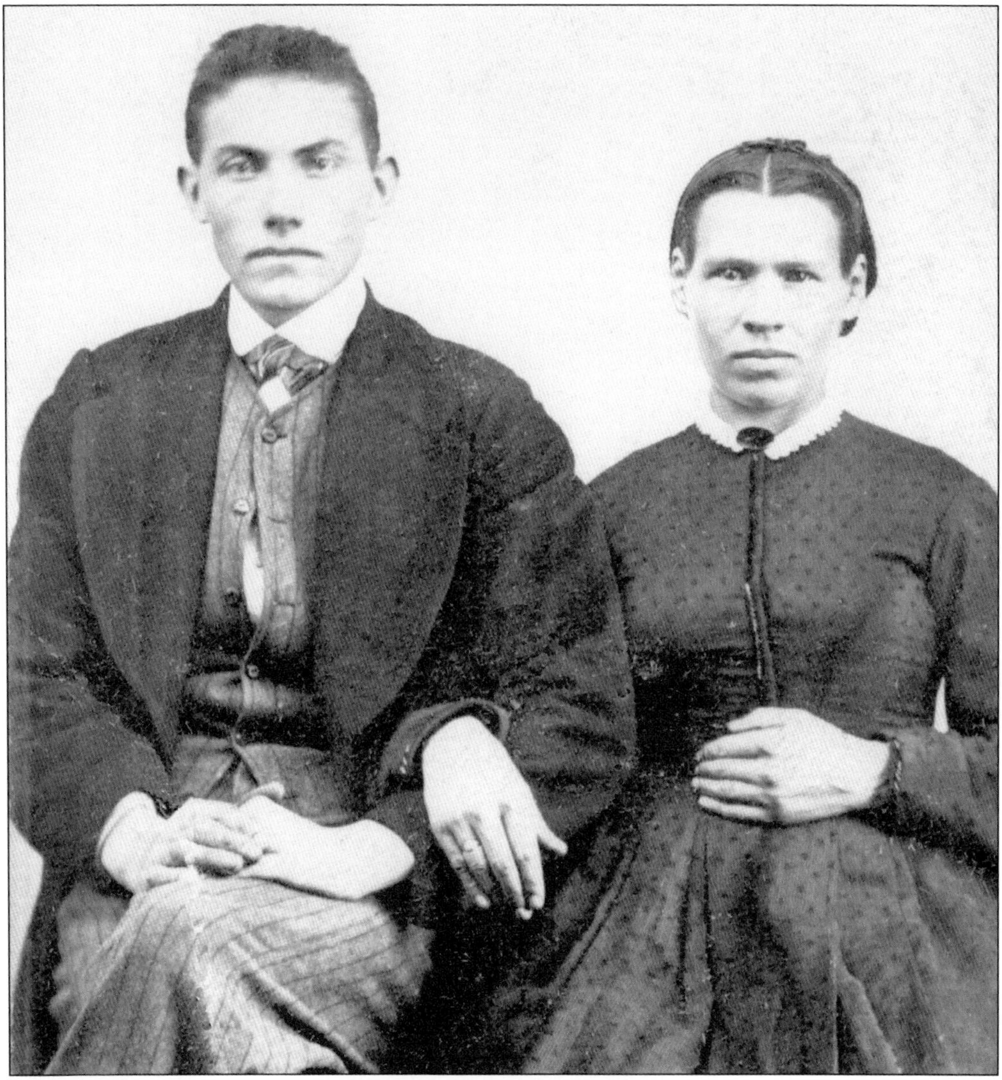

OLE "SYTTEN." From an 1875 issue of the *Decorah Republican*:

> *Suicide at Spring Grove: A Norwegian Blasts Off His Head with a Shotgun. A few days ago, a Norwegian living near Spring Grove, Minnesota, named Ole Oleson, but nicknamed Ole Seventeen, went on a big drunk and spent the night with a lot of his fellows in playing cards and carousing. During the night his wife reproached him, not very harshly, but it aroused his anger. He chased her into another room and would have killed her if the others had not interfered. In the morning he borrowed a shotgun and said he was going to kill a partridge. But the others, after he was gone, suspected there was something wrong and followed after him, and took the gun away. They thought he intended to shoot his wife, as they had had trouble. He finally obtained one from a house, the inmates of which had gone to church. With this he went out into the yard, cut a stick of convenient length, sat down on the ground, placed the muzzle of the gun in his mouth, and fired it off with the stick. At least, appearances indicate this. His head was all blown to pieces and he evidently died instantly. We glean these outlines from Mr. J.B. Smith.*

Because the church did not allow suicides to be buried in the cemetery, Ole Oleson, a Civil War veteran and fledgling politician, was buried in an unmarked grave in the country.

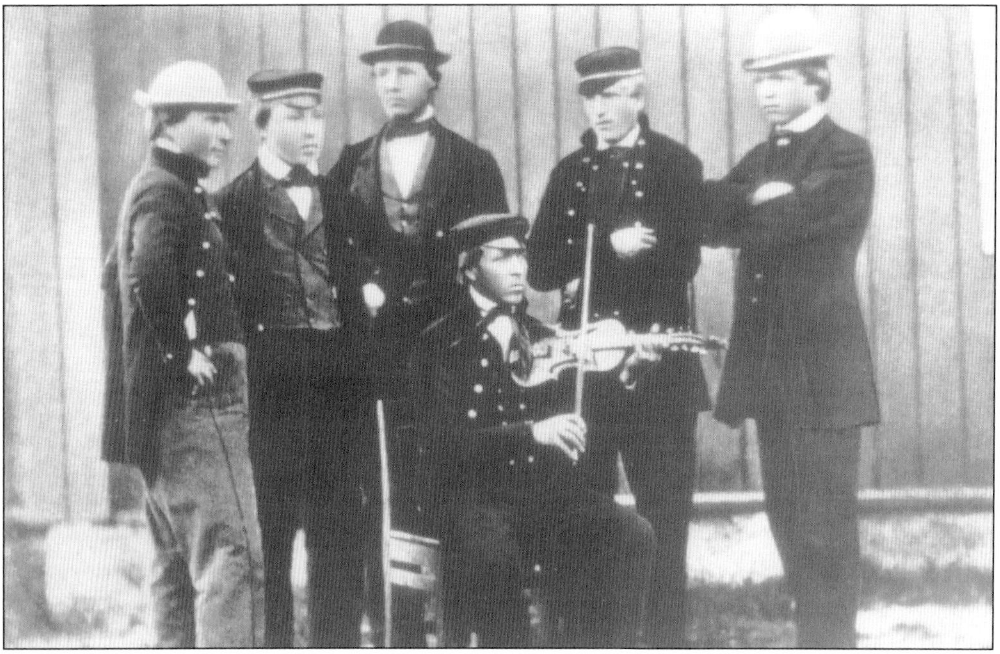

ASLE SUNDET. This group of relatives includes Asle Sundet (second from left), who as a young man immigrated to America from Krodsherred, Norway, with his wife, Aase, and his brother Ole in 1861. The young man with the violin is Hans Sundet, another of Asle's brothers. Hans stayed in Norway and became a renowned fiddle player. He is holding an eight-stringed Hardanger violin, used to play traditional folk music. One of Asle's sons, Hans Sundet, lived in Spring Grove with his wife, Anna Reitan, and children. (Courtesy of Lee and Louise Sundet.)

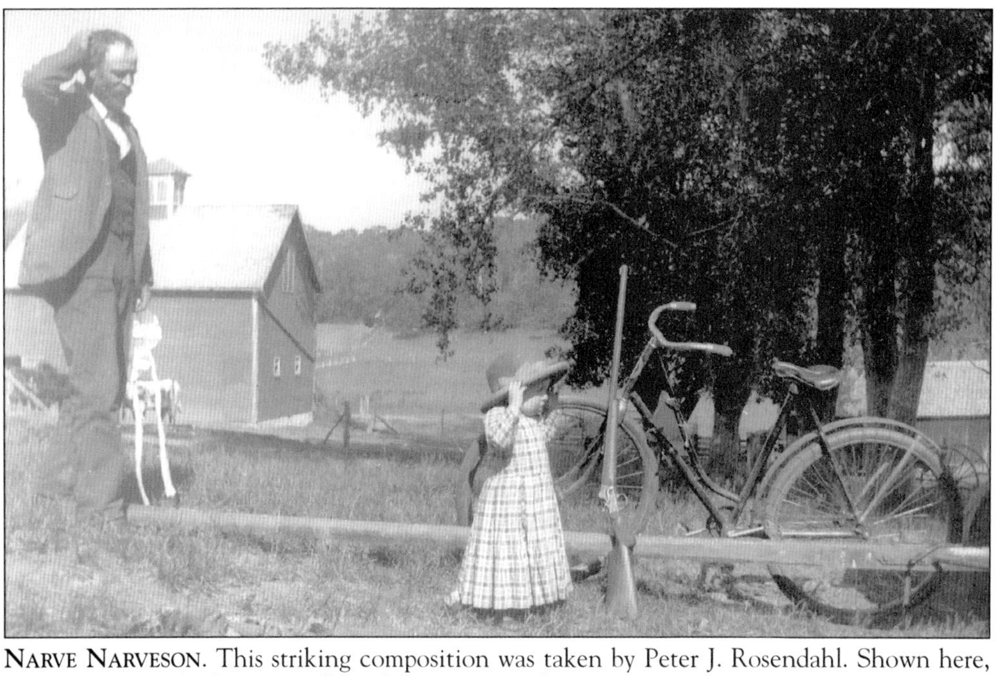

NARVE NARVESON. This striking composition was taken by Peter J. Rosendahl. Shown here, Narve Narveson looks quizzically at his son Percival.

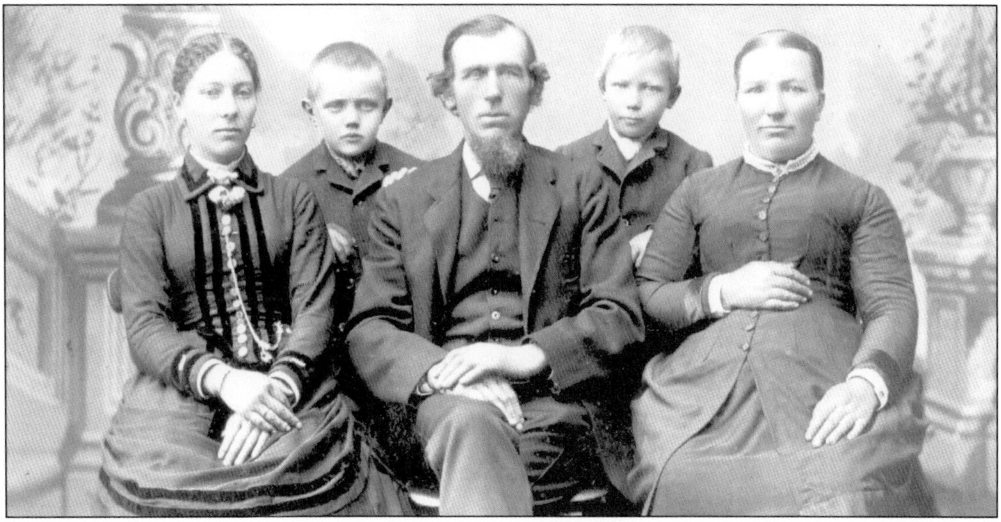

Lars Quinnell. Lars Østedal was born in Trondheim, Norway, in 1836, and immigrated to America in 1859. Before settling in Spring Grove Township, Østedal worked as a lumberjack, rafting on the Mississippi River. In 1867, he married Anne Quinnell and took her last name. Their children, pictured here from left right, are Johanne, Adolph, and Emil. In O.S. Johnson's *Nybyggerhistorie fra Spring Grove og omegn*, Quinnell is described as "one of those noble and faithful workers who came here with two empty hands, but with these hands, along with good health, a strong will and desire and unbending courage to finish whatever he made up his mind to do, worked himself into great riches."

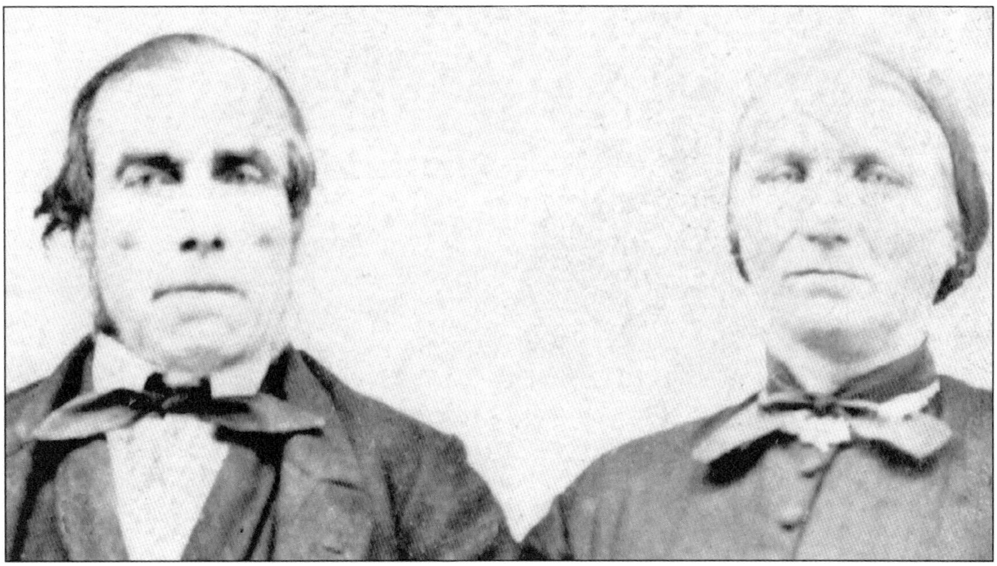

Their Unusual Divorce. Ole Hasledalen, one of the early Norwegian settlers to Spring Grove, was born in 1820. Being that divorce was unacceptable to the church in these days, Ole and his wife, Berthe, decided the solution was to designate a dividing line through their home so that each had half. The *Spring Grove Herald* made this comment about the Hasledalens' arrangement: "Friend O.T. Hasledalen is said to be so happy that our corporate limits will hardly contain him in consequence of the return on Tuesday evening of his good wife Berthe, from the far west." Ole Hasledalen died in 1902, a few years after Berthe.

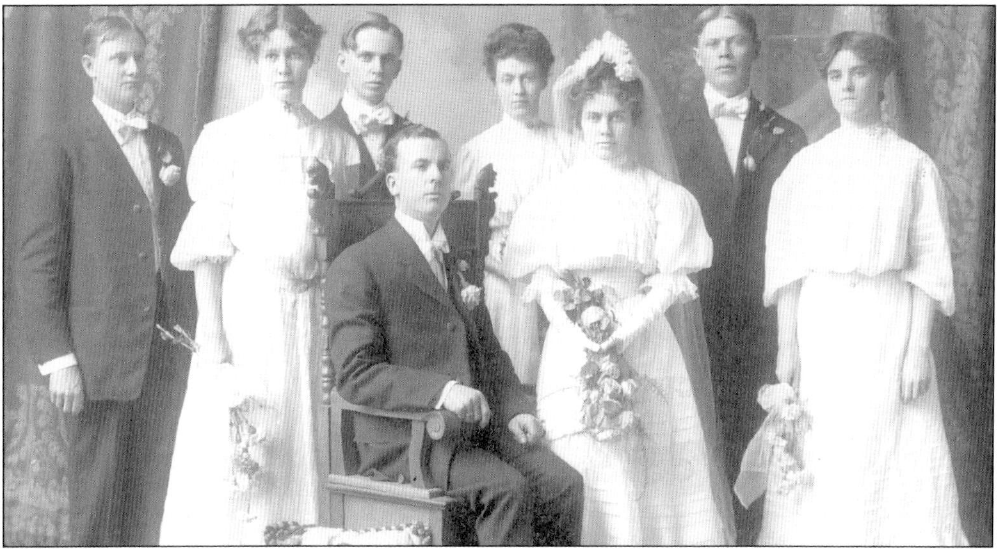

Engell-Bakke. From a 1906 issue of the *Spring Grove Herald:*

> *The largest wedding that probably ever has taken place here, occurred Tuesday, when Miss Anna Bakke and James Engell were united in marriage. . . . She is an estimable young lady, who has been a successful milliner here for several years. . . . He is a popular, energetic and pleasant young man who has pursued the photographer's trade since a young boy, besides having recently passed the Embalmers' State Examination.*

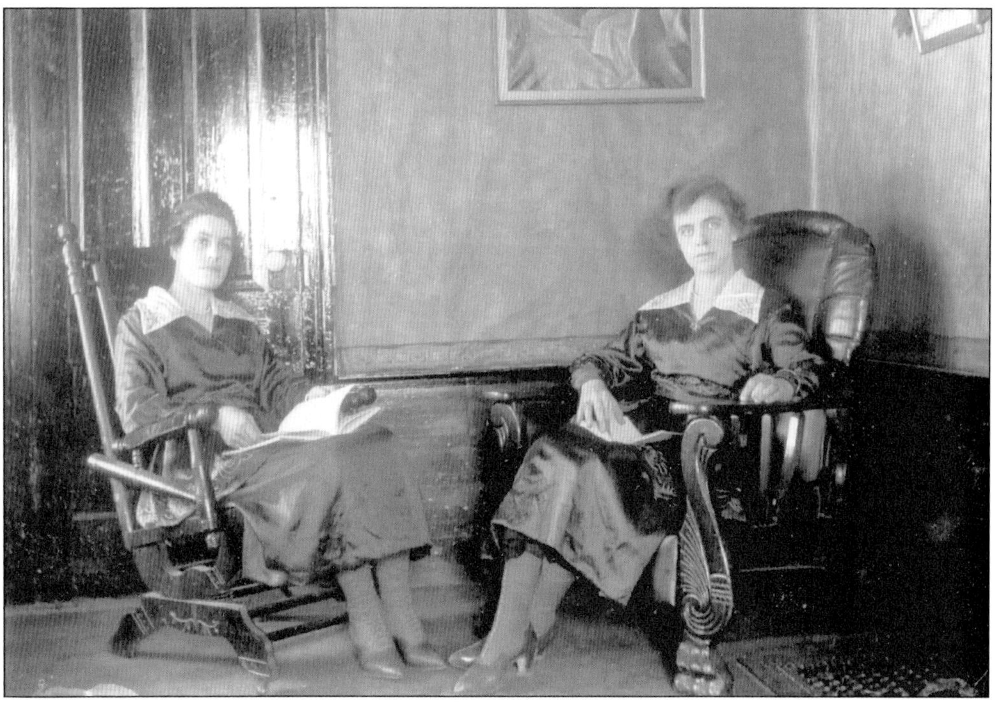

Sisters. Millie and Geneva Ovestrud pause for a moment from their reading to allow their brother Edmond to take a photograph. Edmond was also a painter. The image on the far wall, entitled *Mary and Martha,* is one of his works.

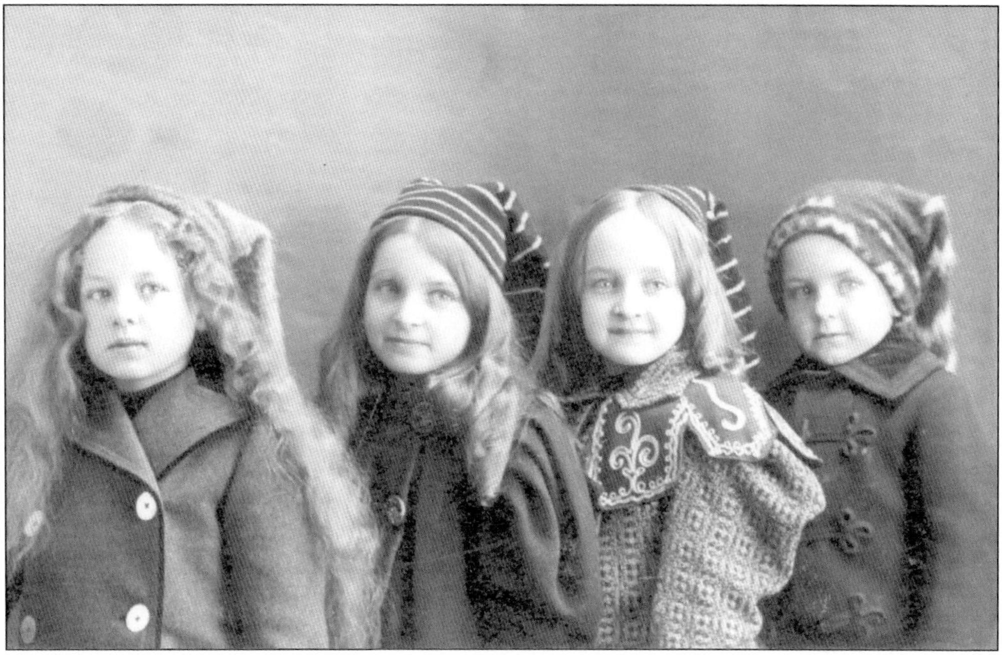

FLADAGER. Shown here are the children of Henry and Caroline Fladager.

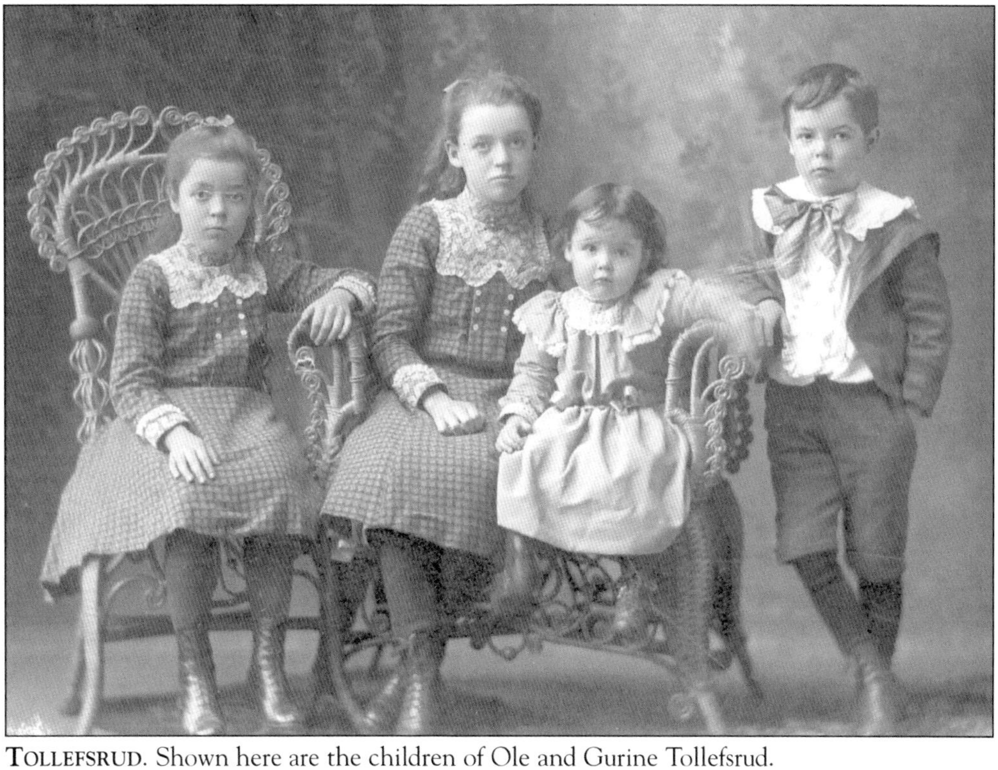

TOLLEFSRUD. Shown here are the children of Ole and Gurine Tollefsrud.

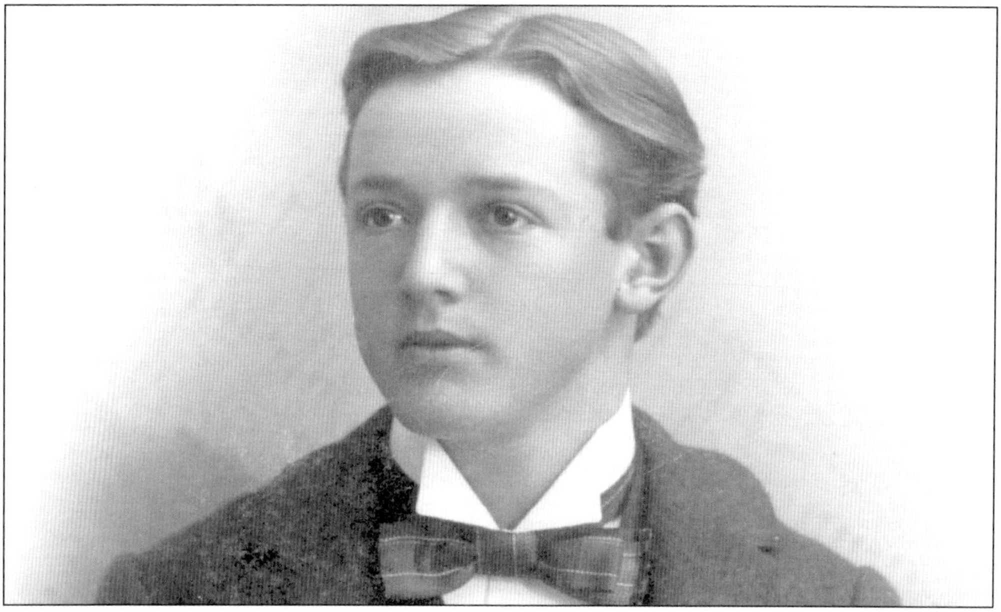

ARNOLD FLADAGER. In his 1927 *Memoir of My Mother, Mrs. M. Fladager*, Arnold Fladager provides some interesting facts about the Civil War: "The only newspaper they had at that time was *Faedrelandet og Emigranten*, and thru the columns of that paper the settlers were able to see issues of the moral battles in Congress regarding Slavery, and the impending Civil War. To be a Democrat was then considered to be a crime, and Democrats were looked upon as pro-slavery men." (Courtesy of Lee & Louise Sundet)

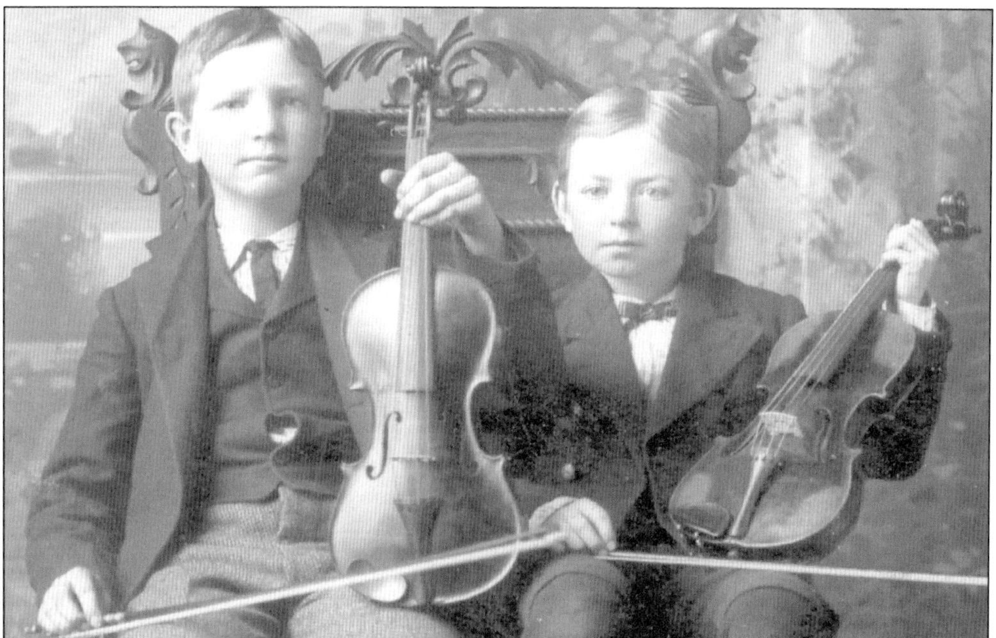

YOUNG FIDDLERS. Maurice (right) was the last Fladager to operate the successful clothing business started in 1860 by his grandfather Mons Fladager. Embrick Hendrickson (left) served in World War I. (Courtesy of Lee and Louise Sundet.)

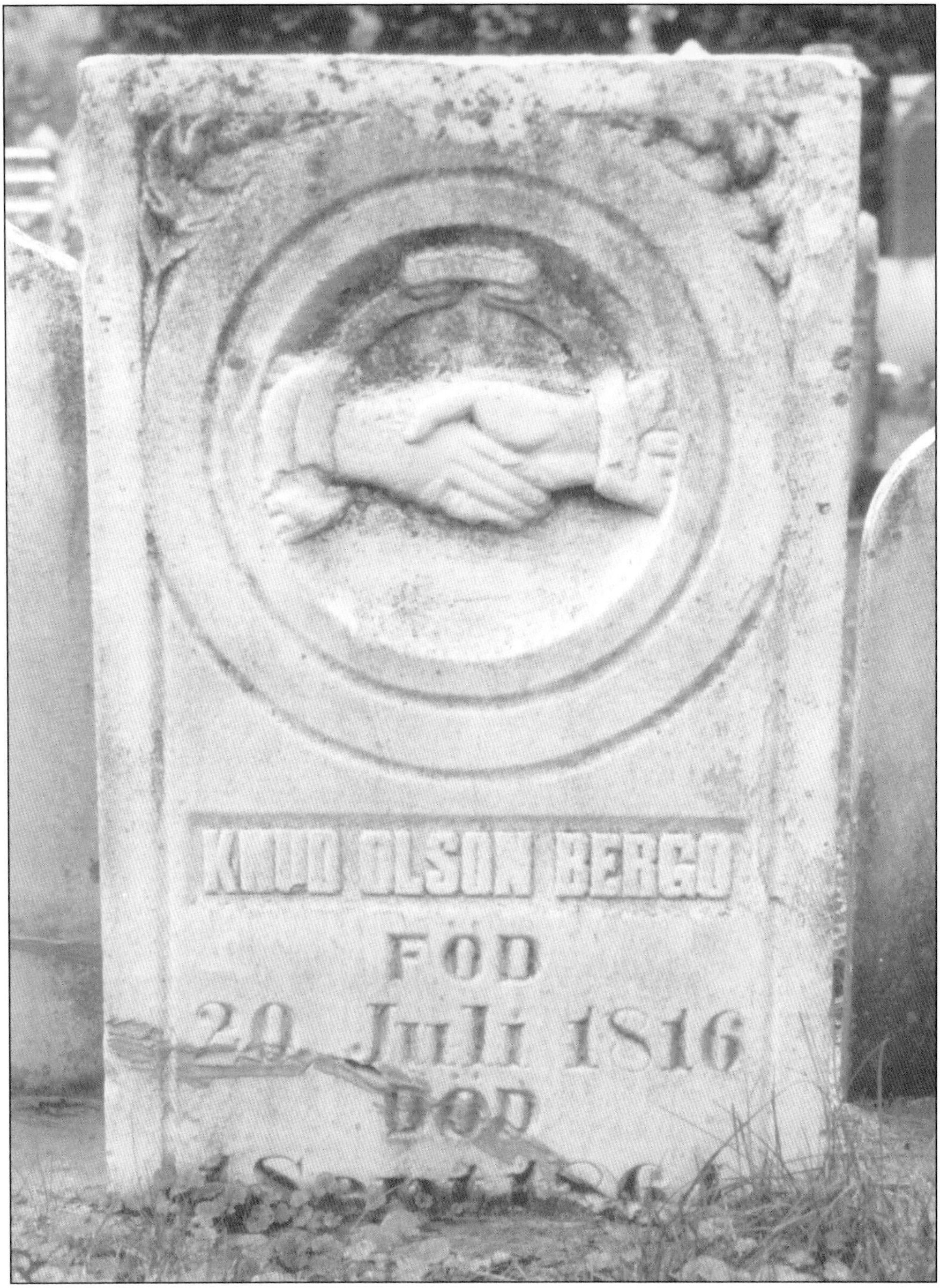

THE NAMING OF BLACK HAMMER. Knut Bergo was born in Valdres, Norway, and is credited with naming the town of Black Hammer, which was part of Spring Grove Township. He woke up early one morning to see a fire blazing over the nearby prairie, charring a large bluff in the distance. The appearance of this reminded Bergo of a similar bluff in Norway, and he exclaimed, "*Sort hammer!*"—Norwegian for "black bluff." The merging of Norsk and English words was common among new emigrants.

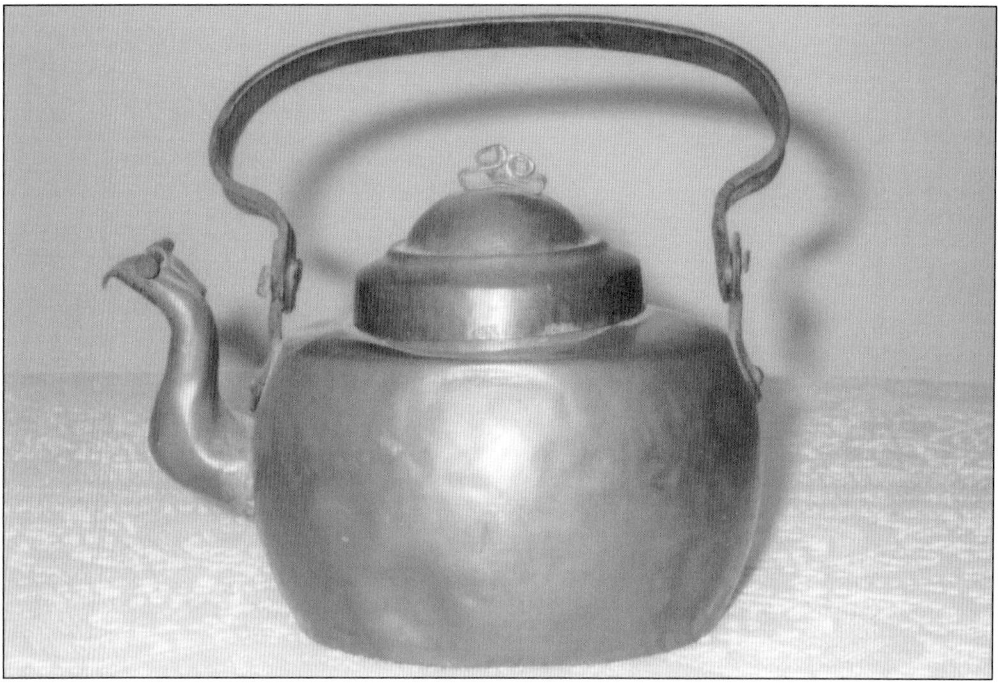

Norwegian Copper Kettle. This kettle was hand-forged in Norway and belonged to the Anders Foss family. This is just one of the many household items the family brought with them on their voyage to America. (Courtesy of Lori Foss.)

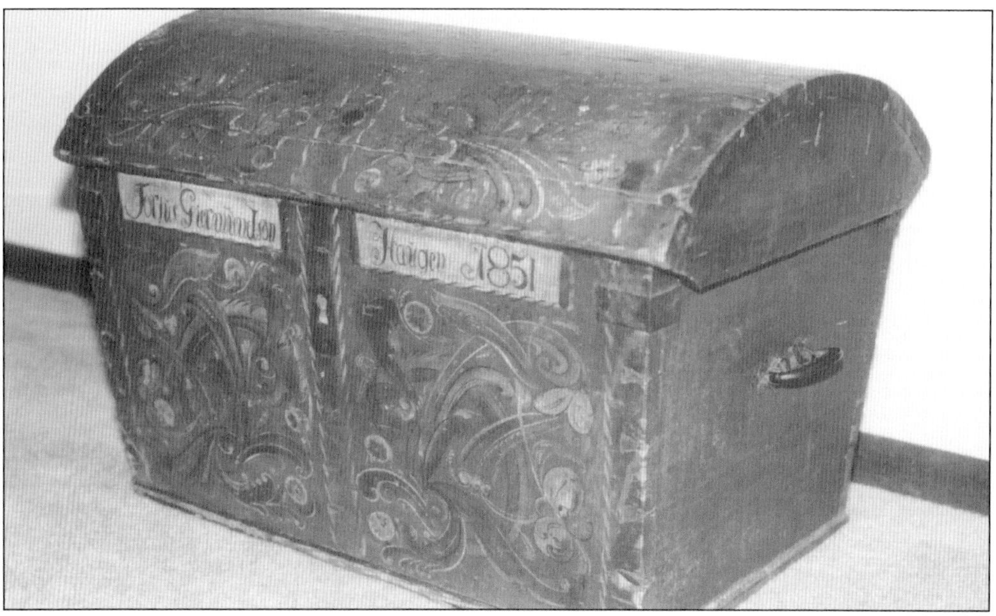

Norwegian Emigrant Trunk. This small emigrant trunk was given to Sigurd Moen and his family when they left for America in 1851. The trunk is painted in typical Norwegian reds and blues. The *rosemalling* (flower painting) was most likely done by the famous Telemark artist, Thomas Luraas, who was said to have been one of the best floral painters of his time. (Courtesy of Howard and Arlene Van Minsell.)

Two

GROWTH OF THE SOIL

In an early newspaper called *Emigraten*, pioneers living in Wisconsin and Iowa found enticing articles advertising available land in southern Minnesota. Many of the settlers had been tenants on large Norwegian farms called *gaards*. Coming to America afforded them the opportunity to finally become landowners. However, immigrant life was not easy; they had to adapt to new climates, soils, insects and pests. If a family did not arrive early enough to build shelter and plant their first crop, surviving the harsh Minnesota winter was extremely difficult. For example, when the Nels Kjome family arrived near Spring Grove, in 1854, they resorted to living under a rock outcropping for the entire winter. Miraculously, everyone survived and the following spring they built a house and opened up their land for planting.

From 1850 to 1870, subsistence farming was the norm and farmers sought land near a stream and grove of trees. These natural resources, along with food crops and a garden, were all the pioneer family needed to survive. Early on, it was common to see a pioneer in his small field guiding an unruly plow through the soil and steering his oxen by a shout of "gee" or "haw." From this simple beginning, farming began to develop year by year as new implements were introduced and American agriculture changed.

From 1870 to 1895, wheat was primarily grown. Farmers thrived until crop failures forced them to become more diversified. Since 1895, most farmers have raised a variety of crops and animals, including dairy and beef cattle, hogs, and poultry. Few small farms have survived. In order to succeed in today's market farmers have had to expand their operations.

By the early 1880s, a second generation of farmers, finding it difficult to obtain land in Houston County, began heading west to the endlessly flat prairies of the Dakota Territories.

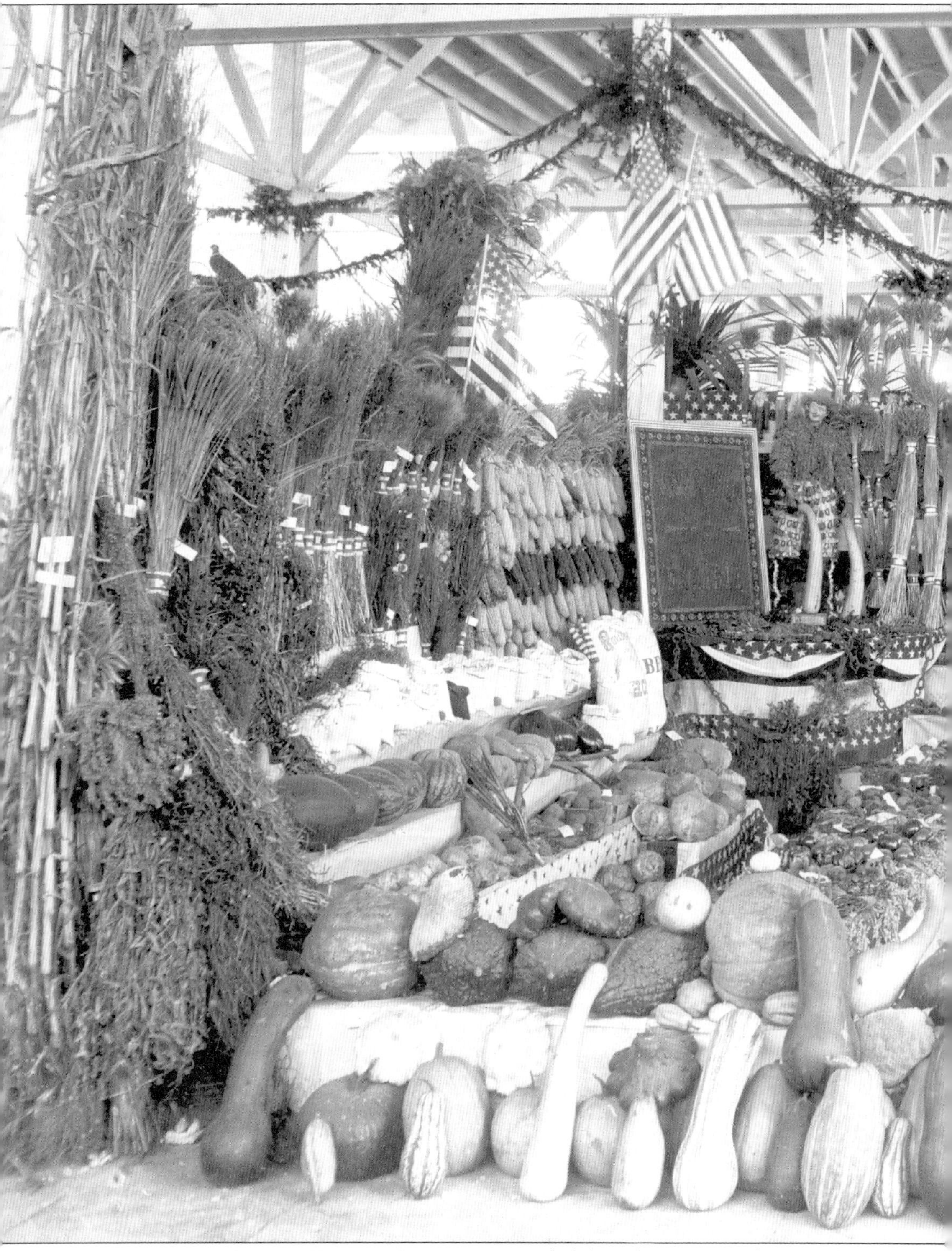

AGRICULTURAL AWARD. Houston County was awarded first-place in agriculture at the 1901 Minnesota State Fair. A town such as Spring Grove was, and continues to be, dependent on

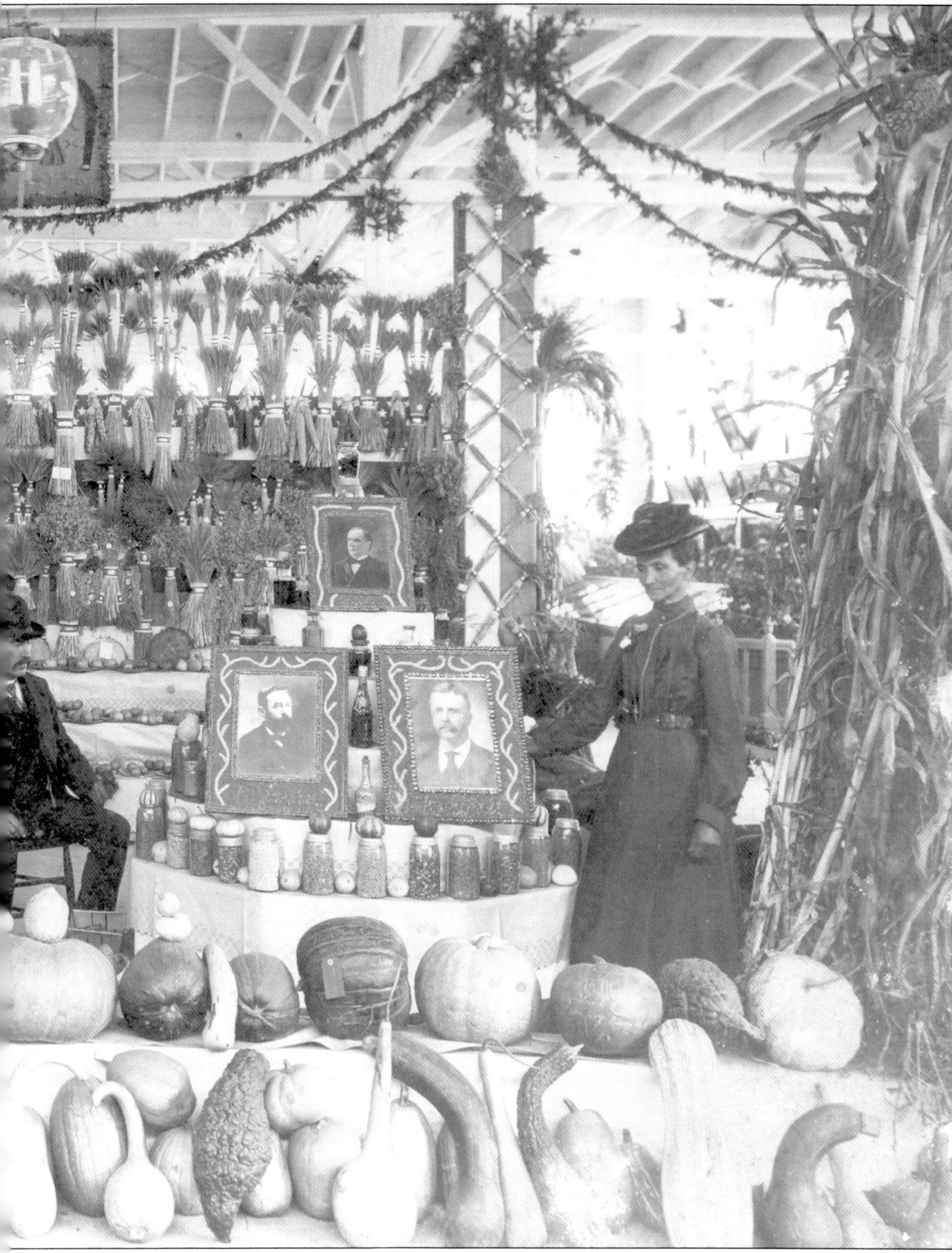

farmers. To quote the American orator and statesman, Daniel Webster (1782–1852): "When tillage begins, other arts follow. The farmers, therefore, are the founders of human civilization."

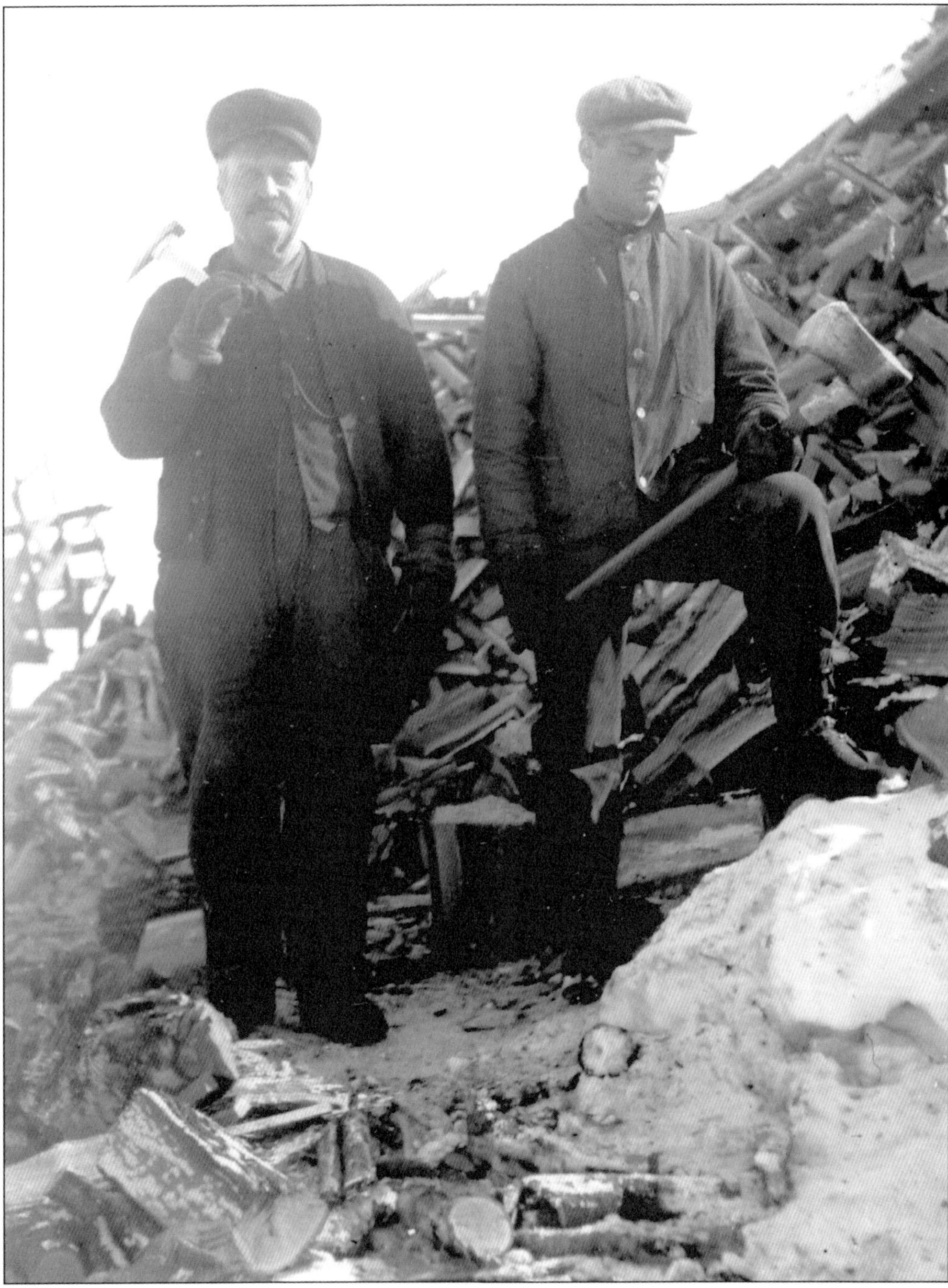

CHOPPING WOOD. Nels Sagdalen and Ernest Ovestrud pose in front of their woodpile. Wood was as important to farm families as making hay or threshing grain, and it was usually chopped in the autumn, before Thanksgiving. Prior to oil and gas fire furnaces, woodpiles were a common sight. The smaller wood chunks were used in the kitchen range, while bigger chunks were thrown into the parlor stove. It was also possible to trade wood with local merchants. This was the case with the Mons Fladager store, as they advertised in 1898: "We have a few men's and boy's overcoats to exchange for wood, either green or dry. Wood must be delivered this winter."

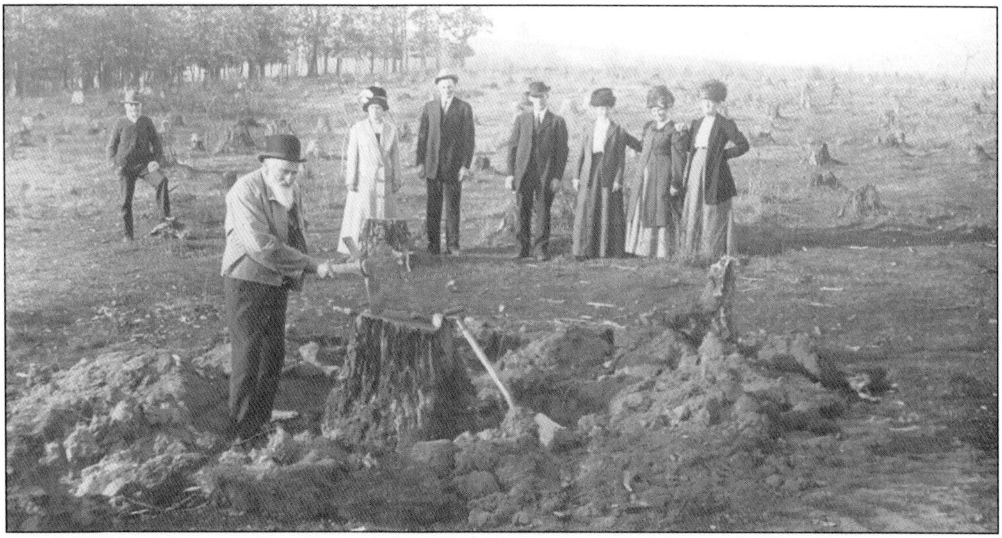

Stump Removal. *Gamle* (old man) Ingvald Muller poses before a stump with his mattock and shovel. After the trees in a field had been cut and hauled away, the stumps would need to be removed. In early days oxen provided the power necessary to remove stumps and their roots. Eventually steam engines were used, and in the 1930s sticks of dynamite usually took care of the job. For smaller stumps, a brush or grub hook was used. The onlookers, seen here from left to right, are Mr. Ramstad, Adolph and Gustava Muller, Hans and Ingeborg Solum, Live Muller, and Anne Engell.

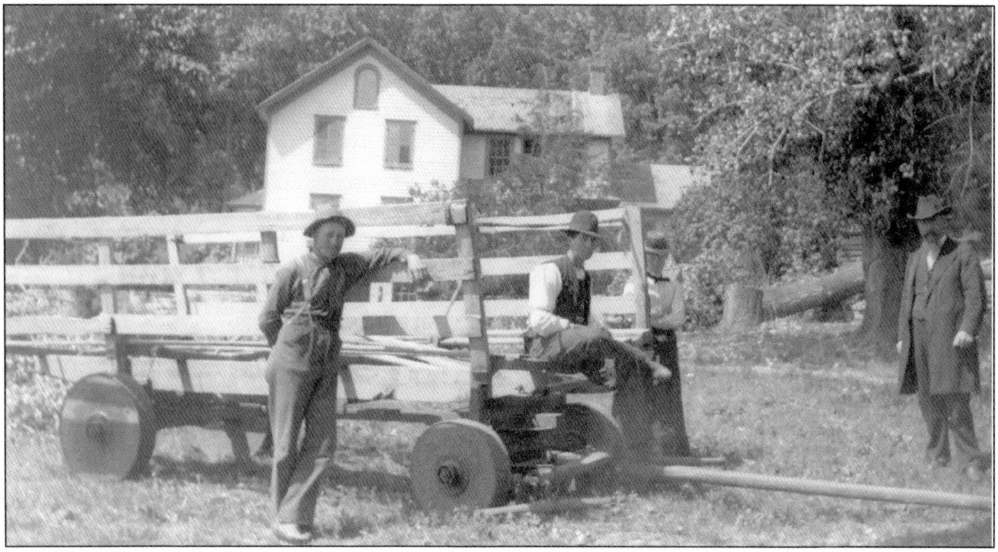

Kubberulle. This ox-cart was a genuine Norwegian construction. Known as a *kubberulle*, it was built entirely out of logs (*kubbe*). Wheels were made from the sawed-off ends of logs, which were then fastened to an axel made from a smaller tree. Quoting from Carlton Qualey, an early resident of Spring Grove and professor of history at Carlton College in Northfield, Minnesota: "When the *kubberulle* had been constructed, the farmer could get along very well. I have heard many pioneers say that the first time they drove with their own oxen hitched to a *kubberulle*, they felt actually independent, if not rich." The party gathered here, from left to right, are Oliver Rosendahl, unidentified, Julia Rosendahl, and Reverend Edward Peterson.

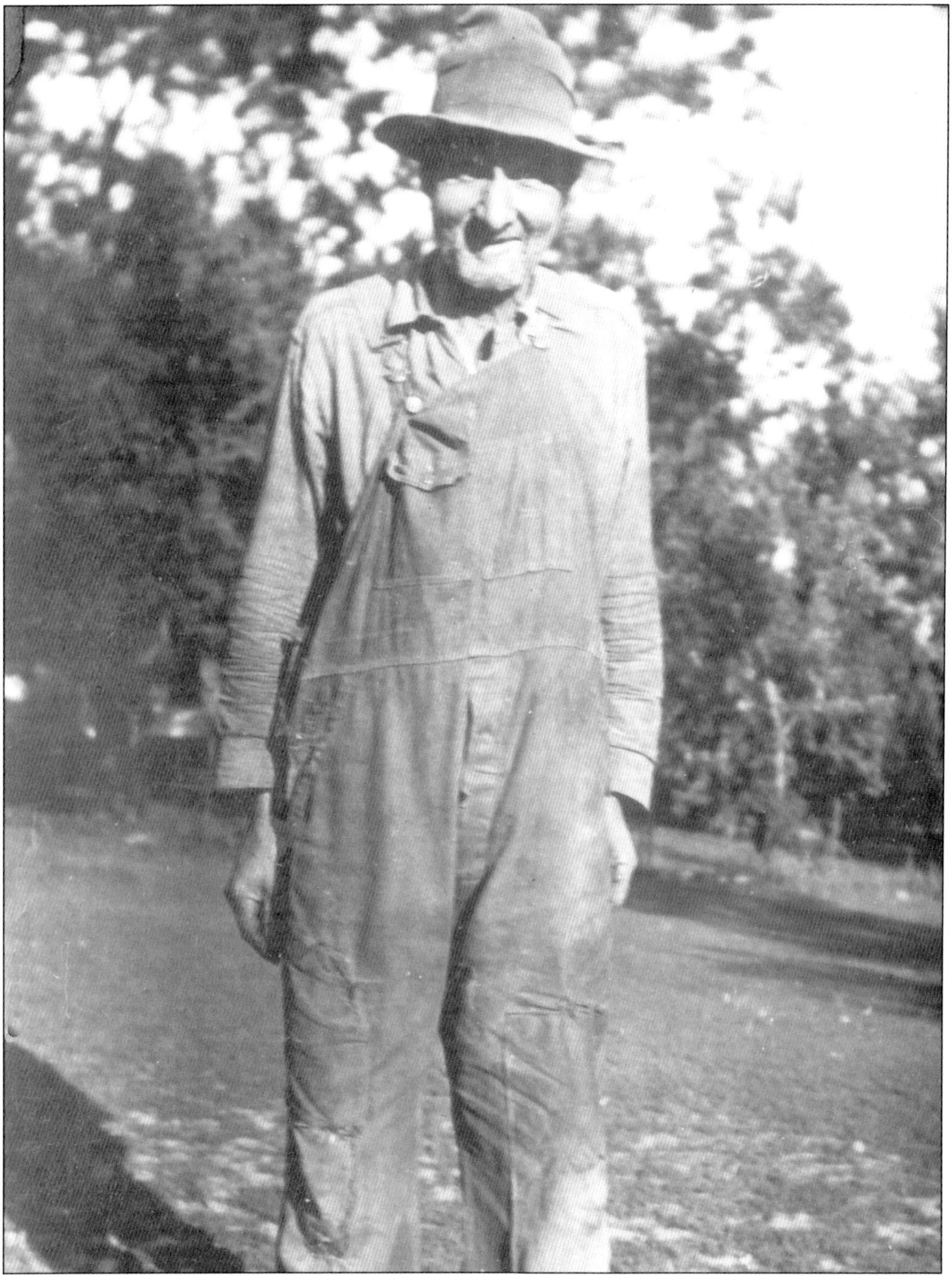

OLE FLATIN. From a 1936 issue the *Spring Grove Herald*:

> *Ole Flatin, a son of Fingal and Guri Flatin, was born in Spring Grove, August 3, 1871. He spent the greater part of his life at the parental home working on his father's farm. As a young man he was blessed with good health, but at the age of thirty he began failing. A head injury suffered in an accident in infancy, which for many years lay dormant, began to cause trouble after he had attained the age of manhood and his mental condition was somewhat impaired.*

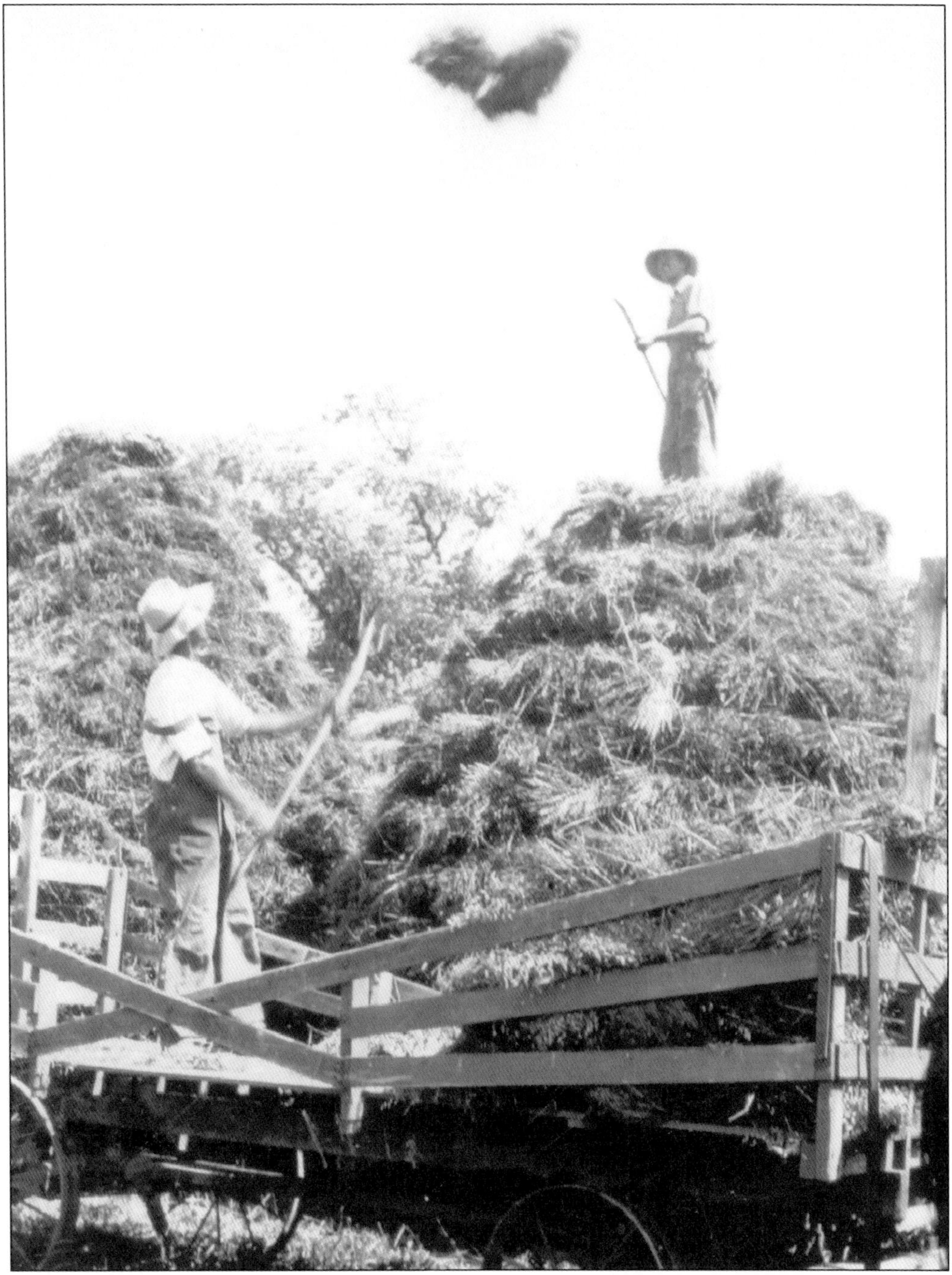

MAKING HAY. Seen here, two unidentified farmers pitch and stack hay. Wild grasses were once cut with a scythe, but gradually new implements such as the horse-powered mower and rake came into being. After the grass was cut it would be gathered up into small piles called windrows until the hay was dried. Hayracks, like the wagon shown here, would be brought out to the field and filled up with hay. The wagons were then pulled to a designated haystack and, as shown, pitchforks were used to unload the hay. There was an art to making these stacks this high. If they leaned in any way, they were bound to topple. Hay was stored in a barn for winter fodder.

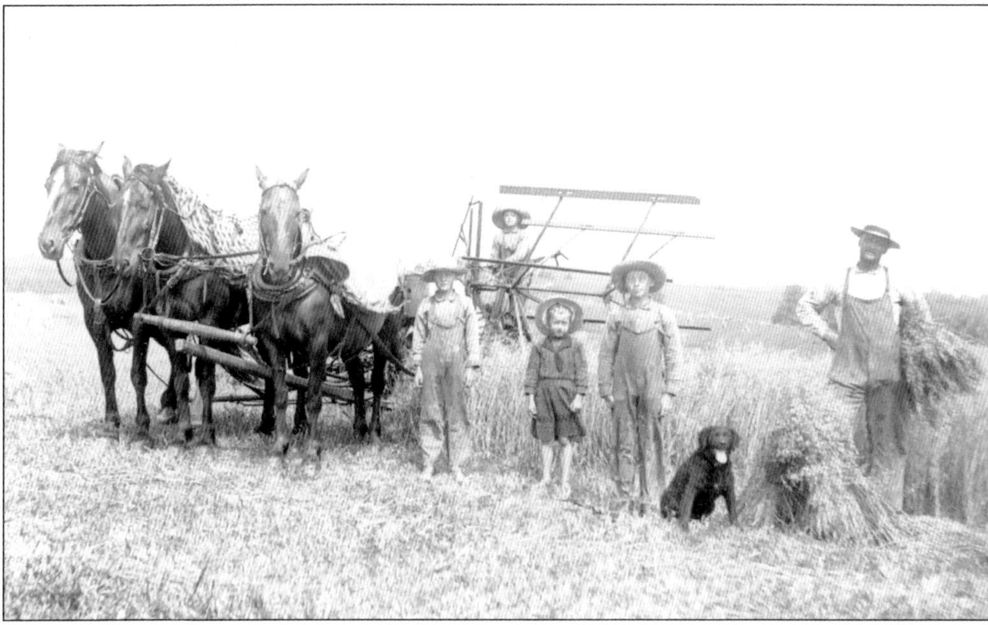

Grain Binding. The Tollefsrud family, shown above from left to right: Oscar, Henry, Theoline, Leonard, and their father, Hendrick, with a bundle of grain under his arm. As the horses pulled the grain binder forward, the paddle-like wheel rotated, bending the grain stalks toward a sickle that would cut the stalks a few inches from the ground. A cloth canvas would convey the stalks to a knotter, which put them together in small bundles that were then dropped off the machine. Workers following close behind the binder would pick the bundles from the ground and prop them up into what were called "shocks," just like the one next to the Tollefsrud's dog. Below are Percival and Clifford Narveson.

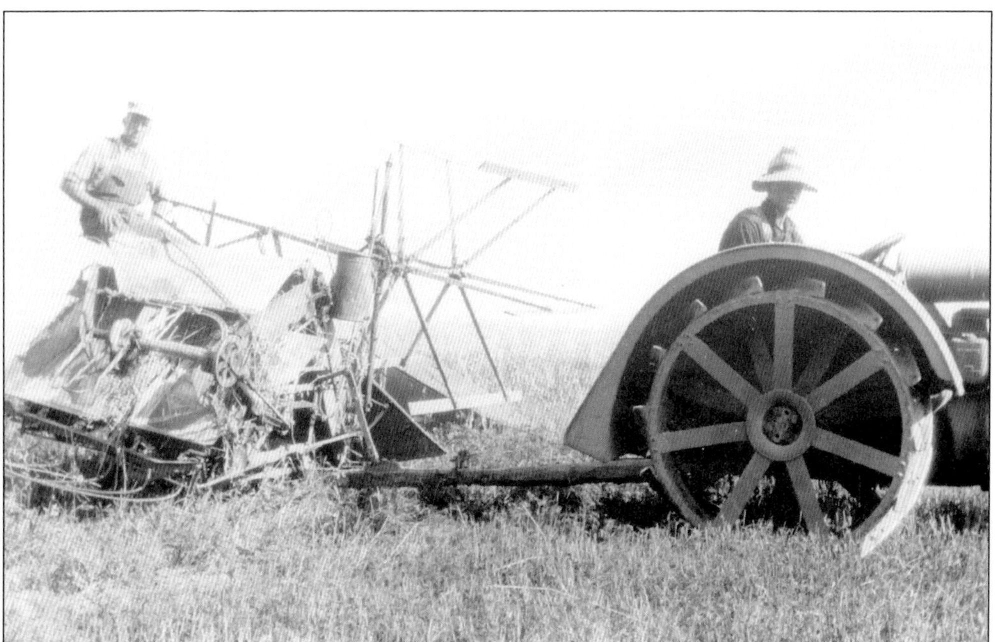

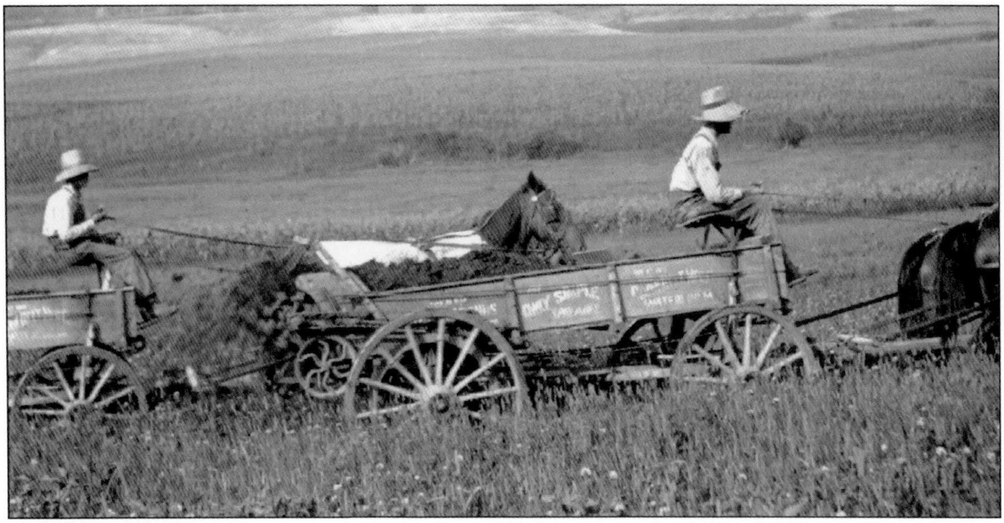

MANURE SPREADER. From a 1907 advertisement in the *Spring Grove Herald*:

> *Just write me today and let me send you a catalog of the Only Simple Wagon Box Manure Spreader. It is always a pleasure to demonstrate the Only Simple machine. You can take it right to your barnyard, load up with any sort of manure, straw stack bottom, corn-stalk mixed, hard or soft, and you will see what can be done with the only successful wagon box manure spreader made. It is just the spreader every farmer in this section has been looking for. I have it ready to show you any time—that is my business. Just drop me a postal. I am agent for four counties. Write me: O. A. Kroshus, Agent. Don't buy a Spreader of any kind without you first see the Only Simple Spreader in action. Get my price. Terms can be made to suit any purchaser.*

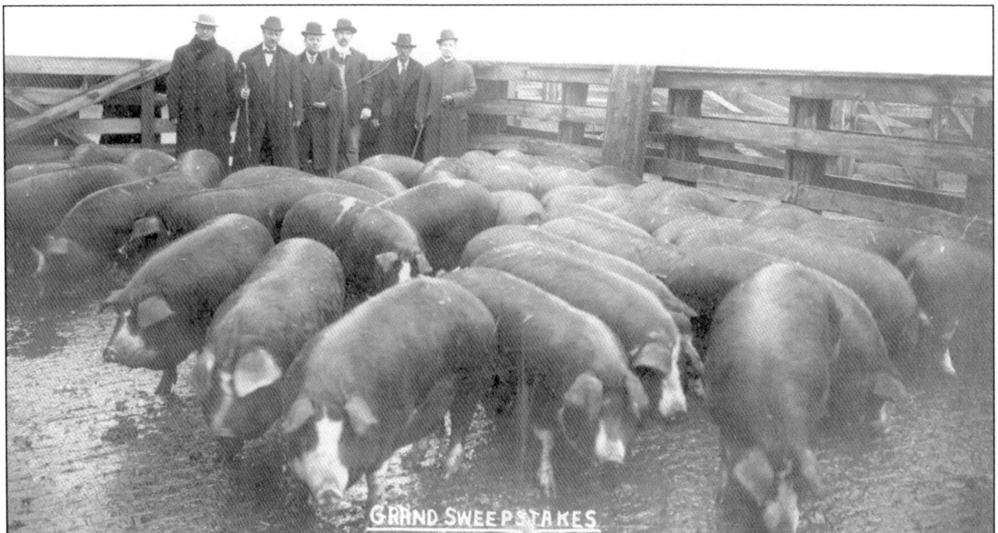

RAISING HOGS. Having been "bred and fed" by George Peter Arnston of Spring Grove, these Poland China hogs won the grand sweepstakes at the 1912 Carlot Hogs International Livestock Exposition. Their ages were seven and a half years; their average weight 261 pounds. Pork was one of the staples of the pioneer diet. It was often served fresh, salted, pickled, or canned. A typical meal consisted of bacon with boiled or fried potatoes and onions—and coffee, a most cherished drink among Norwegians. (Courtesy of the Ballard House).

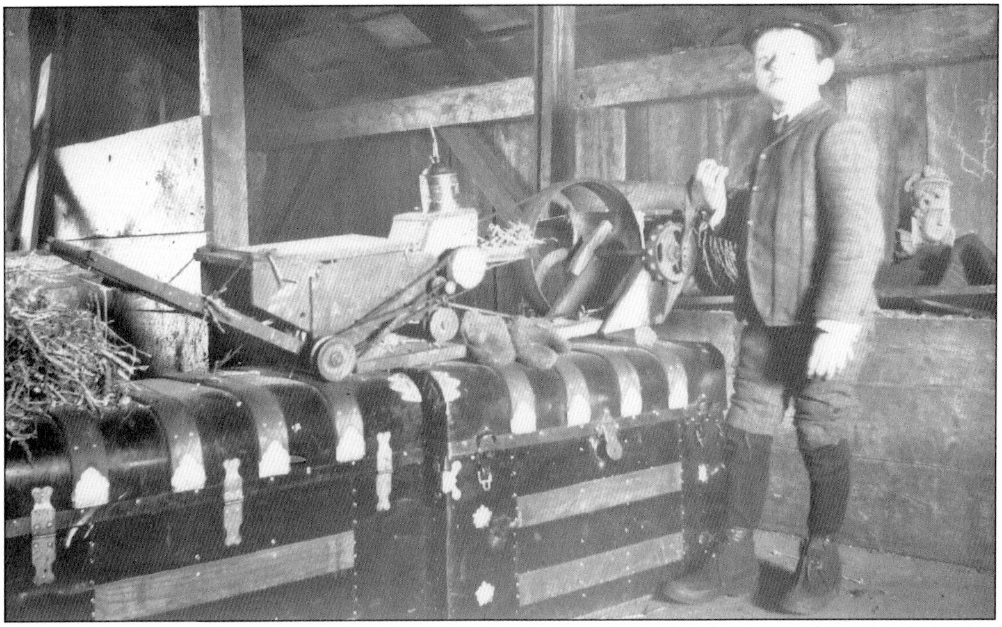

GRANARY BARN. Ernest Ovestrud demonstrates a miniature threshing machine built by his brother Melvin. Larger threshers were at one time run by horsepower, and later by steam engines. Ernest operates his machine with a hand-crank in the family's granary barn. A granary barn consisted of a number of bins where grains such as flax, oats, wheat, and barley were stored.

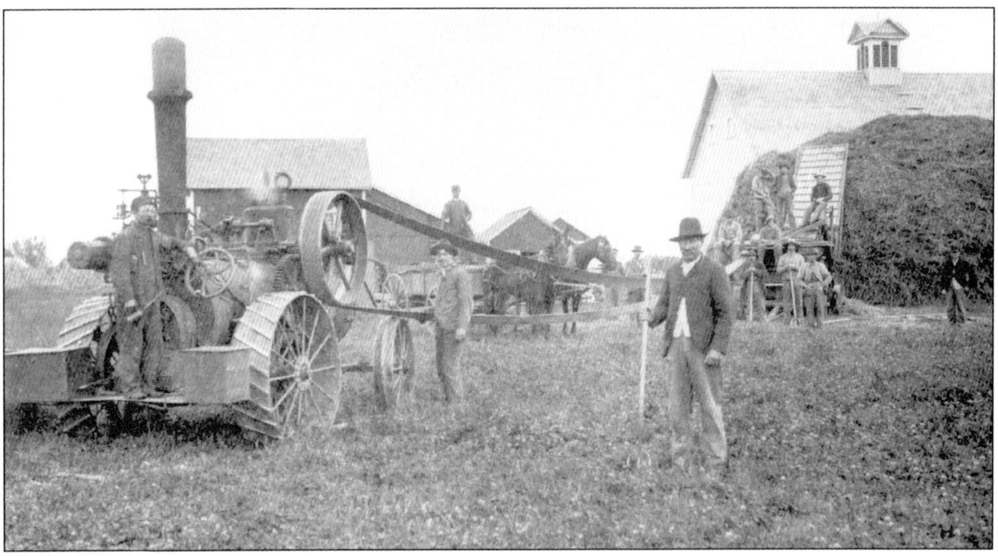

THRESHING CREW. Farmers who needed their grain threshed would work collectively on each other's farms. Farm wives would also help each other cook meals. The steam engine was used to power the threshing machine on the far left, spinning the mechanism through the use of massive conveyor belts. These steamers were extremely loud and cumbersome. Wood, which was thrown into a compartment near the chimney of the machine, was used to keep its engine roaring. When the water level was too low in the engine, the boiler would often explode. Men stand on top of the stacks shown in the background, pitching down bundles into the thresher. These machines could jam easily, so bundles had to be set into the machine very precisely.

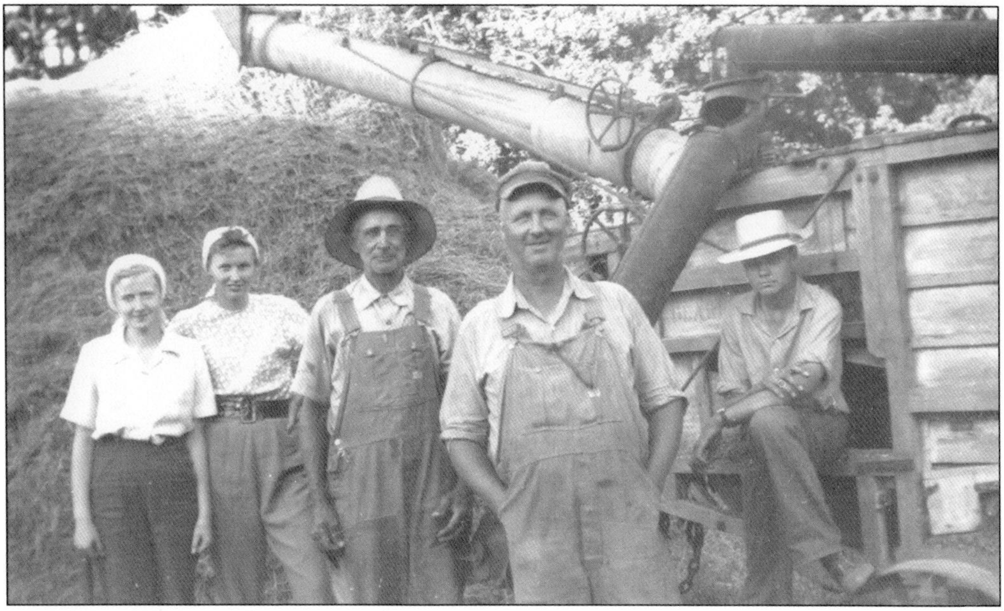

THRESHING GRAIN. The group of threshers shown here at Henry Larson's farm in 1949, from left to right, are Marie Ann Sandemoen, Georgia Kroshus, Henry Larson, Oscar Kroshus, and Allen Kroshus. When grain bundles were pitched into the threshing machine, the grain would be separated from the stalk and fall down a pipe and into bags. The remaining stalk would be blown out another pipe and onto a haystack. This straw would be used as bedding for cattle, chickens, and hogs.

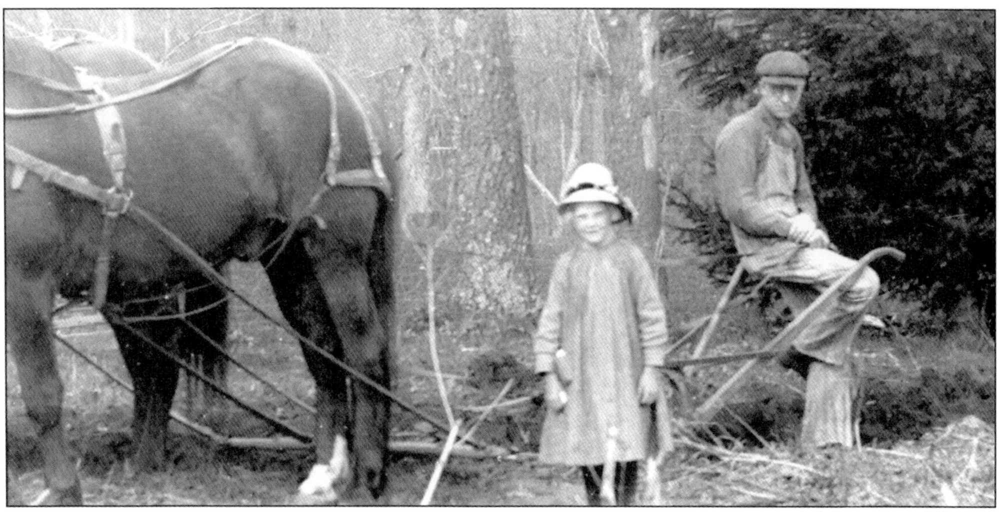

WALKING PLOW. Shown here are Peter J. Rosendahl and his daughter Gladys in their small field with a walking plow. Early pioneers practiced what was known as subsistence farming, growing only enough to feed their own families. The first planting typically consisted of potatoes, rutabagas, or some other root crop. The plow was the most effective tool for burying weeds and aerating the soil. The earliest pioneers used a larger breaking plow to till the virgin prairies, but in the following years the much smaller walking plow could be used. The breaking plow consisted of a coulter that cut a thin strip of earth, a ploughshare that sliced into the soil, and a mould-board that turned the soil over.

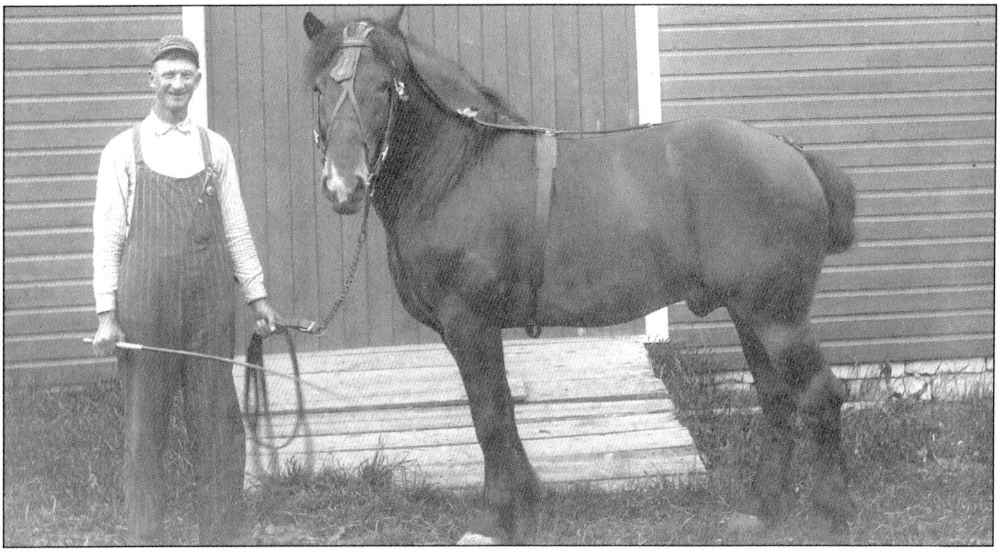

Horse Versus Oxen. Here is an unidentified man and his horse in front of O.O. Roppe's barn. After the 1870s, horses began to replace oxen for work in the field. Though oxen were stronger and could out-pull a team of horses, they were often much slower. The ox needed less care than the horse, feeding off of rough hay and ears of corn, but the horse was much more versatile. It could keep up the right momentum to accommodate reapers, harvesters, and mowers. Oxen were used well into the 1860s, but they were nowhere to be found in the farming community by the 1880s. (Courtesy of the Ballard House.)

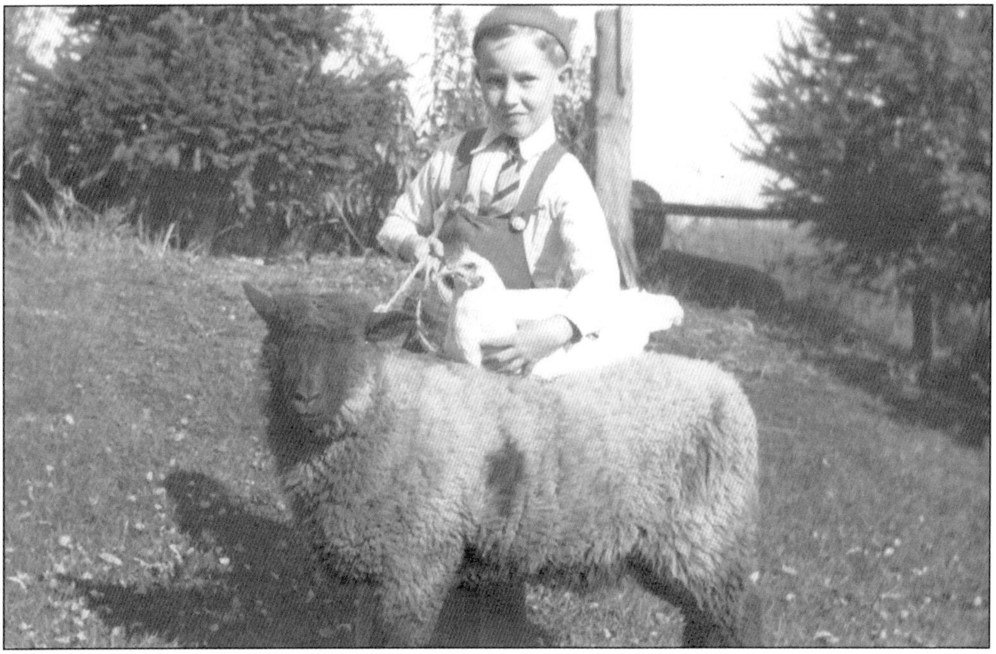

Farm Boy. Harold Muller, the son of Ole and Anna Muller, poses with his hen and ewe on the family farm. Sheep were common on many farms, raised for their wool, which was sheared in spring. And every farm wife had chickens. The hen was used for egg production, while the rooster shrilly announced the beginning of a new day.

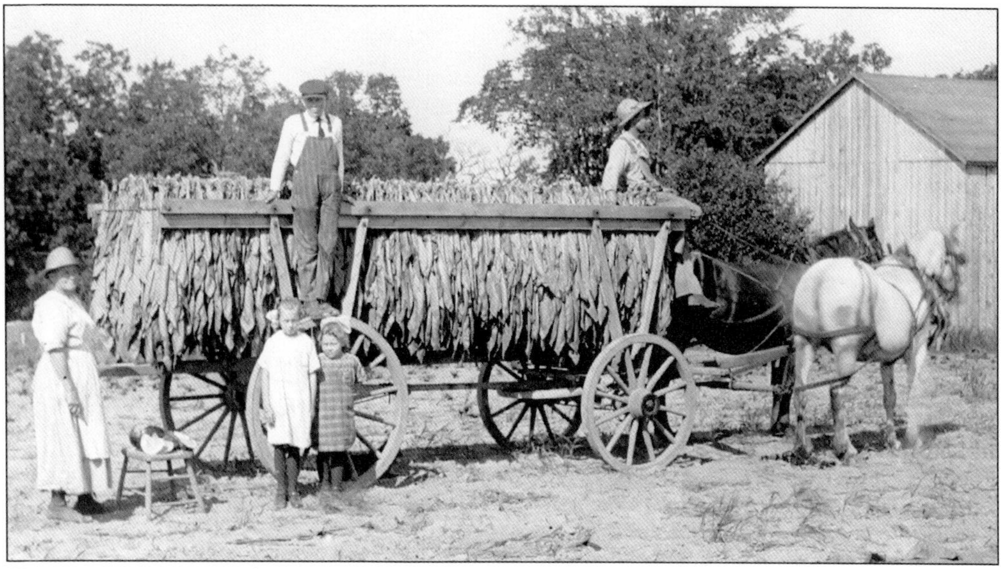

TOBACCO FARMING. The Narveson family is shown here with their tobacco-wagon. Tobacco was a common crop raised in the 1920s by Houston County farmers. The tobacco plants were cut and then spread onto wooden lathes. A special frame was constructed on the tobacco-wagon to accommodate the lathes so as not to damage the leaves. The plants were then transported to a drying shed, shown in the background. An undamaged leaf of tobacco was worth considerably more than one with a hole burrowed into it.

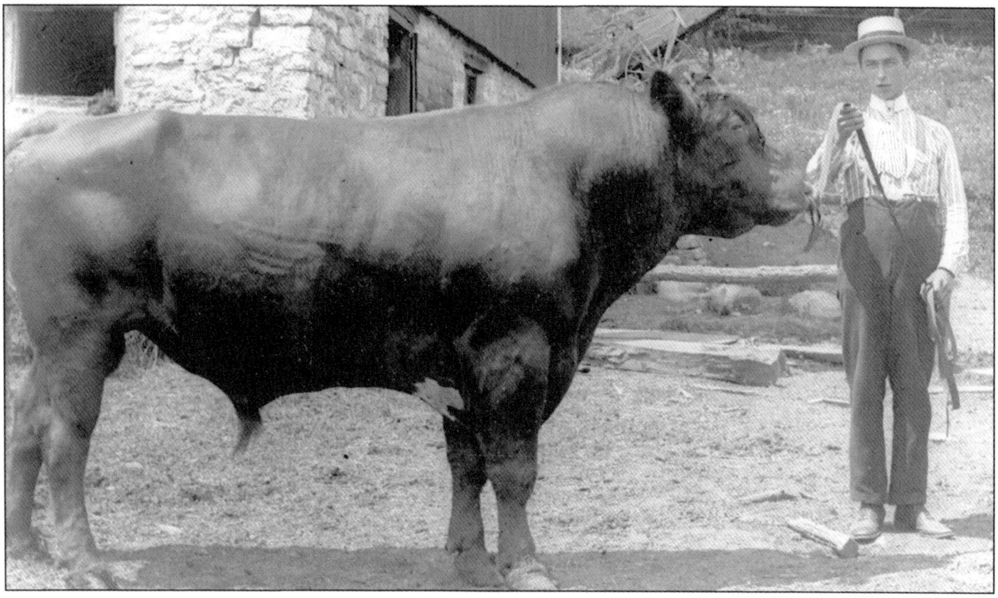

CATTLE. An unidentified man poses with a full-size bull on the Kroshus farm. Cattle were first imported into this country for draft-work, and later developed into either dairy or beef cattle. Heifers such as the Holstein and Jersey were, and continue to be, used for producing milk, while bulls such as the Angus or Hereford are used for breeding and beef. Notice the nose-ring and strap. Depending on the bull's demeanor, a long stick could be attached to keep the animal at a reasonably safe distance.

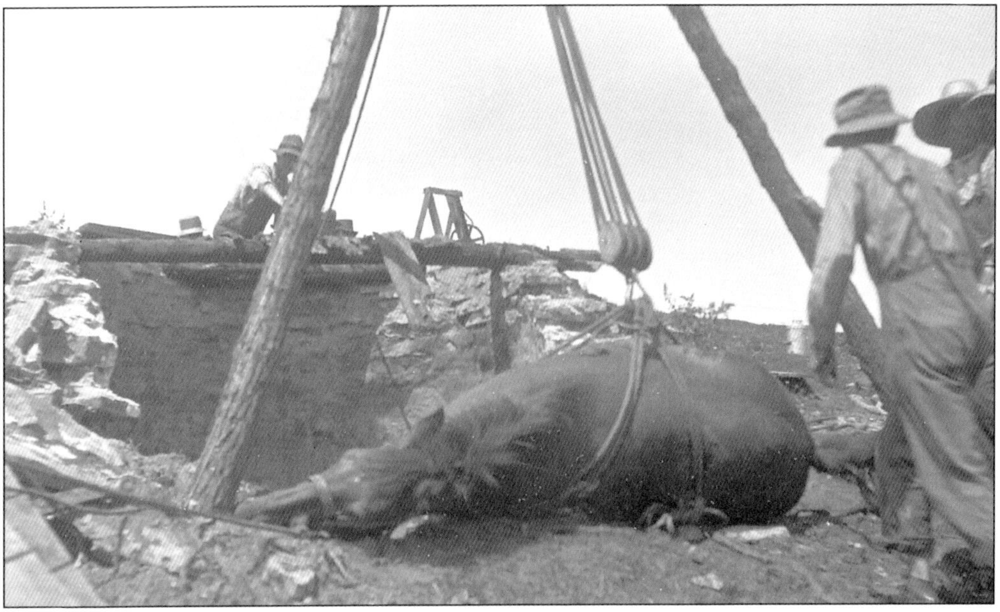

HORSE IN CISTERN. Three unidentified men pull out a horse that has fallen into a cistern on Thor Kolsrud's farm in 1917. Essentially, cisterns were reservoirs for collecting water from rainspouts or water-wells, and were common on most farms because they provided a good water supply. They were usually built next to a house, barn, or windmill, and were about 10 feet in depth. They were also built inside farm homes and used for cold storage.

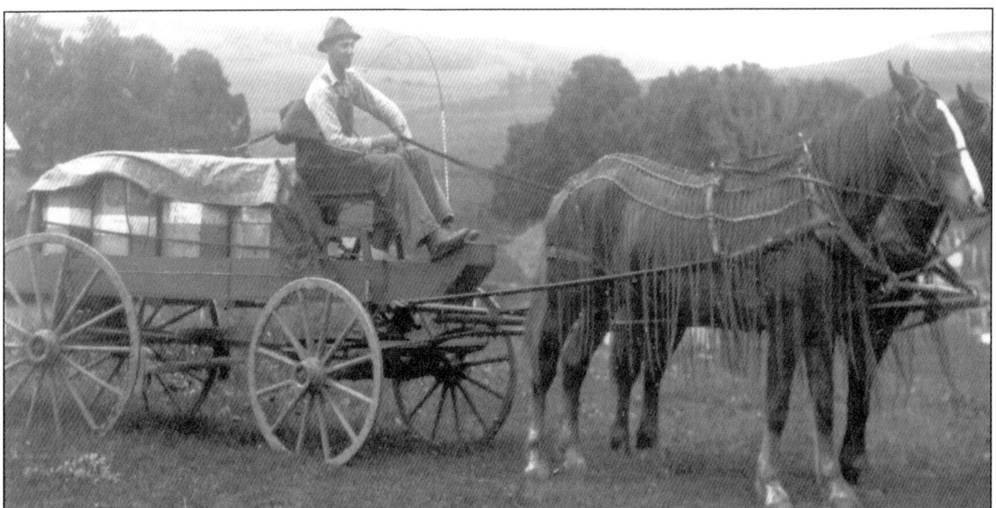

TRANSPORTING CREAM. This unidentified driver transports cream containers from area farms to the town's creamery. Farmers were once paid by the inch for their milk. Nels Onsgard opened the first creamery in Spring Grove in 1883. The business went through a number of owners in the succeeding years. By 1923, area farmers had organized a cooperative to counteract the poor compensation they were receiving from previous owners. Their resolution is clearly stated in this advertisement: "Sell your cream to us and receive just what it brings less the actual cost of manufacture. Buy your butter from us and get the best there is at actual cost. Do not use Substitutes. There is no substitute for Butter."

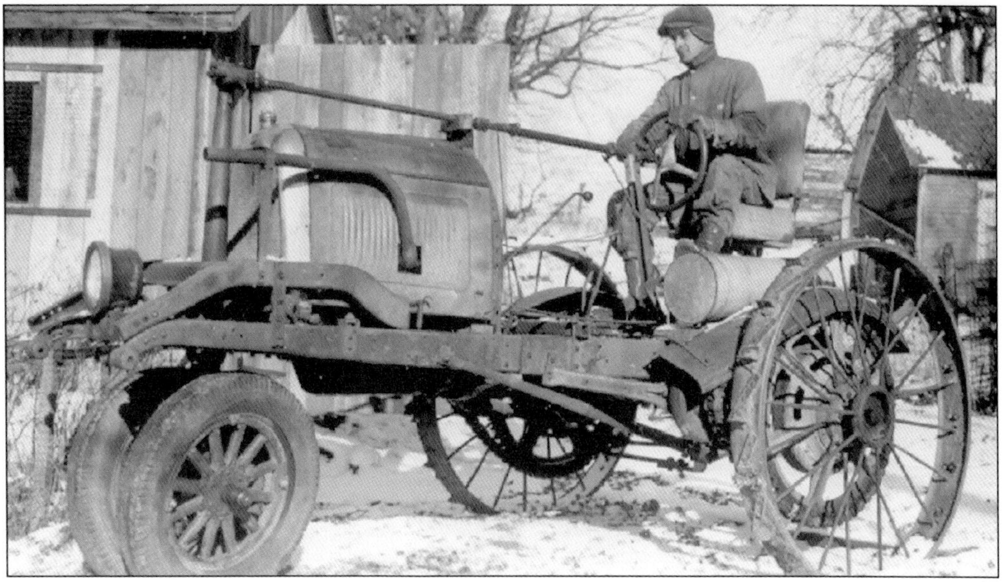

A NEW KIND OF TRACTOR. The Whippet had a short life in the annals of automotive history. It was introduced by the Willys-Overland Company of Ohio in 1926. It was named after the Whippet dog because the vehicle was small but swift. The inventive Melvin Larson used a Whippet engine as the power-source for this homemade tractor. He also built a wood-splitter, in which he attached an axe-head to a slowly revolving wheel. On particularly hot days, Larson was known to take long breaks from his farm work in order to cool off in a water trough.

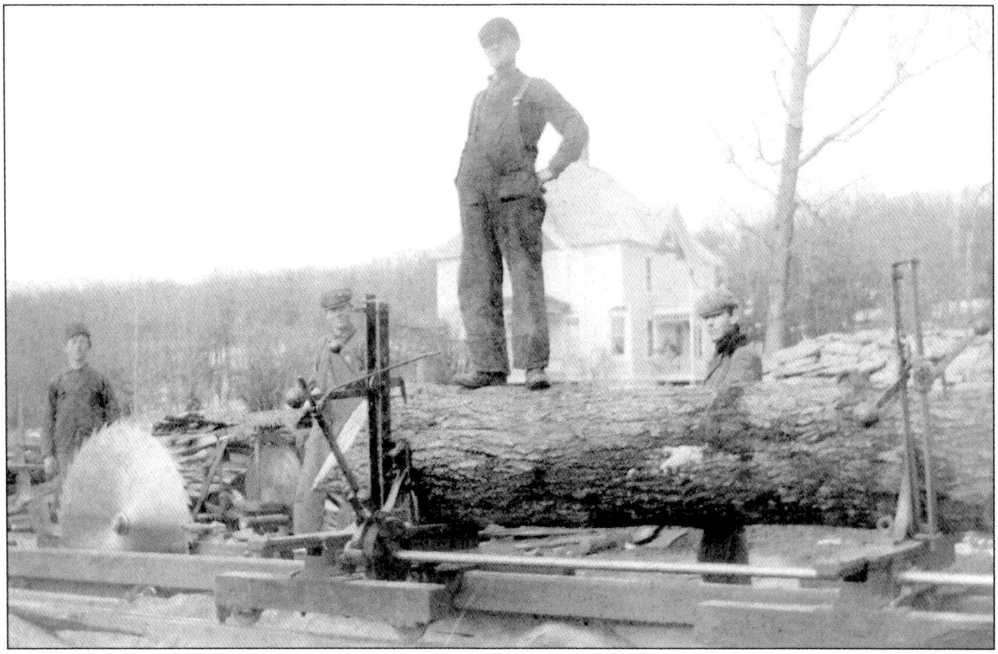

PORTABLE SAW MILLS. Three unidentified men saw logs on the Andreas Hallan farm. One way farmers could get extra income was by selling their timber. Early on, it was easier to have someone come out to the farm and cut logs with a portable saw mill, rather than hauling them to the town mill. These machines were powered by a steam engine or tractor.

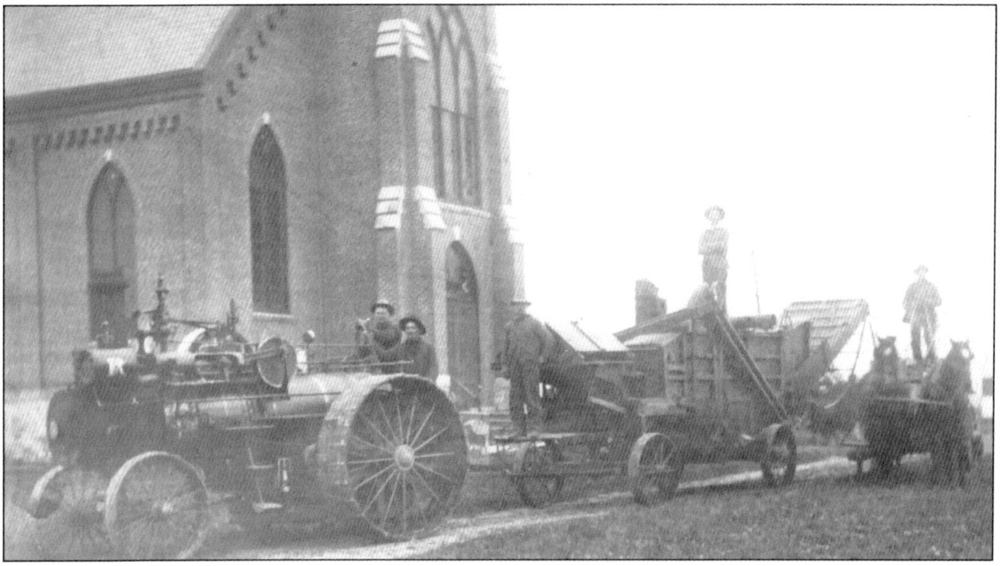

SOLIE'S STEAMER. Carl Solie and his men demonstrate a Russell Steamer and thresher in front of the Spring Grove church. From a 1917 issue of the *Spring Grove Herald*:

> *It is necessary in every community to have a supply of good water, and in order to get this it is necessary to have a man who understands how to get that supply. In this respect Mr. Carl Solie can be referred to as the man for the job. He not only has the experience in drilling and driving wells, but he has the necessary equipment to do the work quickly and in the proper manner. In connection with his well-business Mr. Solie handles a line of pumps and the Ideal, Samson and Woodman windmills. Besides supplying water for this community Mr. Solie has a portable saw mill, and is ever ready to saw lumber. Mr. Solie also sells Russell & Company's threshing machines and the Garden City self feeders.*

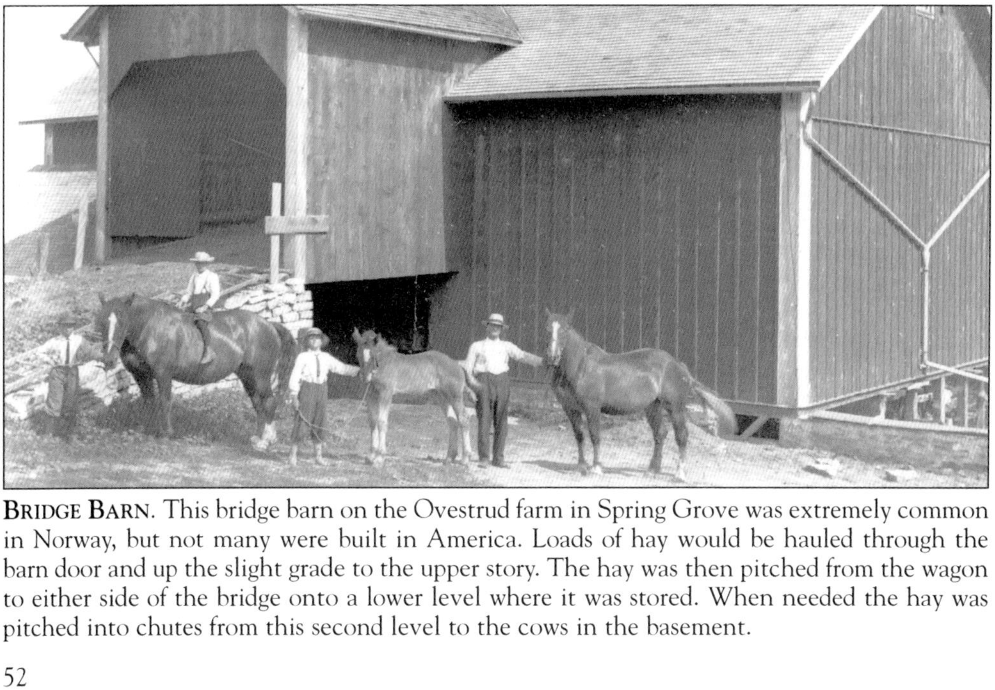

BRIDGE BARN. This bridge barn on the Ovestrud farm in Spring Grove was extremely common in Norway, but not many were built in America. Loads of hay would be hauled through the barn door and up the slight grade to the upper story. The hay was then pitched from the wagon to either side of the bridge onto a lower level where it was stored. When needed the hay was pitched into chutes from this second level to the cows in the basement.

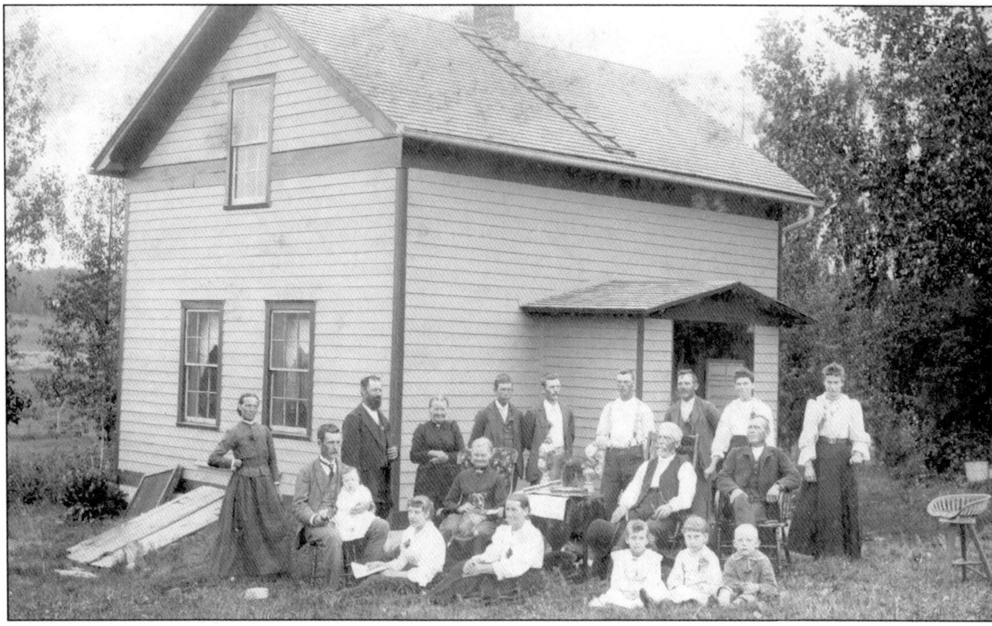

FAMILY GATHERING. A group of relatives are shown here at the farm home of Borger Dvergsten. Dvergsten was born in Hadeland, Norway, in 1825, and immigrated to America in 1866 with his wife, Gudbjor. Notice the ladder built onto the roof. This was used to gain access to the chimney, which often needed cleaning. Homes such as this were usually made up of one or two rooms, as well as an upper loft. Dvergsten farmed his entire life. He placed this advertisement in an 1898 issue of the *Spring Grove Herald*: "Hay for sale. I will sell a quantity of first-class wild hay grown on rich bottom land." Dvergsten died in 1920, at 95. He was, at that time, the oldest man in the history of Spring Grove.

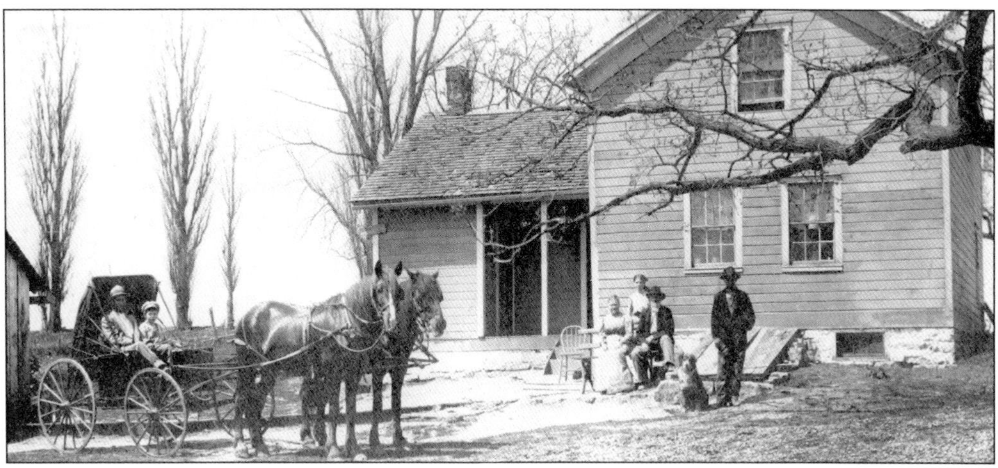

TYPICAL FARM HOME. The Gronvold home gives a perfect example of the common L-house found on many Midwestern farms. An unidentified boy and man sit in the buggy, while Ole and Barbro Gronvold sit next to their children, Benora and Odin. The house has a typical porch and cellar, as well as wooden roof-shingles. These plain-looking homes were subject to various alterations and additions through the years. Decorations such as fancy railings, columns, and windows could be purchased from catalogs. Lightning-rod salesmen were common, and many homes would litter their roofs with these ornate poles.

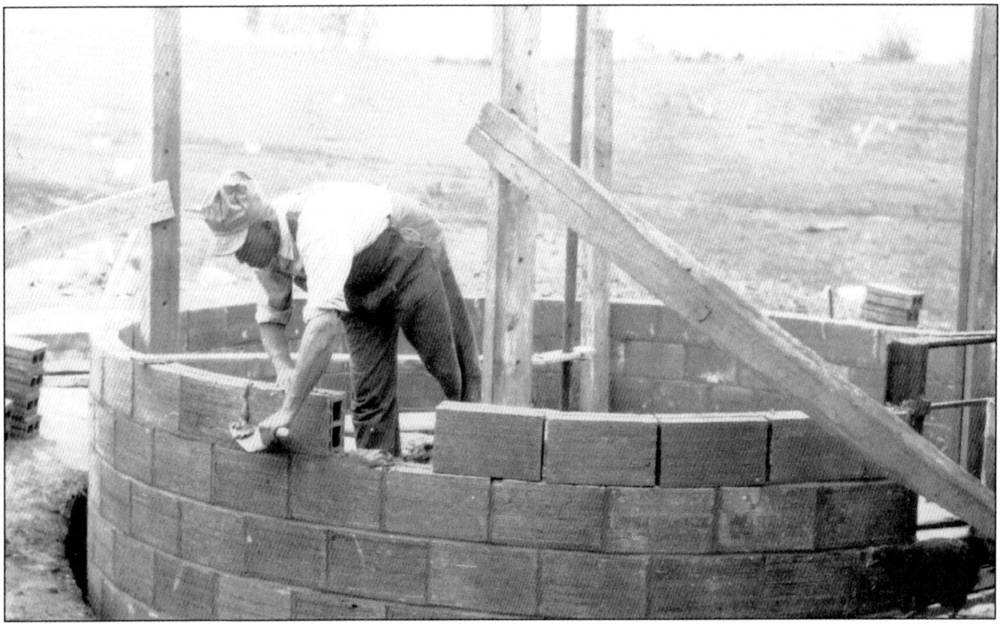

BUILDING A SILO. The *Spring Grove Herald* noted that, "Most farmers feel more or less anxiety about their corn crop this year, but those who feel less anxiety are those on whose farm stand silos. The reason is simple. The silo makes it possible to save corn that might otherwise, owing to immaturity, be almost wholly wasted. The farmer, therefore, who has been thinking of building a silo should get into action." Requirements of a silo were also included: "The walls must be air-tight and smooth inside, the best type of silo is round, the roof should be waterproof, and the structure should be substantial as it has to stand much pressure."

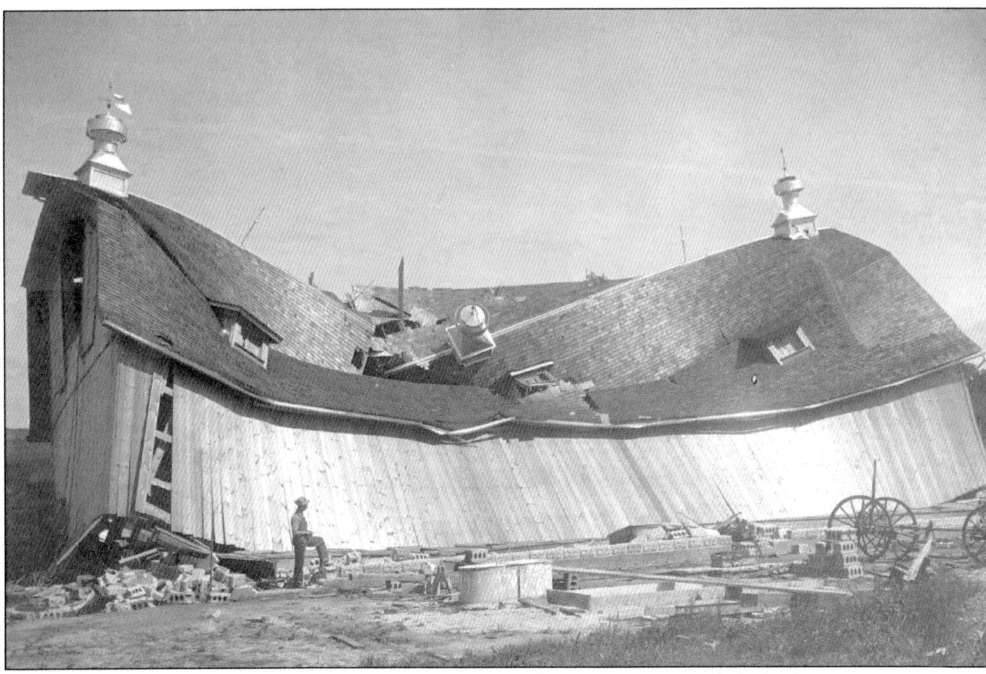

COLLAPSED BARN. An unidentified Spring Grove farmer pauses in disbelief.

Three

Heart of the Community

After building their homes and tilling their lands, the pioneers' next priority was to erect centers of faith and learning. The heart of nearly every newly established pioneer community was the church. It was not only a place for worship, but for socializing and even for business. Residents would trade horses, hire threshers, and take care of other business matters after church services as well as discuss politics and news from the old country. Early Norwegian churches also featured some of the community's first public art. Painters such as Herbjørn Gausta were commissioned to paint altars, like the one pictured in this chapter.

Before a church was built, missionaries, lay preachers, and circuit riders would sometimes come to Spring Grove to preach. One of the first was Ulrik Koren, an ordained minister of the Norwegian Synod who traveled throughout many of the surrounding counties. Because of his extensive mission-field, he visited Spring Grove only twice a year.

In 1855, the Norwegian Evangelical Lutheran congregation was officially organized and became a member of the Norwegian Synod. The congregation's first task was to build a church and find a pastor who could preach regularly. Hans Myrah is largely credited with organizing the construction of this stone church, which was started in 1860, but not completed until 1868, because of the Civil War. Fritz Clauson became its first pastor.

Another important aspect of the community was the school. Before a structure was built, classes were held once a week in various homes. One of the first peripatetic teachers was Cornelius Narveson. He conducted his lessons in a variety of locations, receiving only meals and small compensation. In 1857, the first schoolhouse was built, and James McDonald was hired as its teacher. Many teachers were adamant about speaking only English while school was in session, and Norwegian students were often severely punished for using their native language.

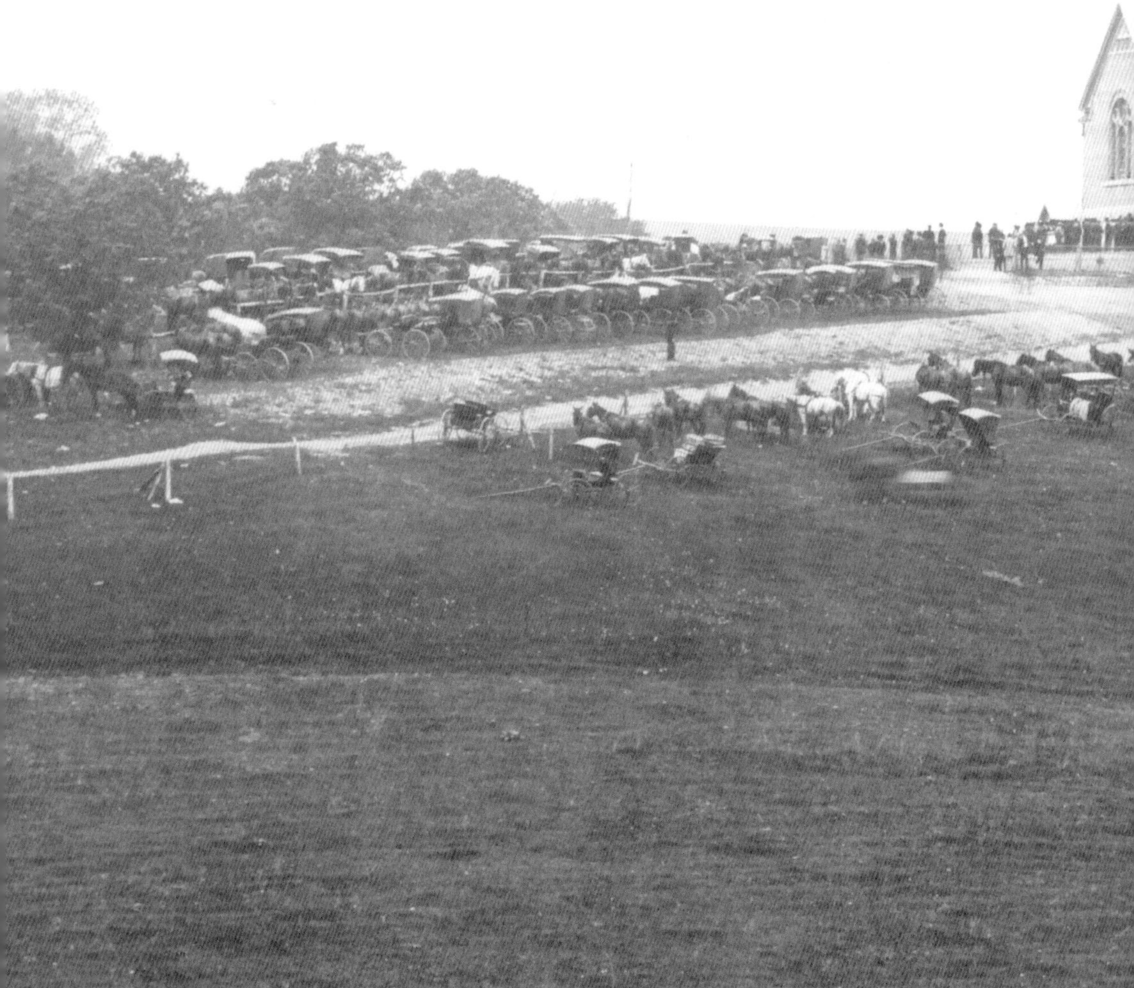

HEART OF THE COMMUNITY. This photograph shows the 1908 dedication of the new

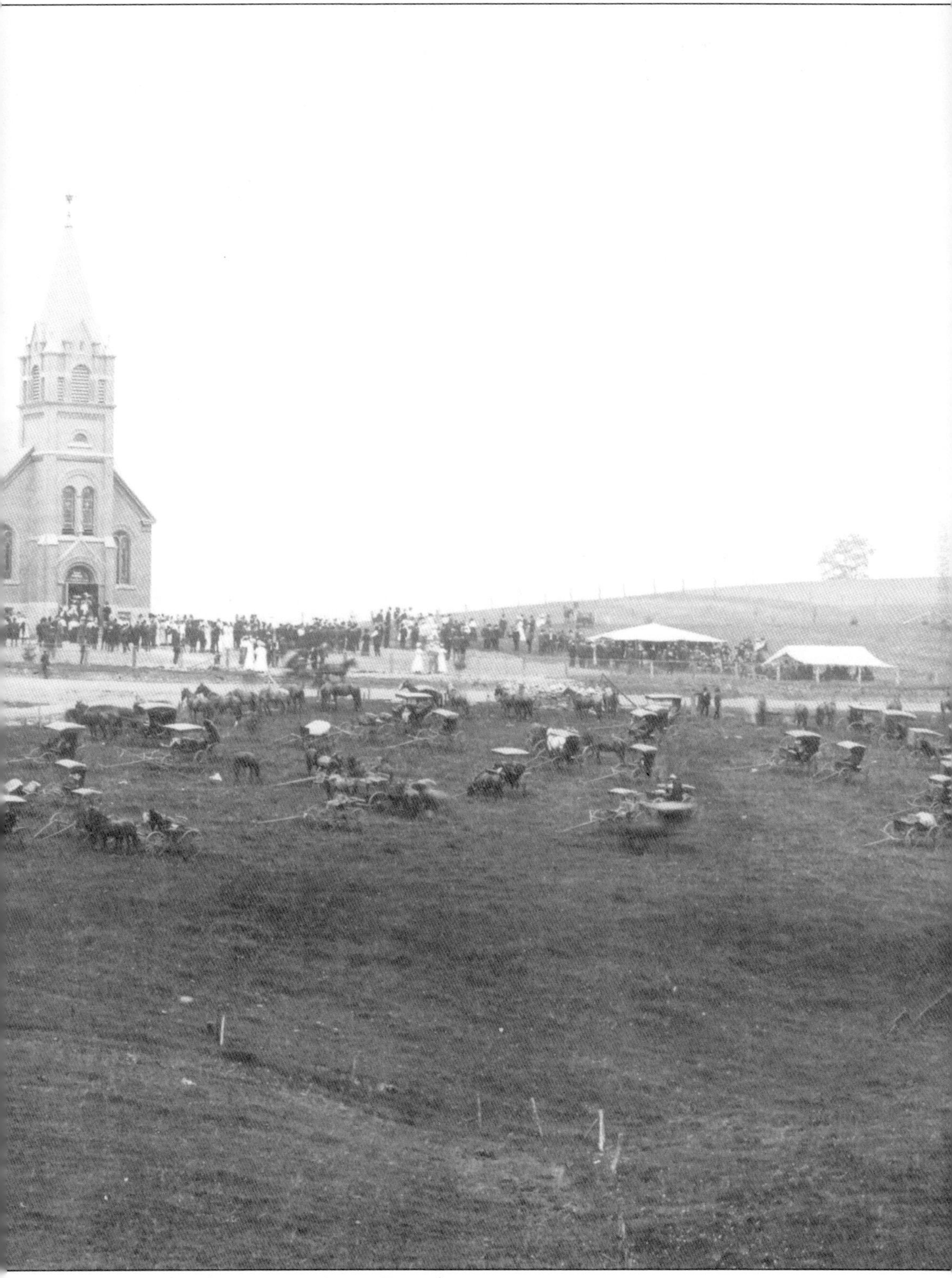

Wilmington church, in Spring Grove Township.

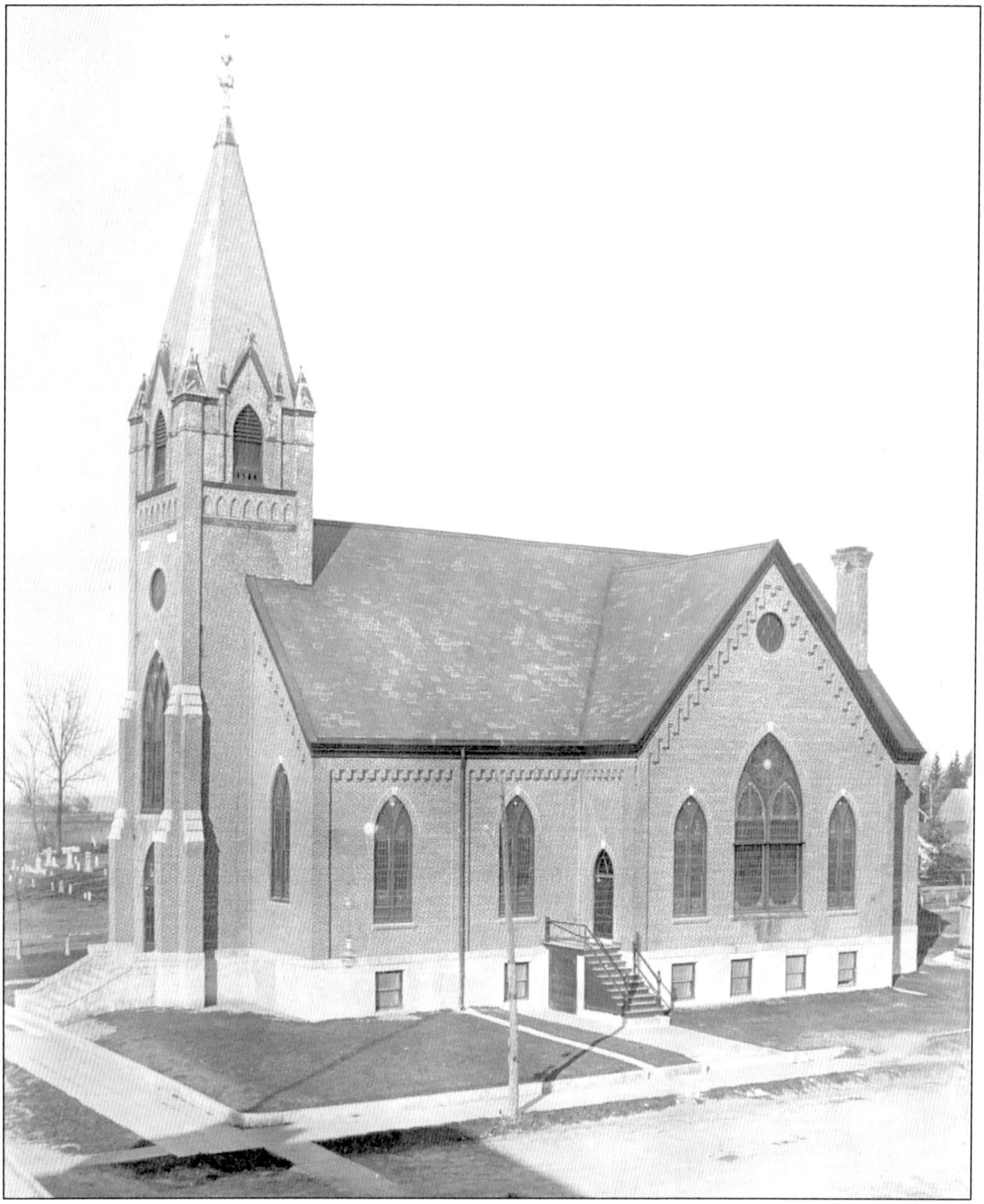

NORWEGIAN EVANGELICAL LUTHERAN CHURCH. This church, built in 1893, stands to this day. From a 1907 issue of the *Spring Grove Herald*:

> *The pioneers came practically empty-handed, but not empty-hearted. Willing hands in obedience to thoughtful brains soon transformed the wilderness to homes. The pioneers progressed materially, but there was something lacking. In Norway they had their churches and pastors, but here they were as sheep without a shepherd. But in February 1854 Reverend Koren, who at that time had a very extensive mission-field, visited Spring Grove and held services in Jorgen Quarve's house. This was the first Norwegian Lutheran service held in Spring Grove. After several other visits, Reverend Koren again held services here June 19th and 20th, 1855 and on this date it is supposed that the Norwegian Ridge Evangelical Lutheran Congregation was organized.*

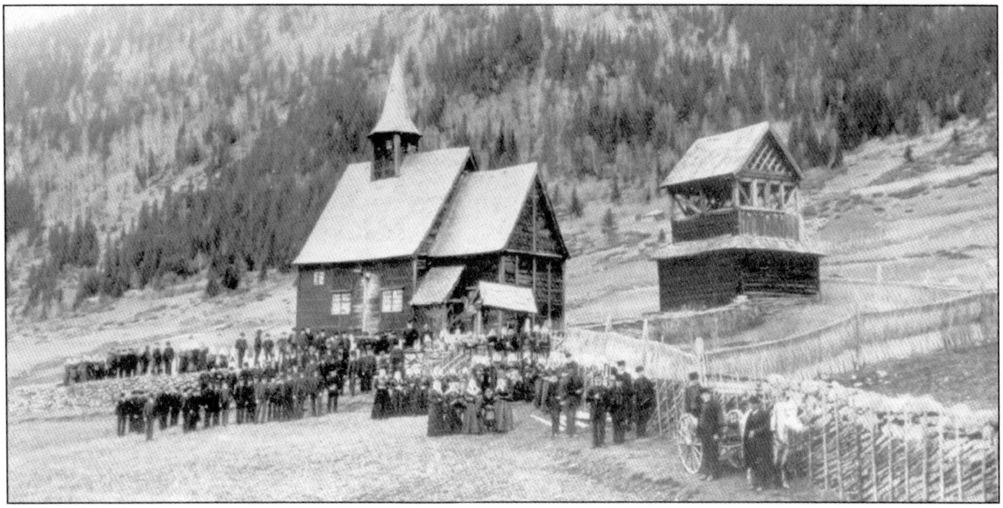

STAVE CHURCH. This is the Lommen stave church in Norway's Valdres Valley. Joren Lommen and her parents came from this area and eventually settled in Spring Grove. This church was built in 1200, just as the Viking Age was ending. In 1015, when Saint Olav ordained that Christianity was to become the religion of Norway, many of these churches were built. The technique of using *staves* (vertical posts) was employed in their construction. These churches became symbols of Christianity, but their design still reflected a pagan past.

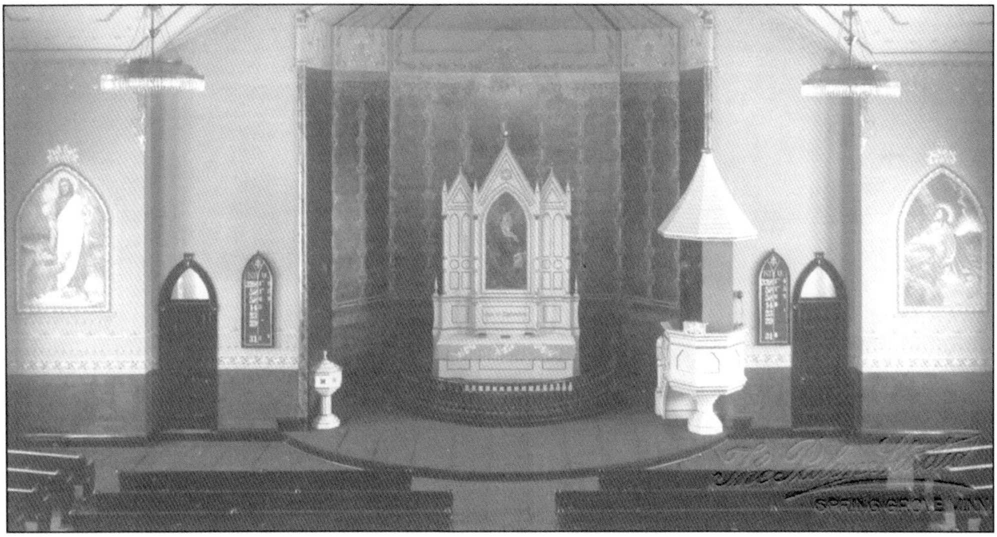

CHURCH INTERIOR. This is the interior of the second church built by the Norwegian Evangelical Lutheran Congregation. Though an interior photo of the first church has been lost to time, an interesting story survives from Pastor A.O. Johnson:

> *It became generally whispered that the church was not safe, and considerable apprehension was felt on that score. On Sunday, June 6, 1875, confirmation services were held and this fact brought together a large audience. Improvised benches had been made in the gallery by laying planks on supports. While the gathering was waiting for the minister to arrive, one of the planks in the gallery snapped. Some one cried out that the church was falling and the people, already nervous about the church walls, lost all reason, and a panic ensued that for a time threatened dire results. Through windows and doors they threw themselves in unreasoning fear.*

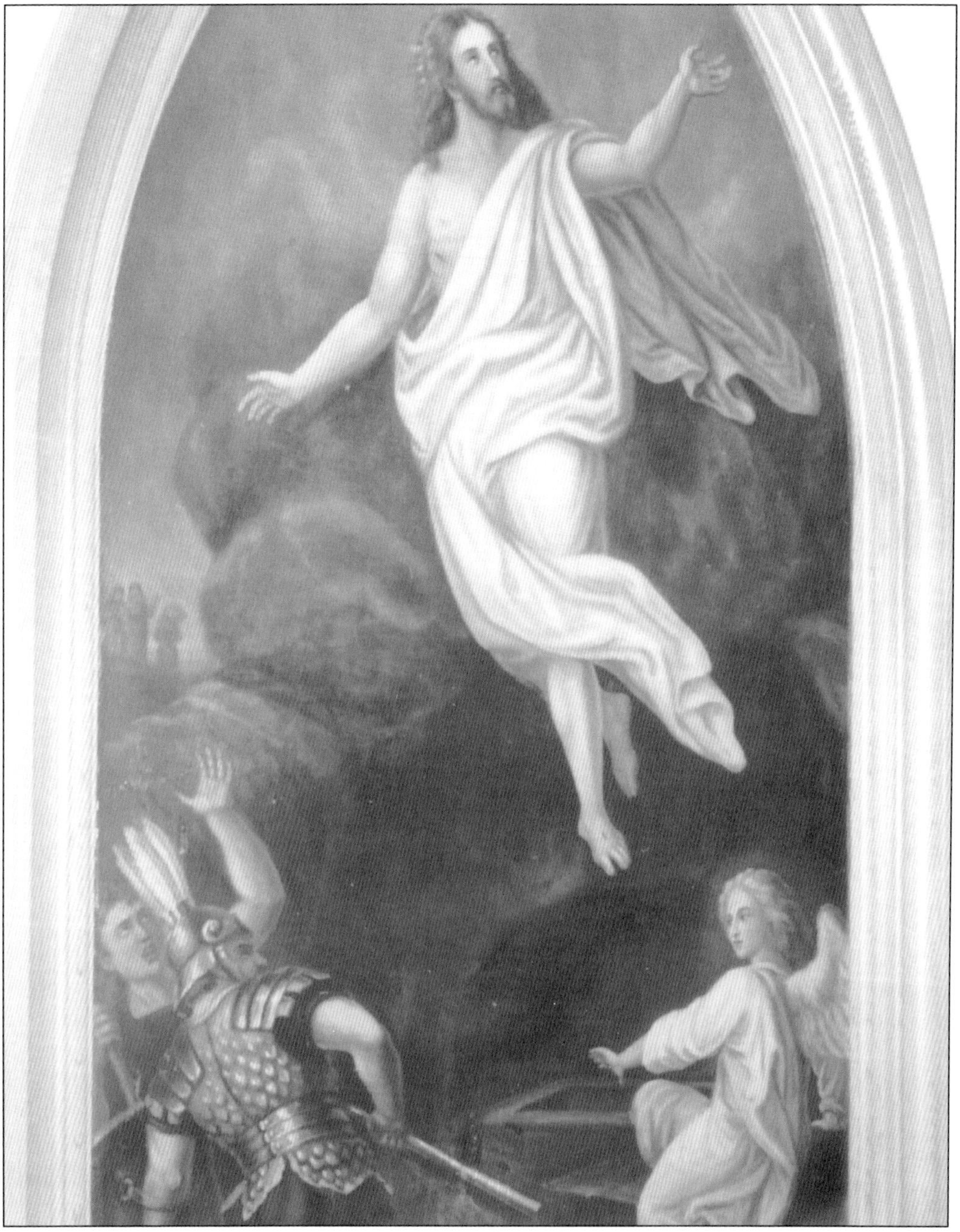

ALTAR PAINTING. Herbjørn Gausta was one of the first professional Norwegian-American artists. Born in Telemark, Norway, he and his family immigrated to Harmony, Minnesota. After attending Luther College in Decorah, Iowa, Gausta was sent to art schools in Norway. Through the efforts of Reverend Ulrik Koren, he received enough money from the community to cover his expenses. The Norwegian community did not support his original artwork, so he resorted to altar paintings, which supplied him with steady income. He produced over 400 of these paintings, ranging in price from $75 to $200, and worked almost exclusively for pastors of the Norwegian Synod, including the Norwegian Evangelical Lutheran Church of Spring Grove. For this congregation, Gausta created the above work, *The Ascension of Christ*.

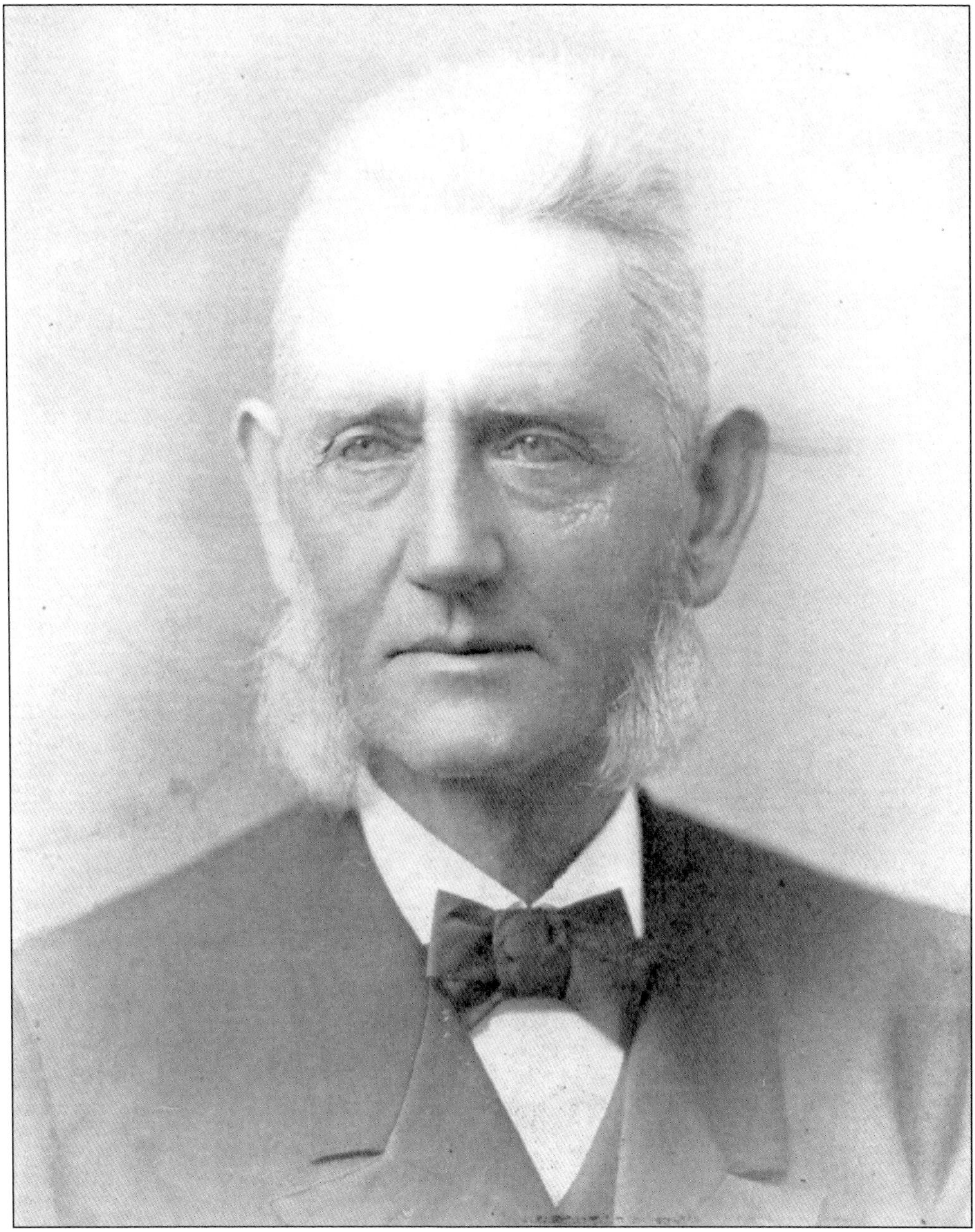

ULRIK KOREN. Koren was the first ordained minister of the Norwegian Synod to conduct services in Spring Grove. Because his mission-field was so large, he held services here only twice a year. During one of his visits, in 1857, he performed communion for over 60 people, christened 21 newborns, catechized 8, held confirmation, and regular church services—all in the course of one long day that extended well into the night. Koren's wife, Elisabeth, kept a detailed diary of her pioneer experiences. Her entry for Sunday, February 5, 1854, describes her feelings while her husband was off conducting his first services in Spring Grove: "Well, I am alone again and will no doubt be alone all week. How I long for the time when there will be a little less traveling, a little more reasonable arrangement, for this one is really all wrong, and, what is worse, is not likely to get better soon." (Courtesy of the Norwegian-American Historical Association.)

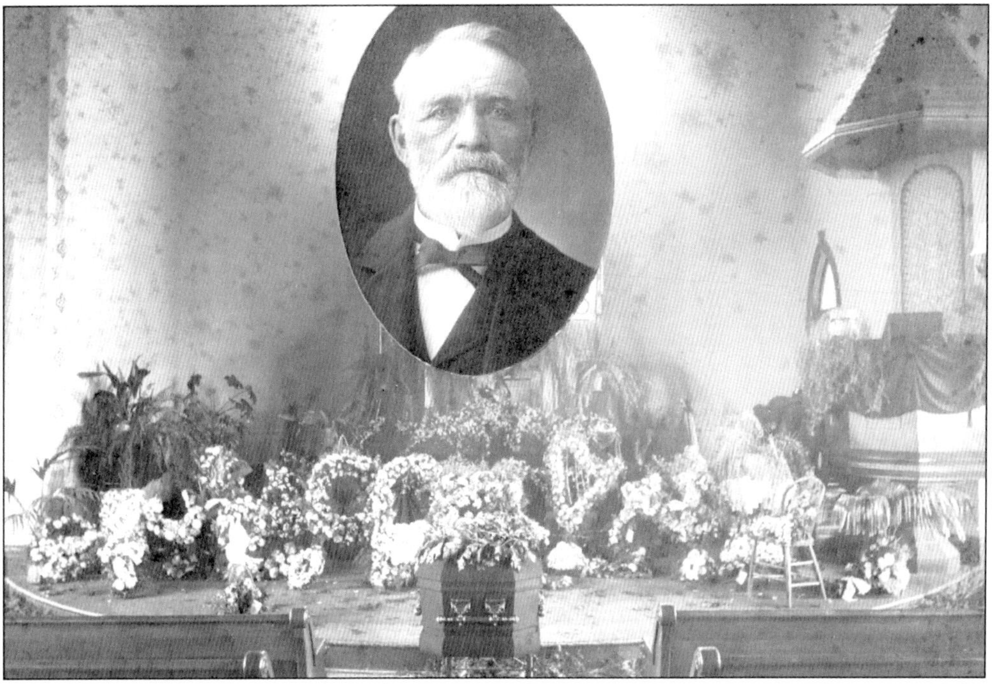

Reverend Reque's Funeral. Styrk Reque was born in Voss, Norway, in 1836. In 1845, he immigrated with his parents to Koshkonong, Wisconsin. He later went to St. Louis where he studied at Concordia Theological Seminary for three years. In 1865, he married Cecilia Anderson and they had nine children. In 1871, he accepted a call from the Spring Grove, Wilmington, and Black Hammer congregations. Quoting from his successor, Pastor A.O. Johnson: "Shortly after his arrival he applied himself to the Herculean task of turning public opinion against the saloon, which he found exerting a cursed influence in the neighborhood. And after five years of fearless work he succeeded in ridding the town of the liquor traffic in 1876, and Spring Grove has since been known as a saloonless town." Reque died in 1910.

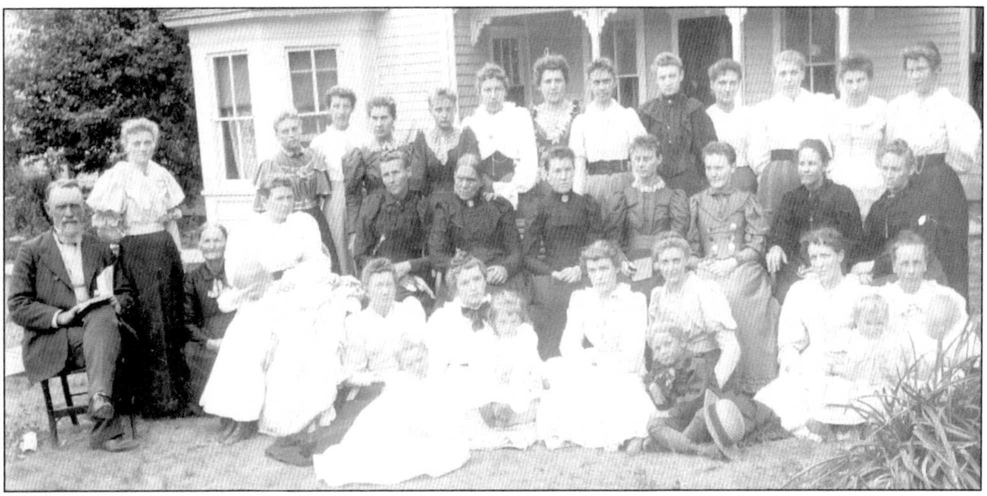

Ladies' Aid. Members of the Ladies' Aid are shown here at the home of Mons Fladager in the early 1900s. The organization held fundraising activities for both the community and missions all over the world. (Courtesy of Lee and Louise Sundet.)

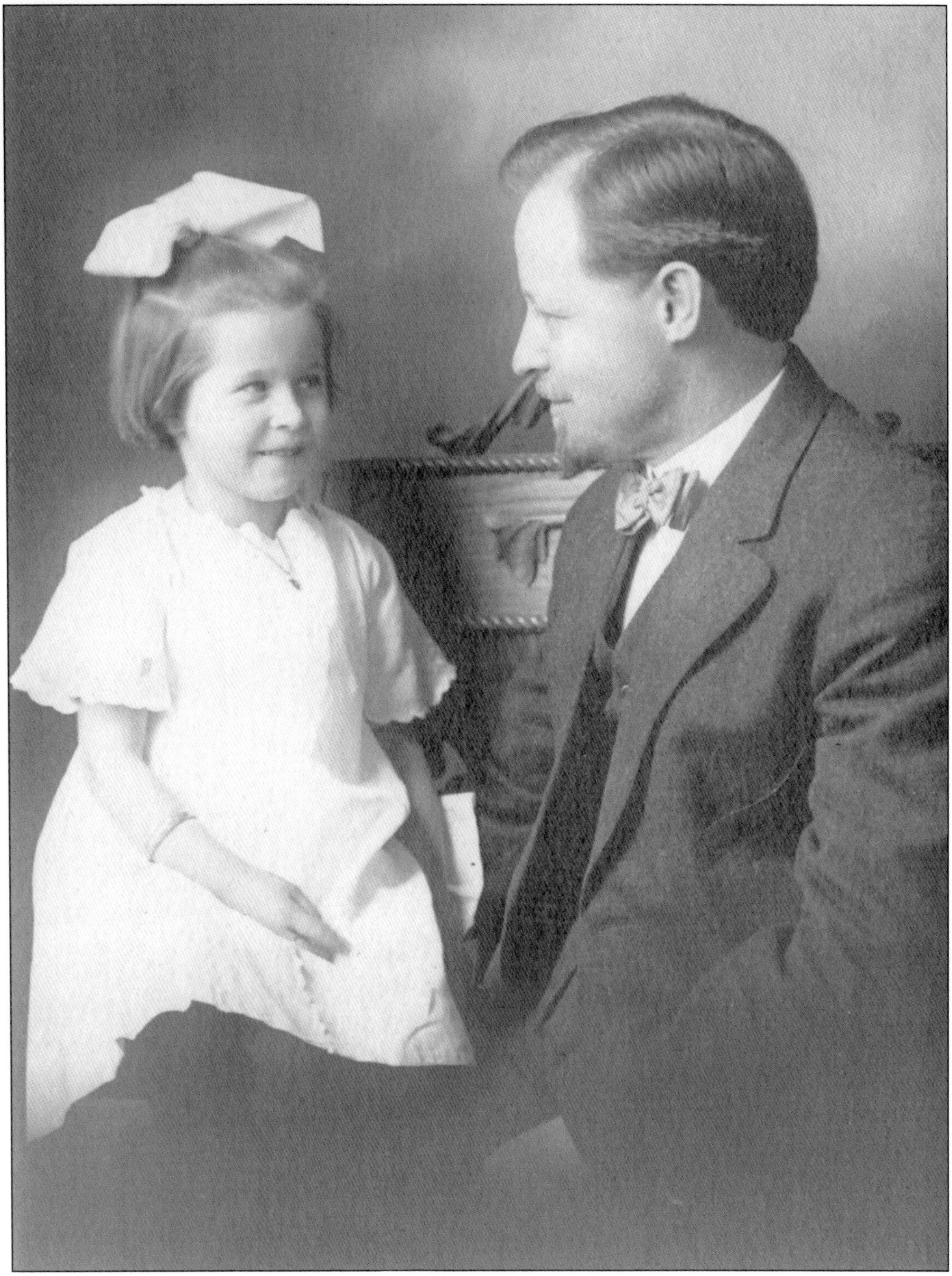

PASTOR A.O. JOHNSON. Pastor Johnson poses with his daughter Clara. Johnson was called to serve the congregation in October 1910. He had previously graduated from Luther College in 1891, training at Luther Theological Seminary. He was ordained in 1894, and began his pastoral work under the president of the Norwegian Synod, H.A. Preus. Johnson's pastorate in Spring Grove lasted 22 years. In 1924, he was the major force behind the creation of the parochial school, which gave children the opportunity to be excused from public school for a few hours each day to receive religious training.

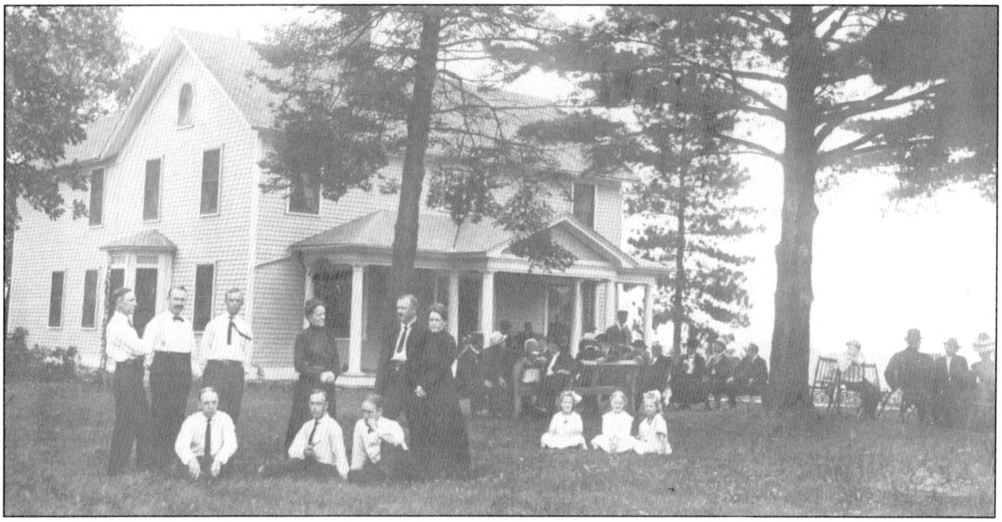

THE PARSONAGE. A parsonage was always provided t the current pastor and his family, and this particular home was built in 1871 for Reverend Styrk Reque. In 1857, Fritz Clauson arrived to become the first official pastor in Spring Grove. The congregation of the Norwegian Evangelical Lutheran Church of Norwegian Ridge purchased 60 acres of land from George Timansen, and the following notice appeared in an 1857 issue of *Kirketidende*: "Vacant charges in America. Norwegian Ridge, Minnesota and Big Canoe, Iowa. Salary $400 and the usual incidents." This included a log cabin, known as the *praestegaard*, which the congregation had ready for Clauson upon his arrival from Norway.

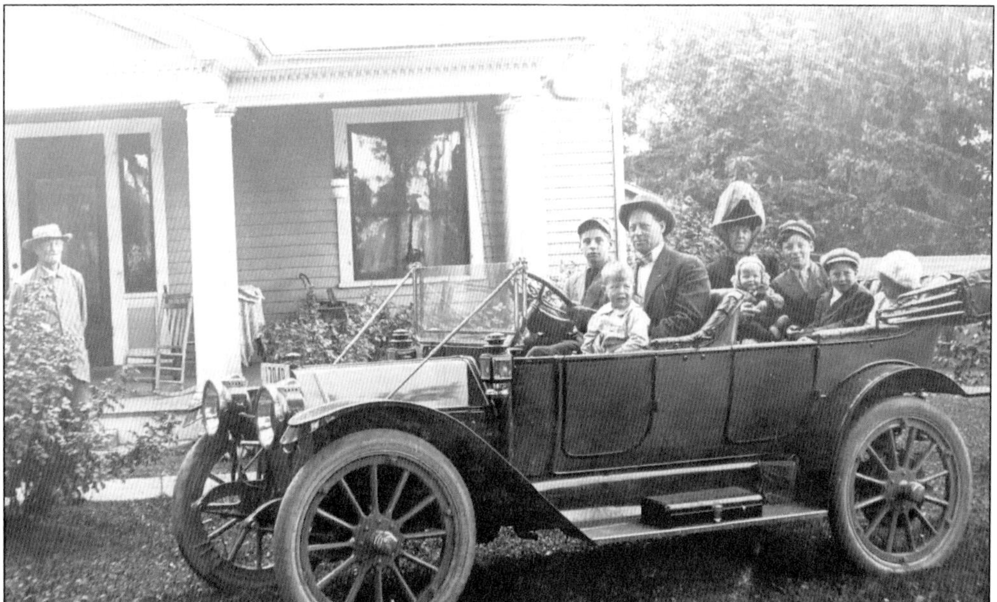

CONGREGATION CAR. This 1912 Buick was given to Pastor A.O. Johnson and his family by the congregation of the Norwegian Evangelical Lutheran Church of Spring Grove. The parsonage, where Johnson and his family lived, is in the background. The man to the far left is the parsonage groundskeeper, Peter Tranby, known to residents as *Presta Per*.

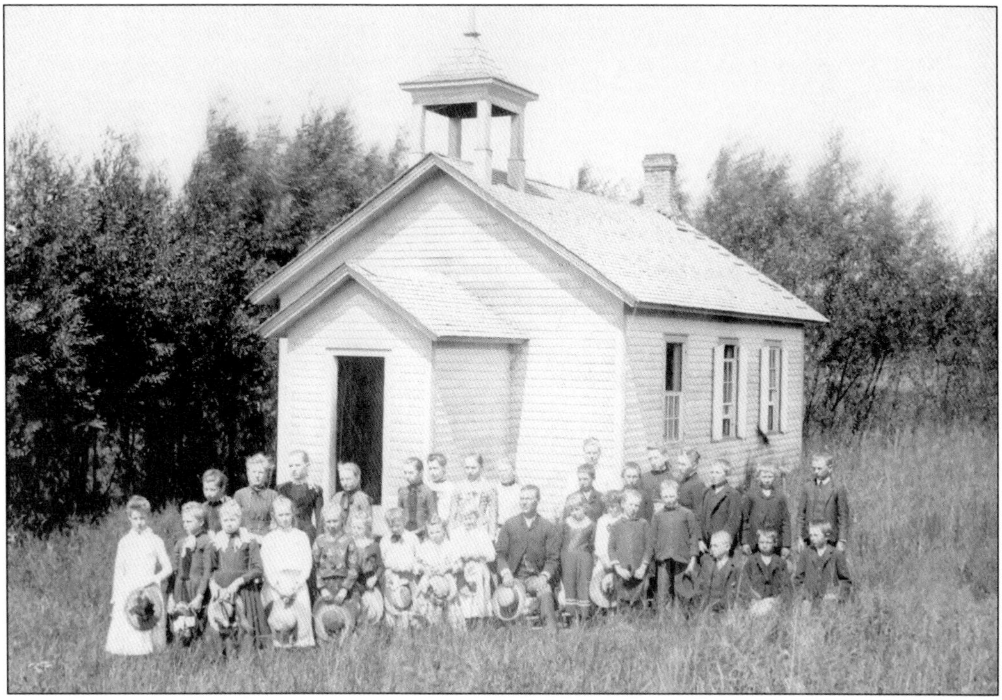

One-Room Country Schoolhouse. Schools were often named after the farmer on whose land it was built. In this case the school was built on land purchased from Embrick Melbraaten, and was therefore named the Melbraaten School. Before schools were erected, teachers and students would often meet in various farm homes in the area. This was known as peripatetic schooling.

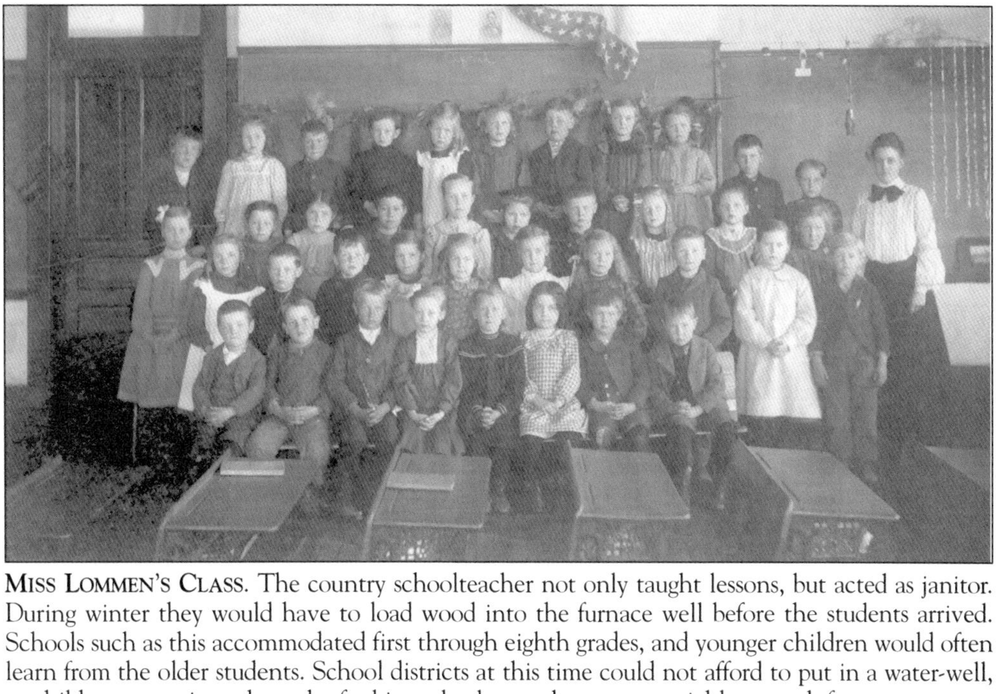

Miss Lommen's Class. The country schoolteacher not only taught lessons, but acted as janitor. During winter they would have to load wood into the furnace well before the students arrived. Schools such as this accommodated first through eighth grades, and younger children would often learn from the older students. School districts at this time could not afford to put in a water-well, so children were given the task of taking a bucket to the nearest neighbor to ask for water.

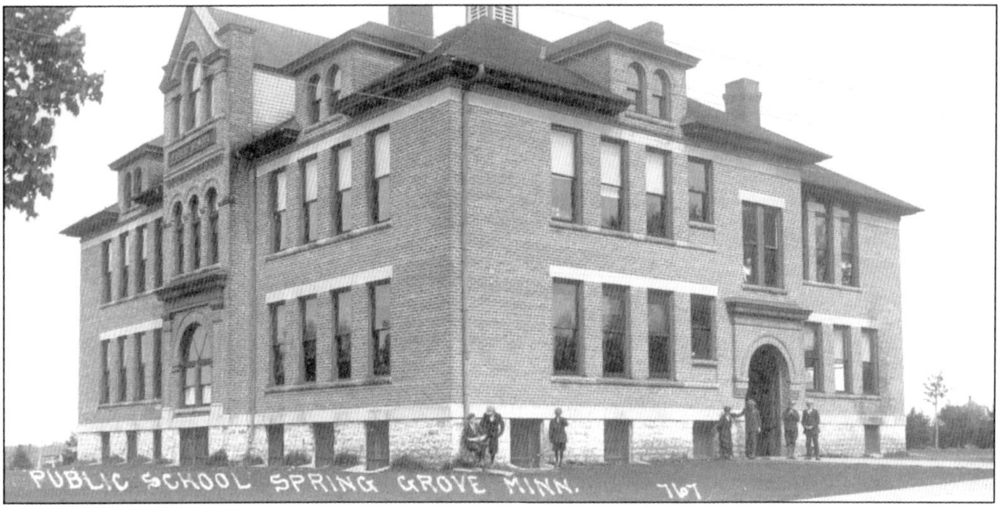

PUBLIC SCHOOL. From an 1899 issue of the *Spring Grove Herald*:

> *Bids for the new schoolhouse were opened last Monday. The work will commence as soon as school closes and the old building can be removed, which will be about the middle of May. The heating apparatus is expected to cost $800, while plans and specifications cost about $150. It will then be seen that the building complete with hot air furnaces will cost within the estimated $10,000, which must be considered very satisfactory especially in view of the great advance that has taken place in the cost of building material. Ingvald Muller of this place has been awarded the contract for furnishing 175,000 bricks to be used in the construction of the new school. This is quite a compliment to the Spring Grove brickyards.*

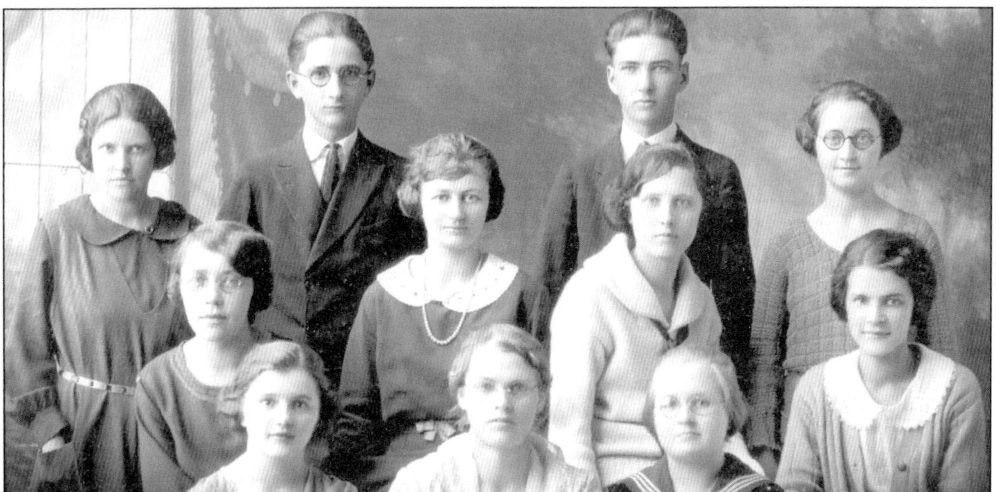

TEACHER TRAINING CLASS. A 1907 issue of the *Spring Grove Herald* stated, "This school will afford an excellent opportunity for the preparation for teaching as well as review of all subjects required for first and second grade certificates. Beginning teachers should make an effort to give perfect attendance during the month." Pictured here, from left to right, are the following: (front row) Alice Halvorson, Miss Nell Bryan (the teacher), and Myrtle Ike; (middle row) Idella Thorson, Minnie Sannes, Norma Rostad, and Julia Glasrud; (back row) Gladys Narveson, Jerome Joerg, Carlton Qualey, and Edna Bagley. Interestingly enough, Carlton Qualey (back row, second from the right) went on to become a professor and wrote many articles on Norwegian immigration.

Four

Merchants and Main Street

Many of Spring Grove's early pioneers were Yankee entrepreneurs. They usually stayed only a few months, or until a better opportunity presented itself in other settlements. The earliest recorded entrepreneur was James Smith, a Pennsylvanian, who established a post-office in 1852. The first town election was held in 1855 at Smith's cabin, and when it was decided that Caledonia would be the seat of Houston County, he promptly moved there.

Other Yankee entrepreneurs soon followed. In 1855, William Banning erected the first gristmill. It was located on Riceford Creek, in the southwestern part of the township. Many interesting stories surround this mill, including one that the millstone was so slow that mice ate each kernel before it was ground. William Hinkley opened a general store in the same year. He was known to sell liquor from his bedroom window at any hour of the night. The following year William Fleming established the Pumpkin Tavern. The name was suggested when Fleming had to build an extra room to accommodate a group of travelers from St. Paul: he ingeniously used pumpkins for the walls.

By the 1860s, after the arrival of an immigrant named Mons Fladager, the business district of Spring Grove became almost exclusively Norwegian. Fladager was to bring prosperity and organization to the town, and his importance and influence will be considered in following pages. Dr. Thor Jensen was a respected physician in Spring Grove for over 40 years. "Calls promptly attended to; night calls must be accompanied by good conveyance," read one of his advertisements in 1900. E.J. Foss, who owned a Ford dealership, did much to bolster Spring Grove's economy with his automobile sales. These and many other Norwegian entrepreneurs soon began to establish themselves in Spring Grove. By 1870, according to a United States census, there were three general stores, one brewery, two shoemaker shops, three blacksmiths, one saloon, one hotel, one wagon-maker shop, and one veterinarian.

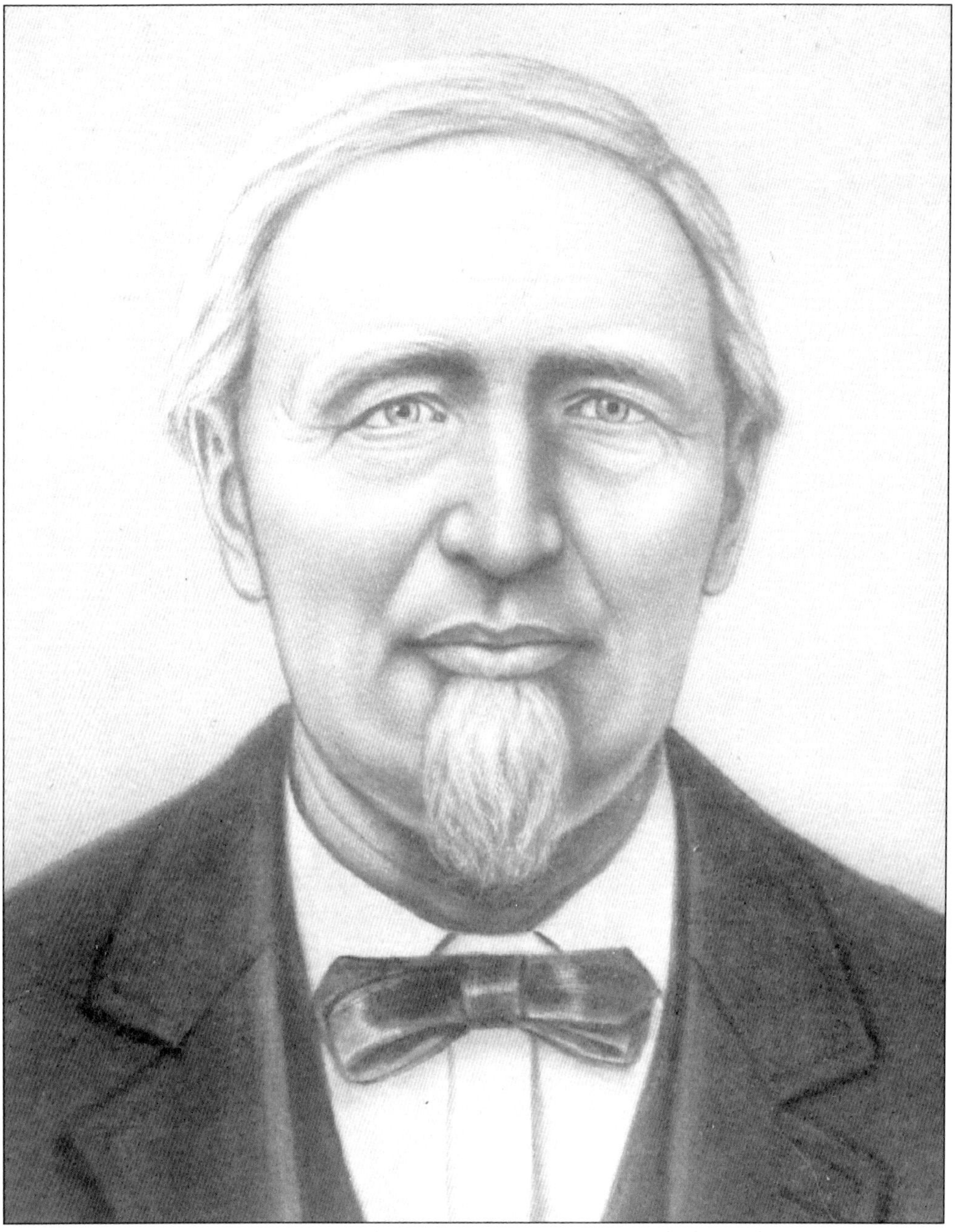

The Father of Spring Grove. The name Mons Fladager will always be associated with Spring Grove business. Fladager arrived in 1859, and opened a general store in the log cabin previously owned by William Fleming. Fladager operated here until 1864, and then moved to a larger building on Main Street. Financial success led to expansion, and in 1881 he built a new store across the street. He worked at this location with his sons until his death in 1905. When it was announced that the railroad would be coming to town, Fladager had the foresight to have his 45 acres of land surveyed and platted. The prospect of the railroad made this land a goldmine, and soon Fladager sold all his lots. There was now a burgeoning business district in Spring Grove. (Courtesy of Lee and Louise Sundet.)

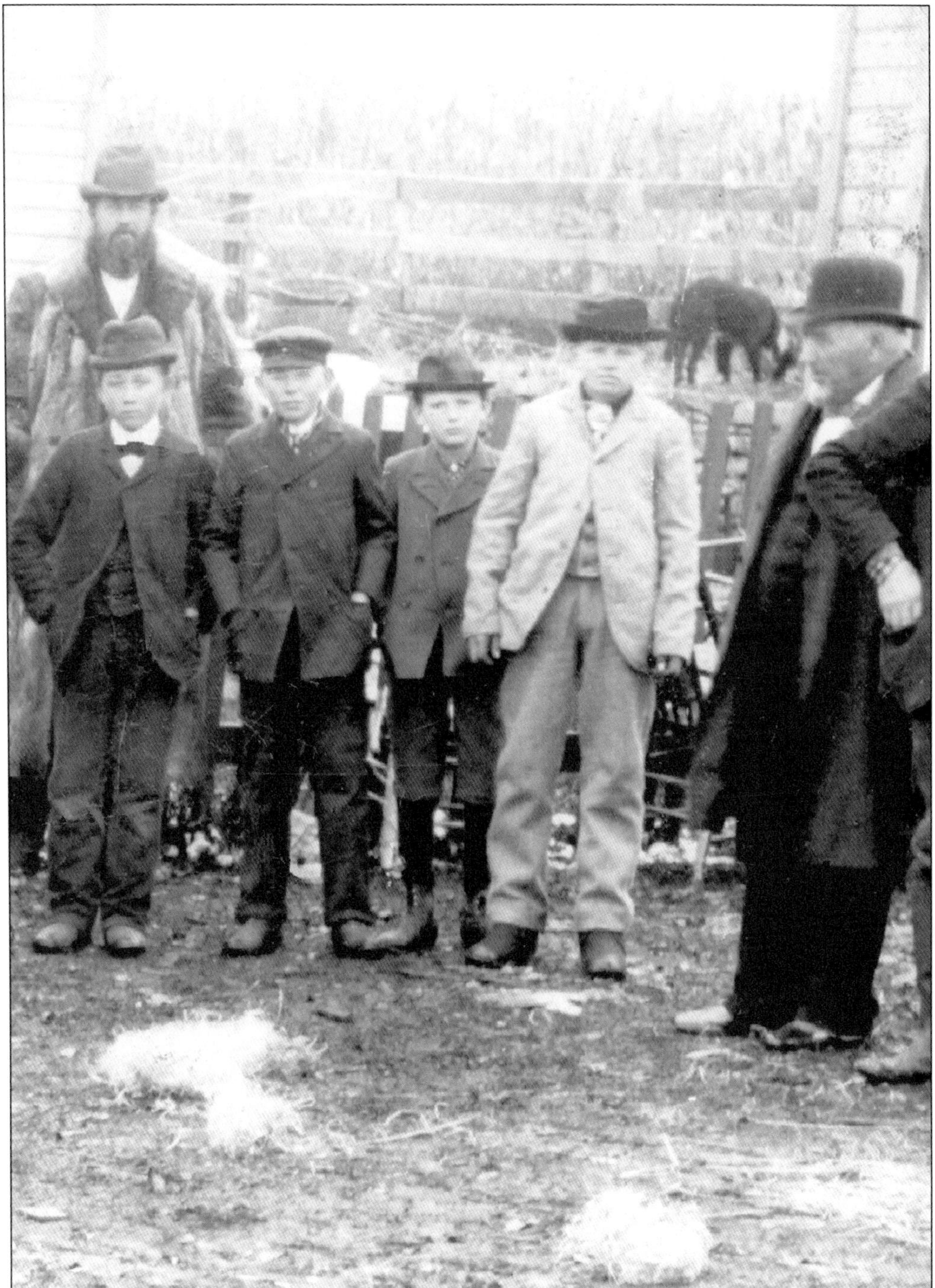

FLADAGER ON MAIN. Here is a rare shot of the diminutive Fladager (far right) interacting with a crowd on Main Street. From his humble origin as a house-painter in Norway, Fladager essentially built the economy of Spring Grove. In 1863, he married Joren Lommen and they had seven children: Henry, Peter, Inga, Edward, John, Martin, and Arnold. The Fladager family operated their business in Spring Grove for 110 years. (Courtesy of Lee and Louise Sundet.)

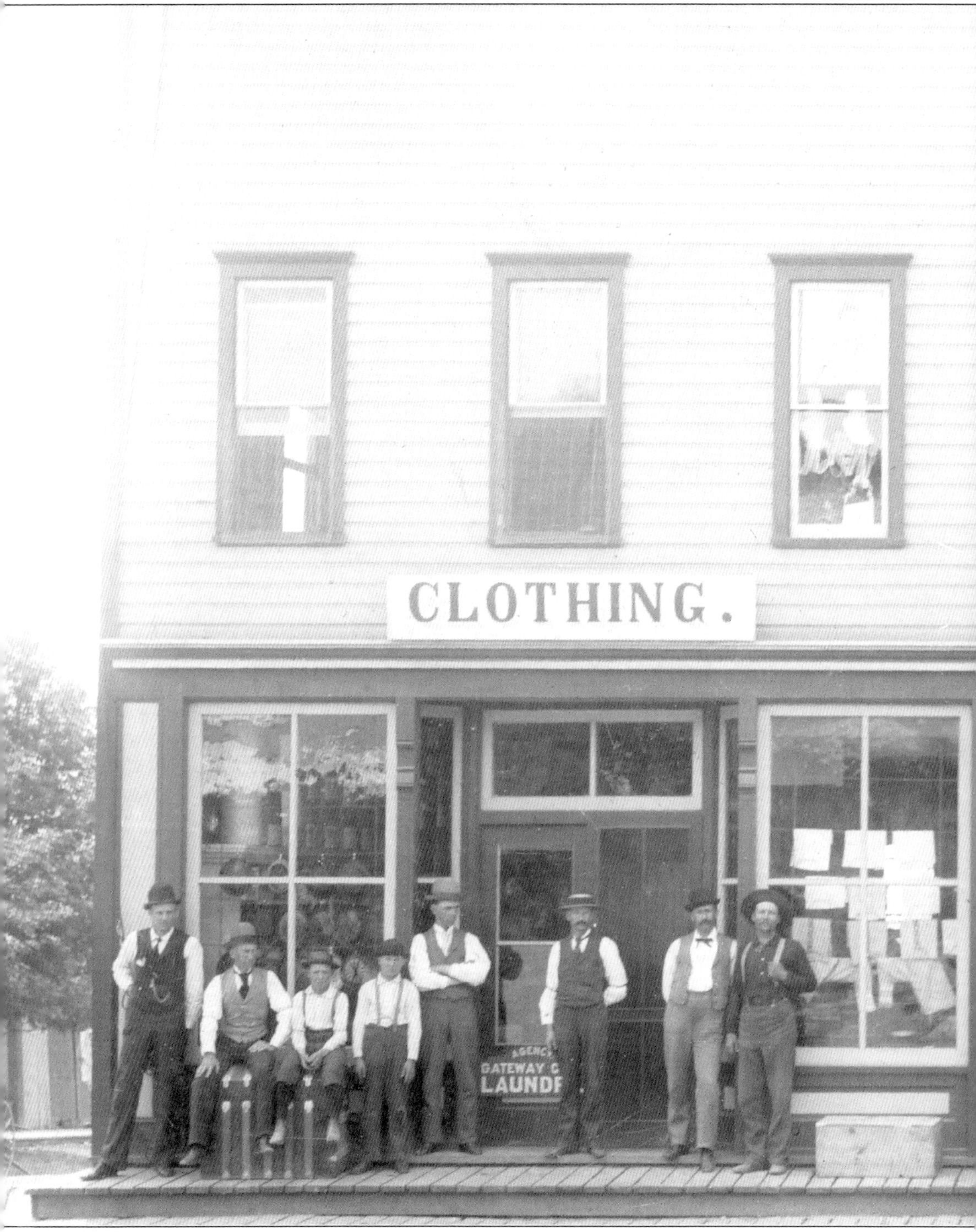

FLADAGER BUILDING. Henry Fladager was the manager of this clothing store. It began as 700 square feet in 1892, and expanded over the next two years to more than twice that size. After his father Mons died in 1905, Henry and his brother Peter continued the business, known then as Fladager Brothers. The City Restaurant was owned by Hans Braaten. Its 1895 advertisement

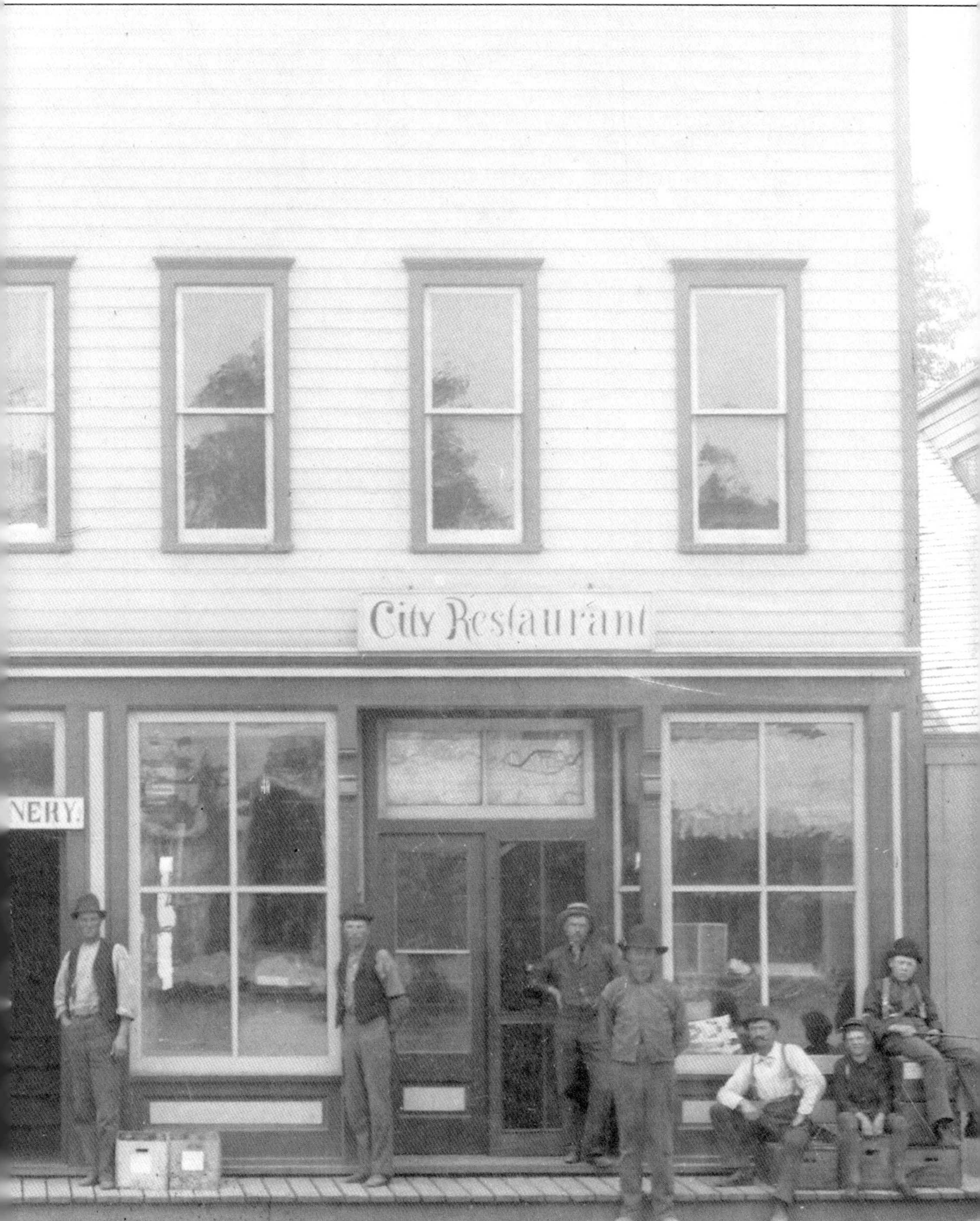

reads, "We are now in our Elegant New Quarters centrally located on Main Street, one door east of Nelson & Tone's. Temperance Drinks, Tobaccos, Cigars, Candies, Nuts and Fruits. Good Lunch Served on short Notice. Your Patronage Solicited." (Courtesy of Lee and Louise Sundet,)

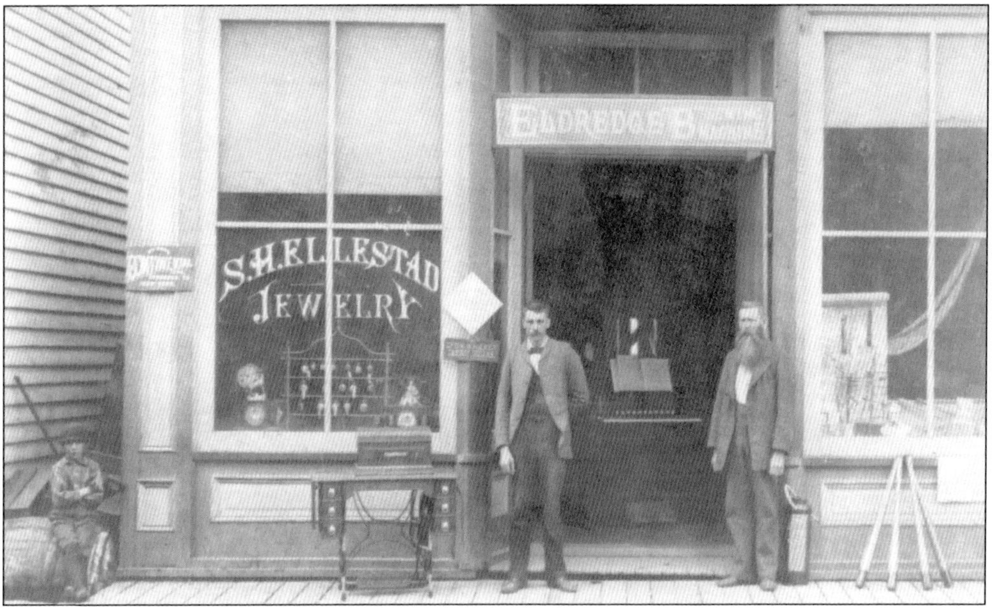

Renaissance Man. Sven Ellested (left) died of consumption at the age of 44, but undertook many endeavors in his short life. As a young man he apprenticed at the *Decorah Posten* in Iowa, and eventually opened a print shop. When he was 21, he published the first issue of the *Spring Grove Posten*, which lasted only one year. After this he studied telegraphy, erecting some of the first telephone lines outside of the city. He was also an accountant, buttermaker, barber, and jeweler. One story tells of Ellested running into the church as it burned in 1873 in order to save the altar painting. The man on the right is Brown Anderson, a popular business owner for over 50 years. His brother was the famous scholar Ramsus B. Anderson.

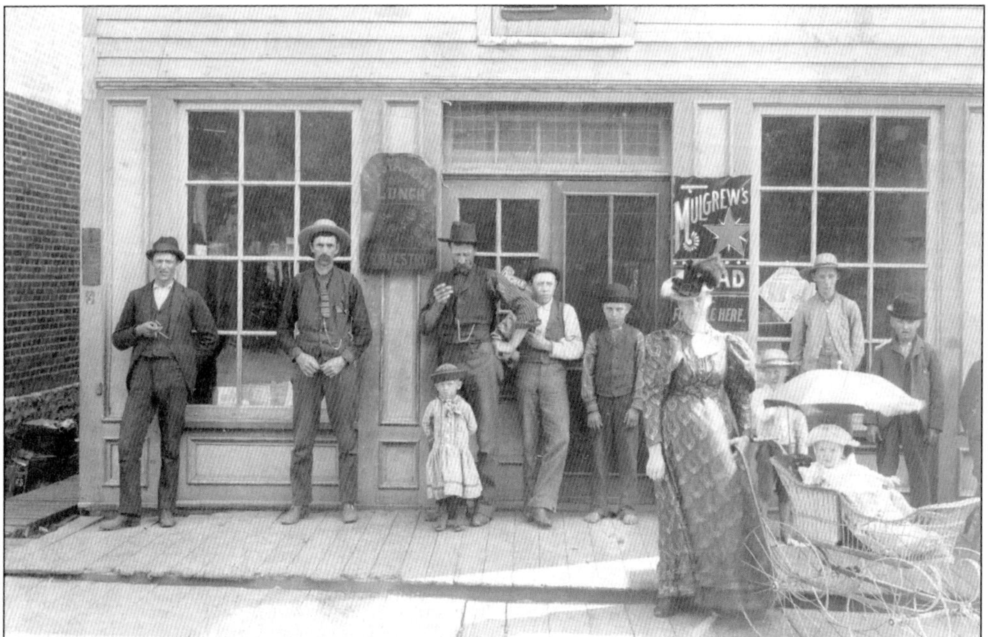

Restaurateur. A group of unidentified residents pose in front of Guul Ovestrud's restaurant.

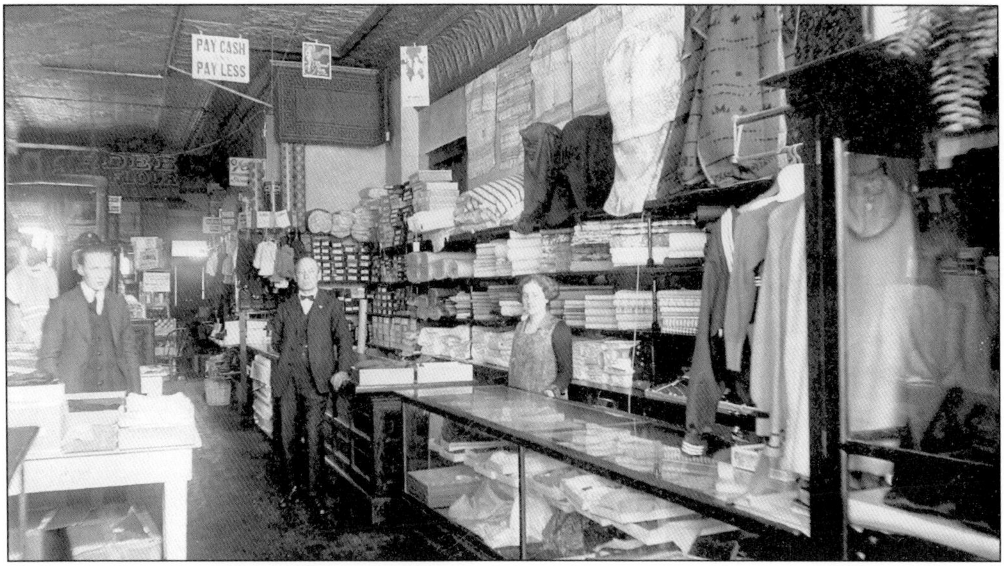

GENERAL STORE. Pictured here are Olaf Larson, Eskild Quinnell, and Jarla Hallan. From a 1917 issue of the *Spring Grove Herald*:

> *Spring Grove is truly proud of several mercantile establishments, all of which are well-kept and ably conducted, but among the foremost of these is the very up-to-date store owned by Quinnell & Clauson. These gentlemen are meeting with unusual success in their business. They aim to handle only the best in their particular lines, and specialize in the better class of merchandise, such as fancy dress goods, ladies' and misses ready-to-wear garments, and a full line of shoes for men, women and children. In addition to these lines they do a large business in carpets, rugs, linoleums, lace curtains, draperies, etc., as well as having a large grocery department.*

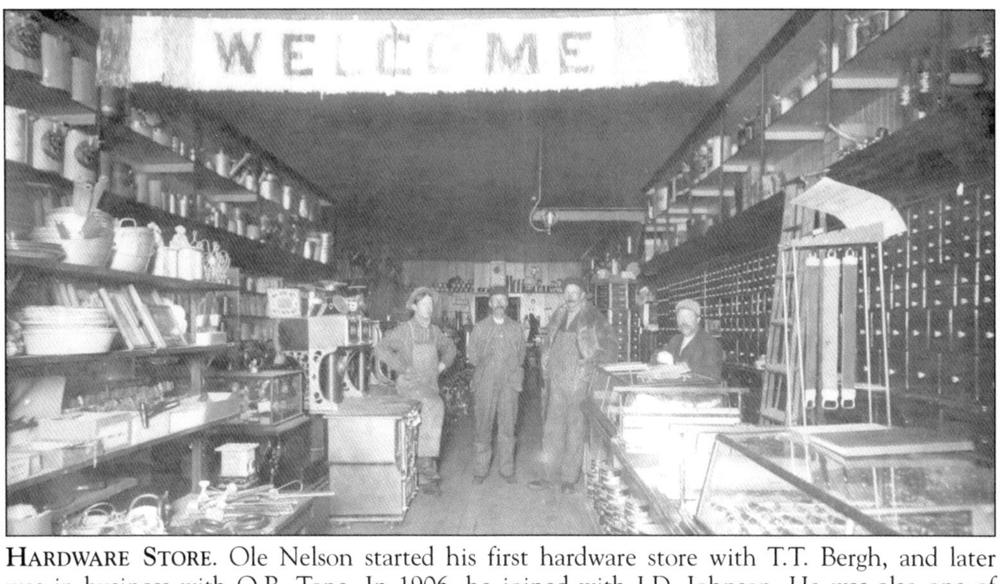

HARDWARE STORE. Ole Nelson started his first hardware store with T.T. Bergh, and later was in business with O.B. Tone. In 1906, he joined with I.D. Johnson. He was also one of the organizers and presidents of the State Bank of Spring Grove. It is interesting to note that Nelson changed his last name from Blexrud to Nelson because there were so many Ole Blexruds in town. Thereafter, he was known as O.B. Nelson.

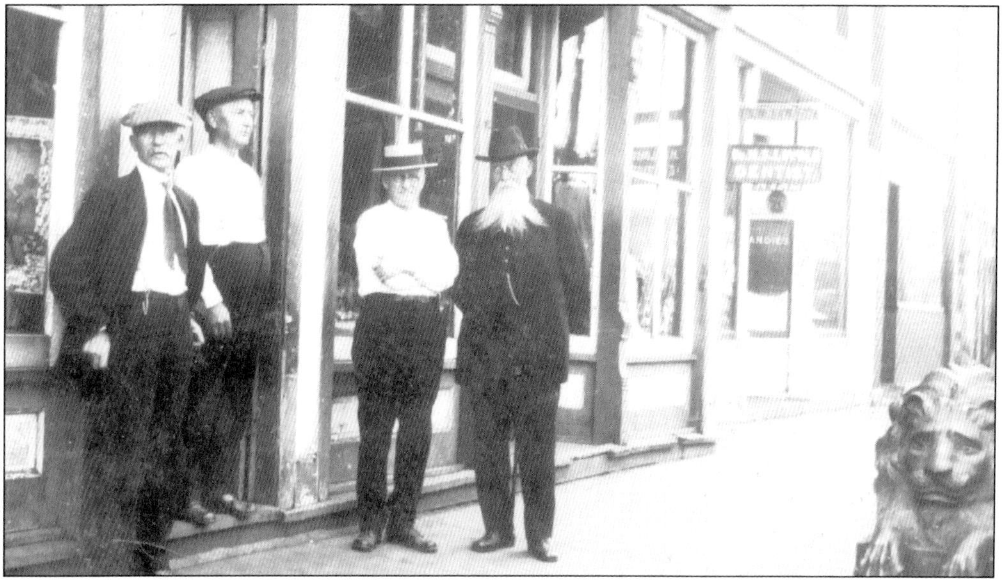

FLADAGER LION. Four unidentified men pose in front of the Fladager store. Notice the lion statue in the far corner. It was given to Mons Fladager by his cousin Mons Anderson of Wisconsin. Anderson owned a successful clothing business and was referred to as the Merchant Prince of La Crosse. His Lion-brand overalls made him a millionaire.

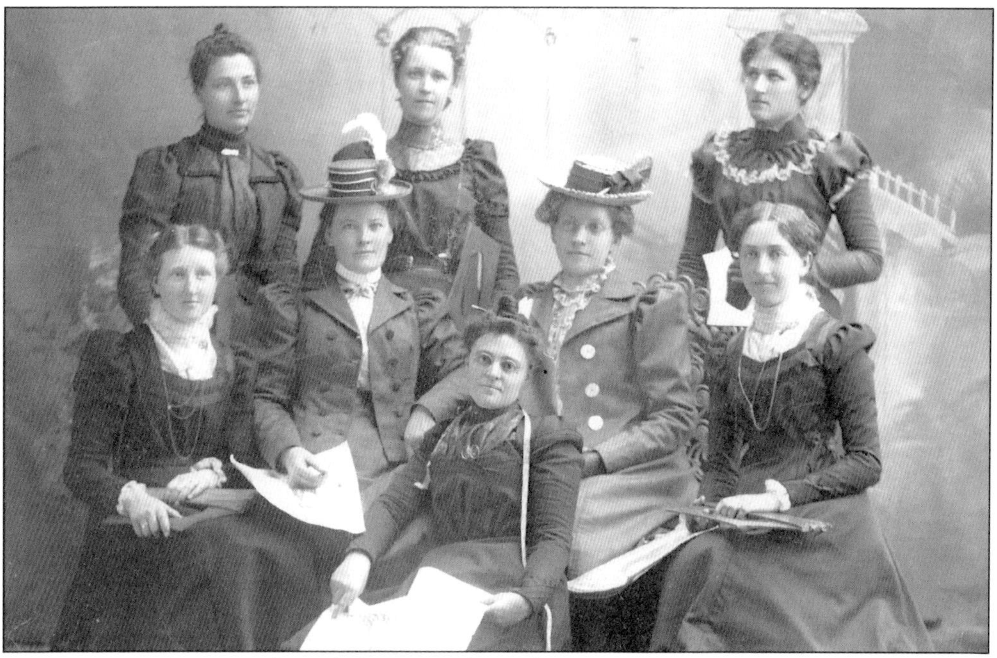

DRESSMAKING CLASS. Before clothing merchants became more prominent, families relied on dressmakers. They would hire a woman to visit their home, take measurements, and make their clothing. Norwegians did not accept the American tradition of buying ready-made clothes, preferring to have theirs "made to order" at home. Emigrant women were encouraged not to bring much clothing from Norway, but to purchase "American" when they arrived. Therefore, native costumes were mostly abandoned, except for special occasions.

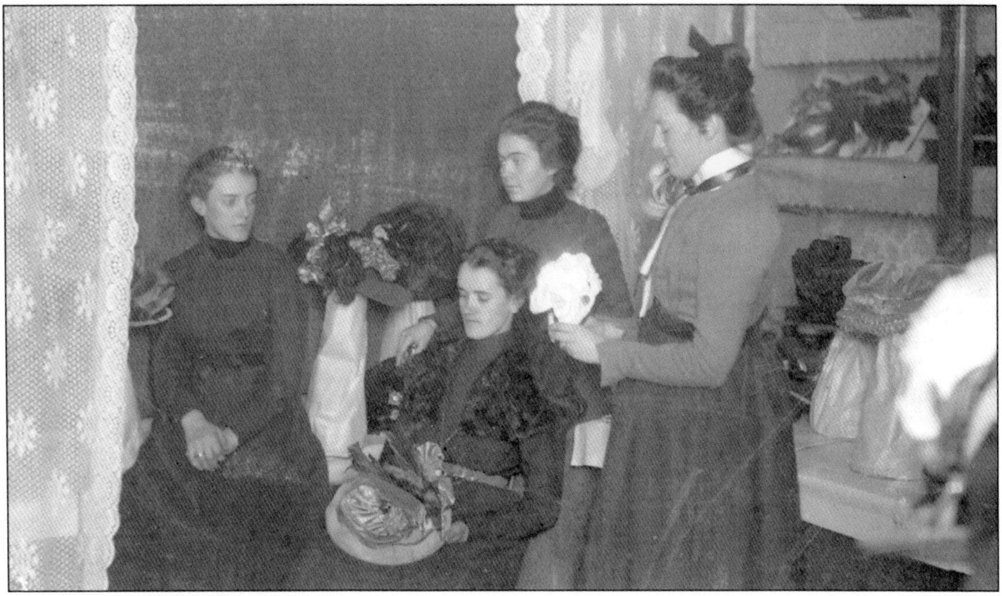

MILLINERY. Anna Engell is shown here with her millinery employees. A milliner is defined as a person who designs, makes, trims, or sells women's hats. The term was first recorded in 1529, and referred to products from Milan and northern Italy such as ribbons, gloves and straws. The haberdashers who imported these items were known as "milliners." Anna's sister, Ida Bakke, also had a shop in town.

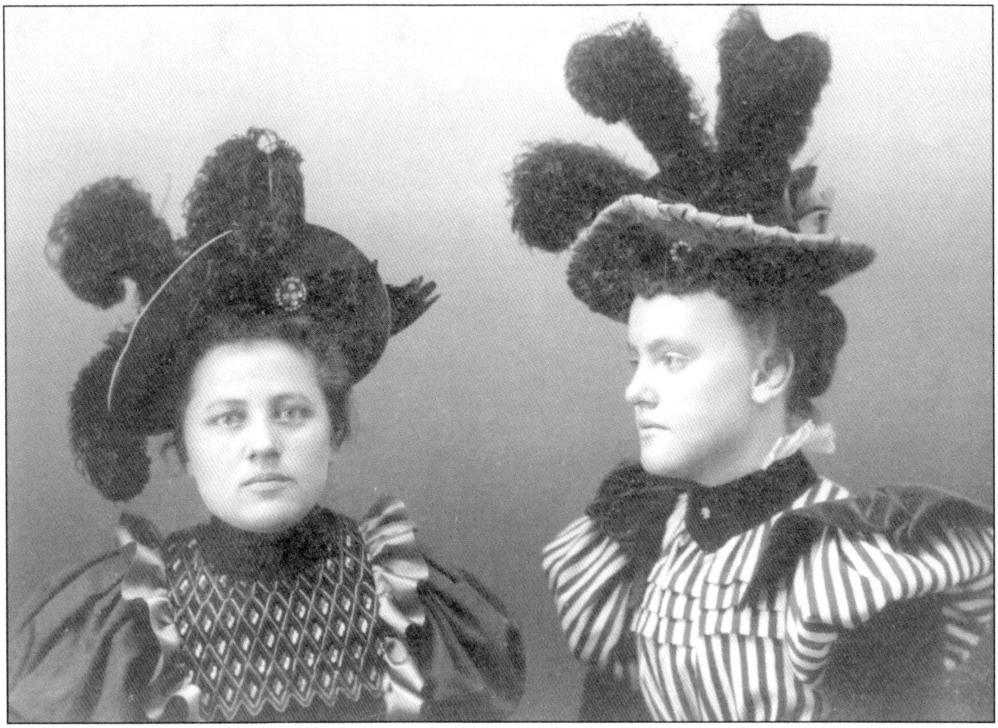

WOMEN'S HATS. This is Maria Engell (right) and an unidentified friend. The photo was taken by her father Christian Engell, who owned a photography studio in Spring Grove.

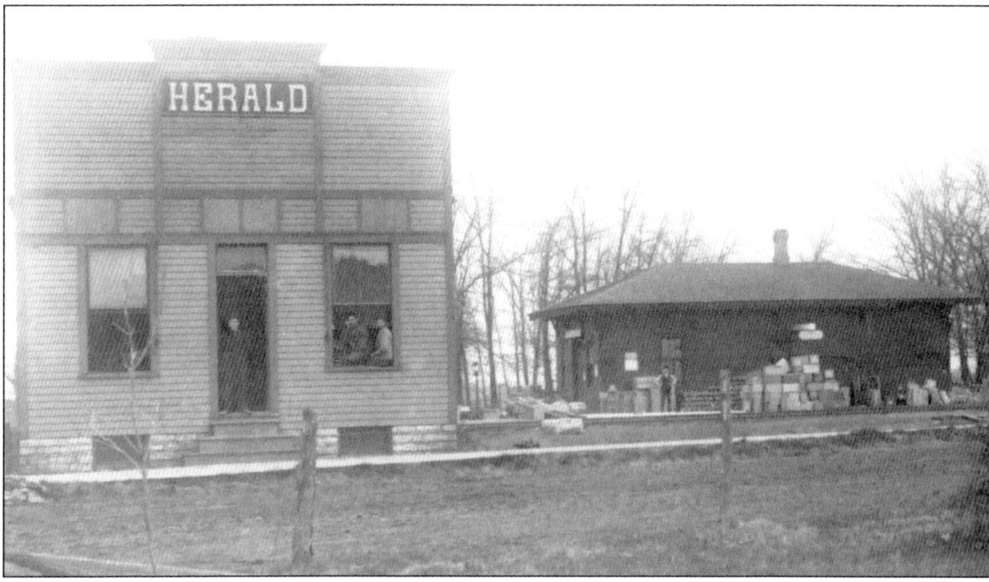

The Herald. W.H. Smethurst published the first issue of what was then called the *Spring Grove Weekly* in November 1891. Years of financial trouble caused Smethurst to sell the publication to Frank Bartholomew. After two years of publication, Bartholomew's building burnt down. He continued for a few more years, but eventually sold to O.K. Dahle, who erected the building pictured above. Dahle also gave the paper a new name: the *Spring Grove Herald*. Through the years the newspaper went through a variety of owners, most notably Bernt Onsgard, whose association with it lasted 35 years. The *Herald* is still in the Onsgard family. Notice the depot to the right. The railroad tracks ran directly behind the *Herald* offices, as shown in the picture below.

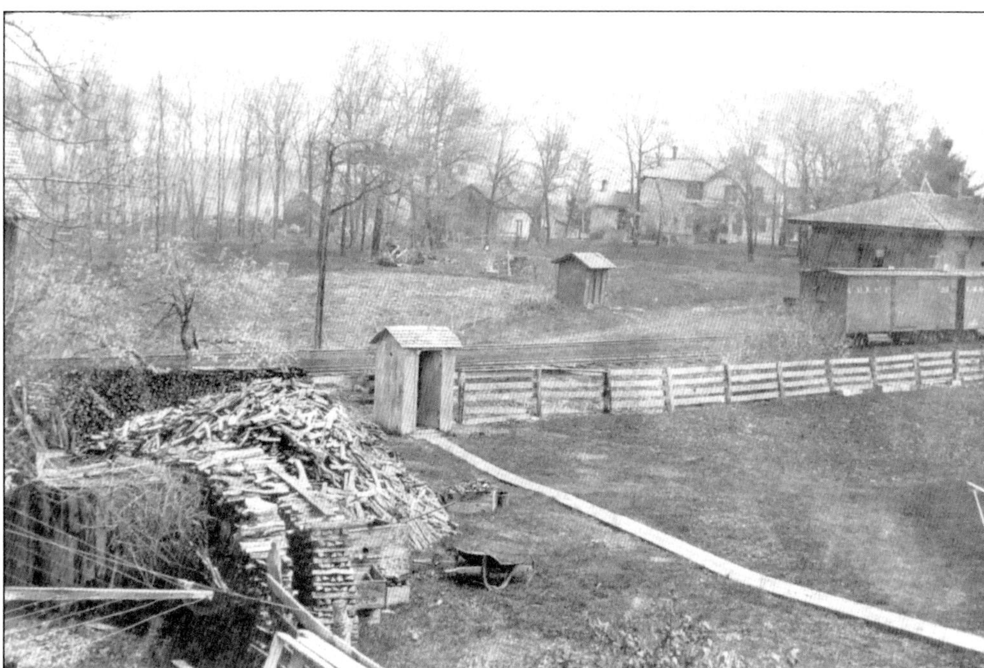

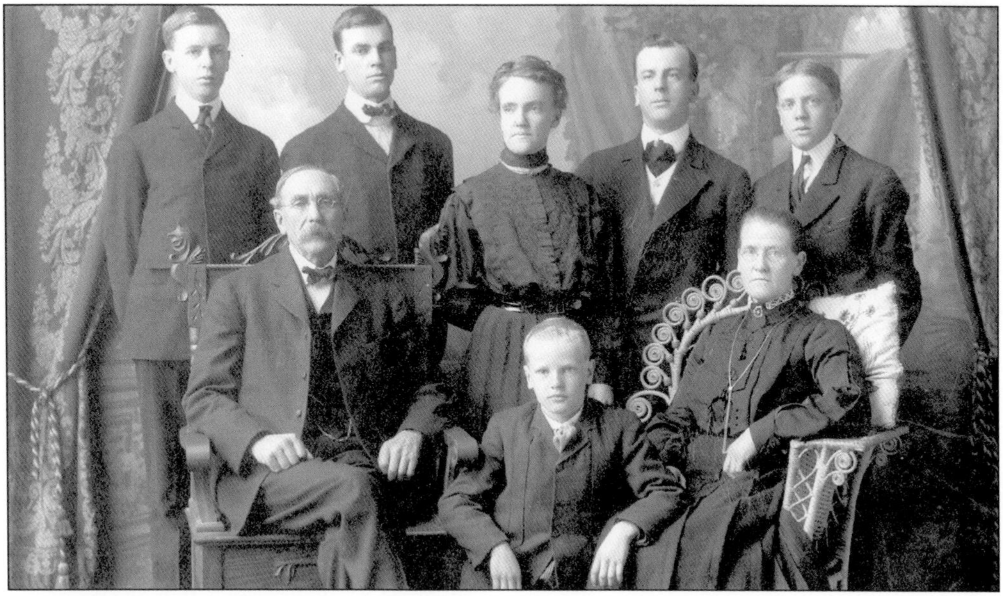

THE NEW STUDIO. Here is a photograph of Christian Engell (seated, left) and his family. From a 1907 advertisement in the *Spring Grove Herald* for Engell & Son's photography shop, The New Studio: "A Sound Argument: We advertise absolute facts. Photography is a modern necessity. It is unwise to delay in having your photography taken. In years to come you collection of photographs will form the most important part of the family history."

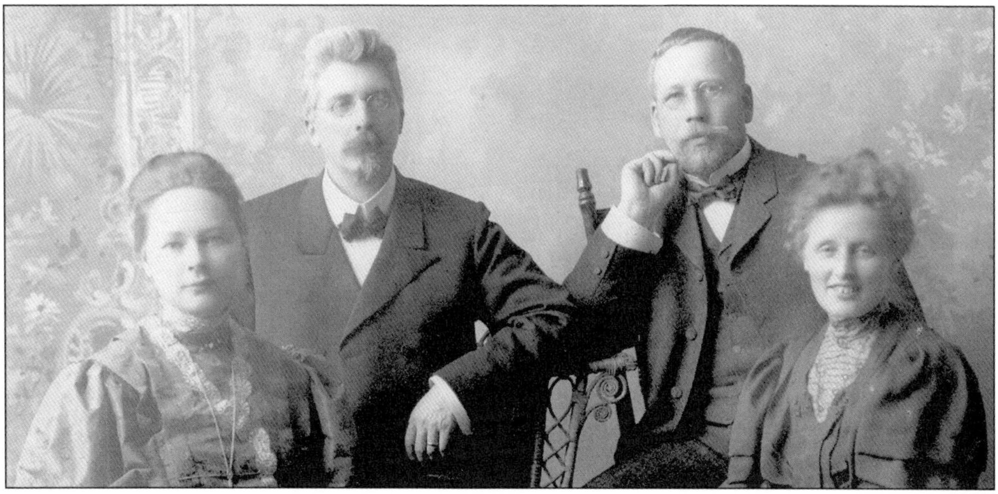

DR. THROND STABO. Stabo (right) was born in Toten, Norway in 1869. He graduated with a medical degree from Christiania University and immigrated to America in 1894 with his wife, Helga Hammerstad (left). He stayed in Spring Grove with the Ingvald Muller family until he could establish himself in town. In 1895, he was licensed to practice medicine in Minnesota. He was one of the first physicians to perform surgical operations for appendicitis, and also owned the first automobile in Spring Grove. In 1907, he moved to Decorah, Iowa, where he continued his practice and became the president of the Luther College Board of Trustees. In 1914, the Knighthood of St. Olaf was bestowed upon him by King Haakon of Norway. Stabo was also the Norwegian Vice Consul from 1917 to his death in 1946. This position gave him the opportunity to meet many famous Norwegians, most notably polar explorers Fridtjof Nansen and Roald Amundsen.

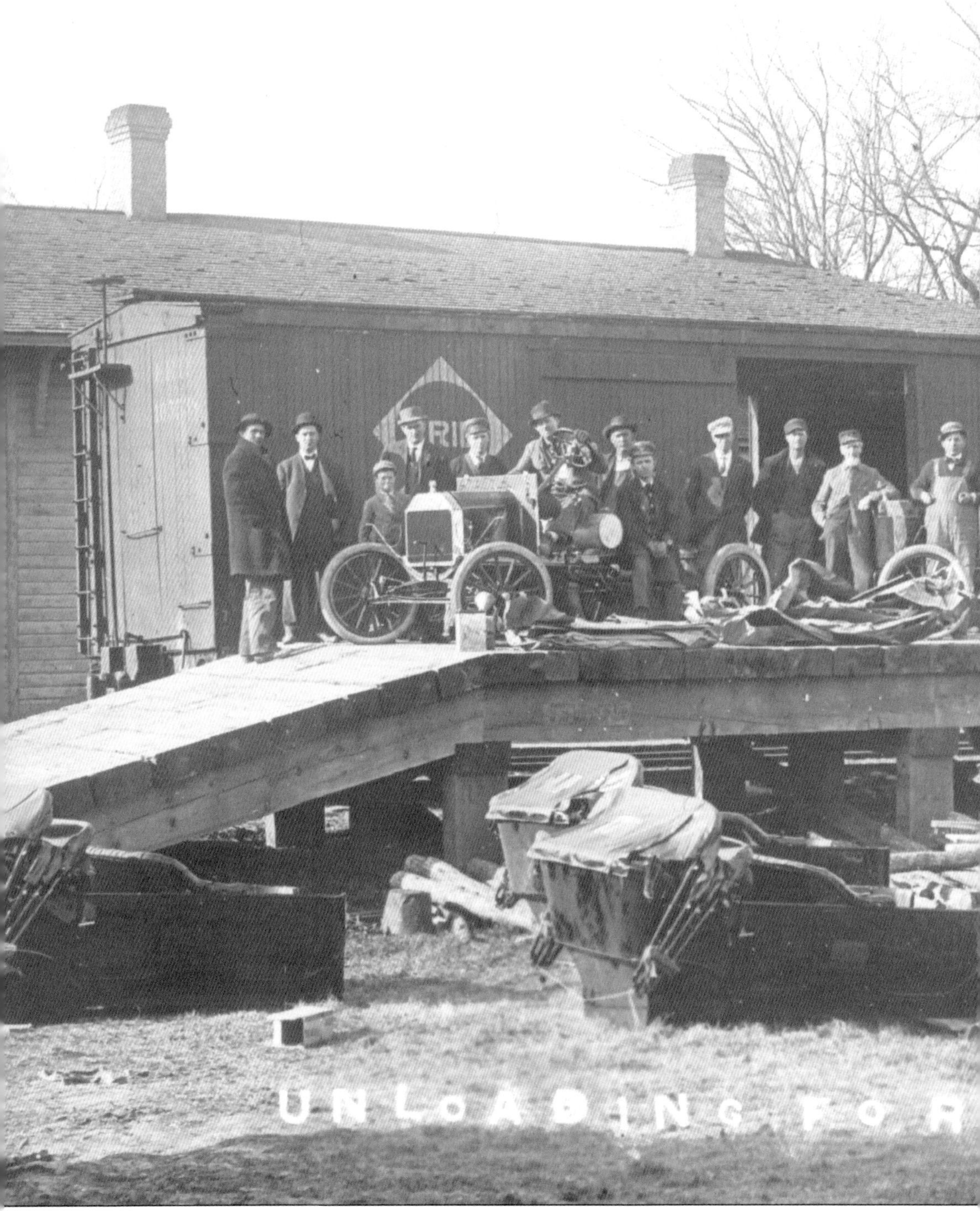

Unloading Model Ts. Employees of the Foss Garage unload 1912 Model Ts from boxcars at the depot. After the vehicles were quickly assembled (so as not to fall apart) they were driven to the garage where final adjustments were made. Fenders, wheels, chassis, lights, and running

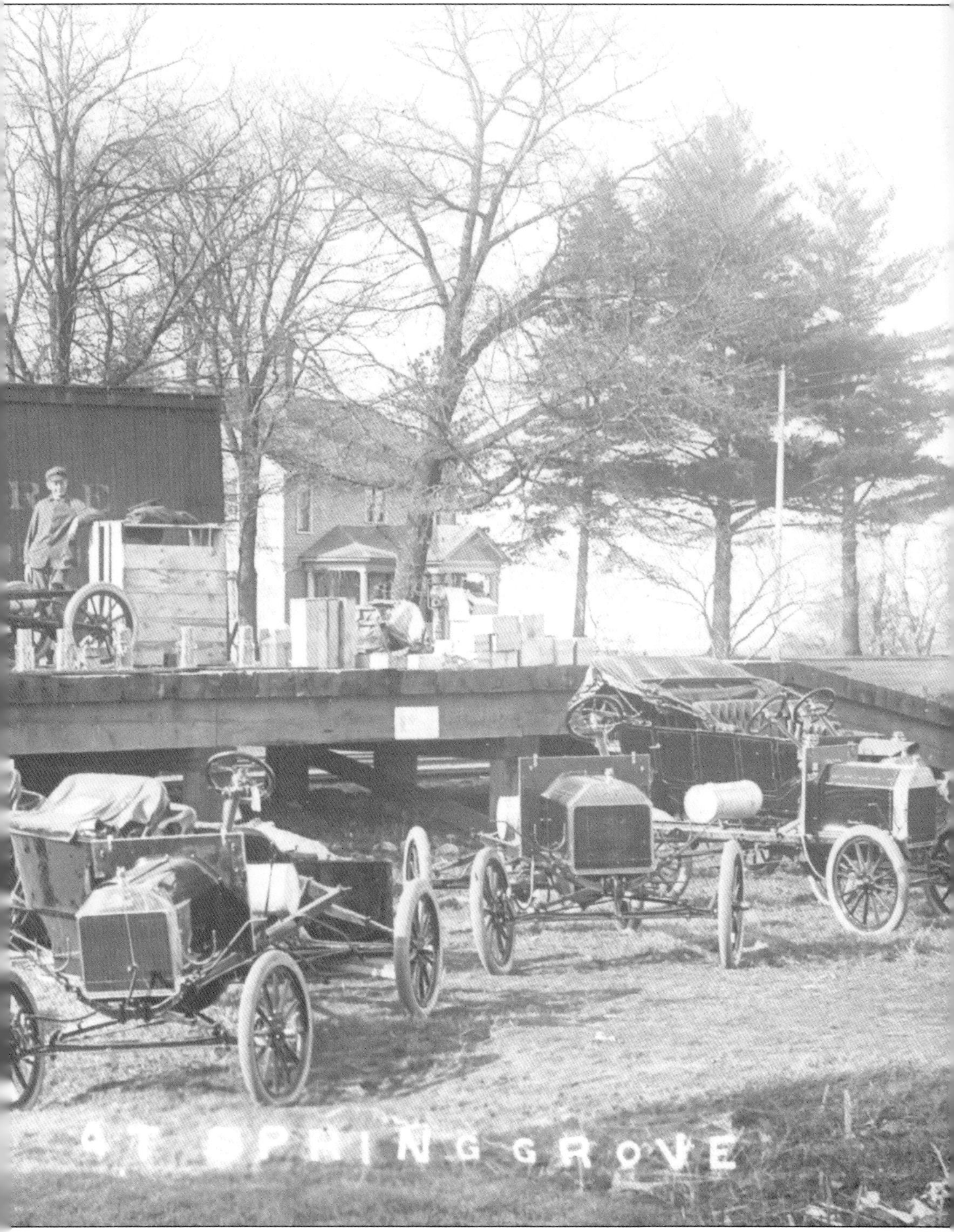

boards were all packed onto the train. Typically there were eight vehicles in each boxcar. In 1915, the Ford Runabout cost $390, and the touring model cost $440. The freight fee was $20.45. Spectators and prospective buyers often gathered to watch the unloading and assembly.

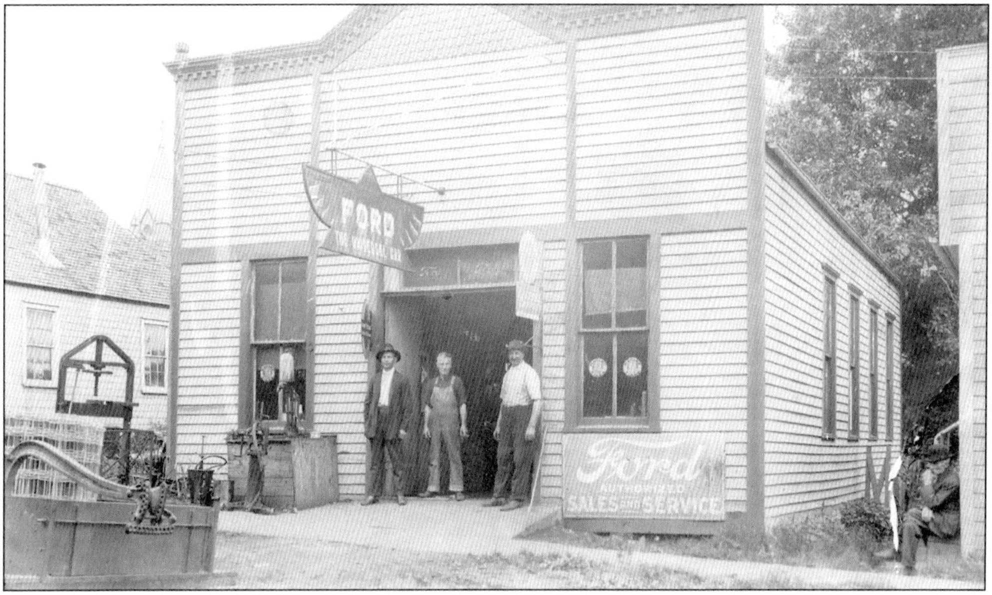

THE FOSS GARAGE. From thea 1917 issue of the *Spring Grove Herald*:

> *A good barometer of the prosperity of any community is the automobile business, and when a stranger sees a number of automobiles in a village or in the public highway he is at once convinced that he is in a productive territory, and that the farmers are of a thrifty character. And when one sees a number of automobiles in a locality, if he is a close observer, he will find that a very large percentage are Fords. Realizing all these facts and the universal demand for Ford automobiles, Mr. E.J. Foss easily decided what his line of effort should be in the business world.* (Courtesy of Patricia Ashman Foss.)

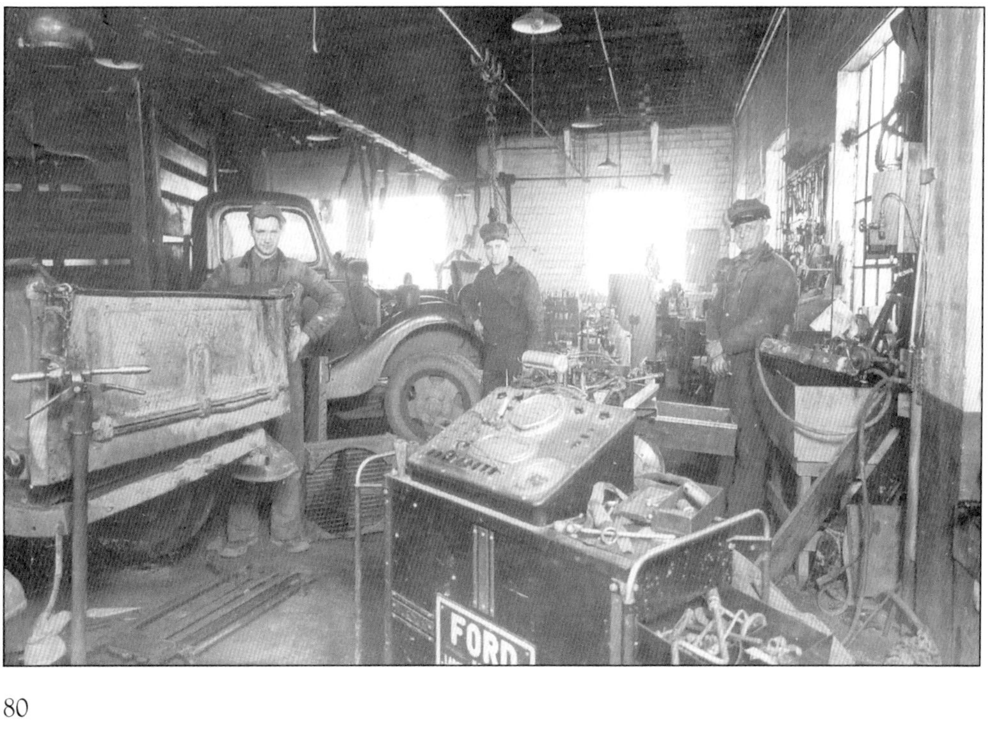

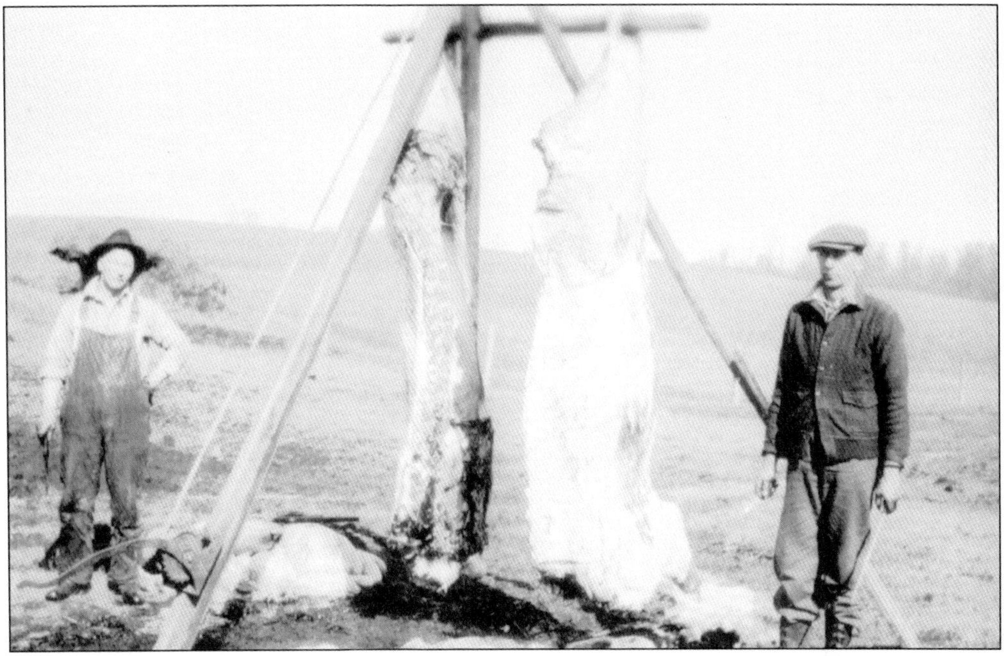

MEAT MARKET. Ingemon Muller (left) is shown here with an unidentified man. Muller was the owner of the local meat market in Spring Grove, along with his brothers Gustav and Gilmar. The business was first known as Schansberg & Muller. Their men would go from farm to farm, butchering animals. Besides providing this service, Muller also rented cold-storage lockers at his business on Main Street. "Schansberg and Muller received part of their ice for the coming summer," the *Spring Grove Herald* reported in 1920. Blocks of ice were packed in sawdust so that they would last longer.

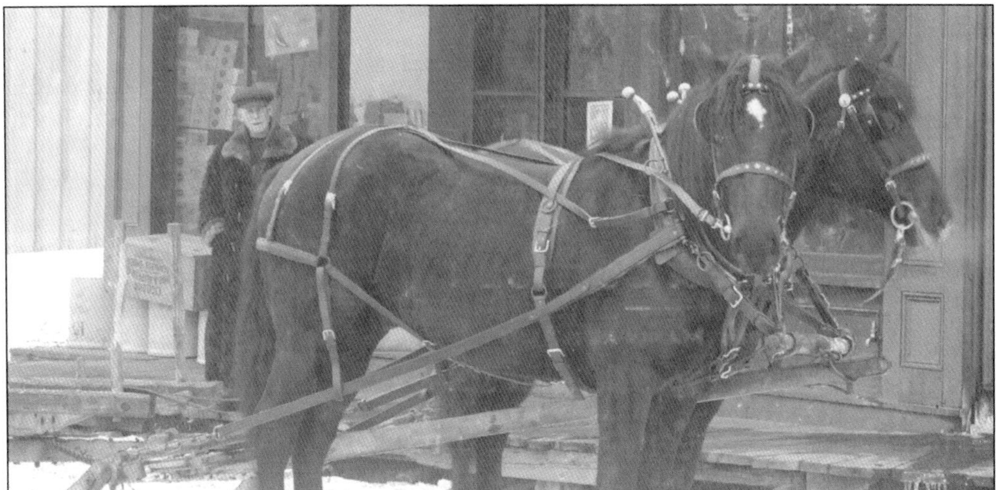

HARNESS SHOP. A 1909 advertisement for Nelson & Goergen Harness Manufacturers of Spring Grove read, "Bridles 3/4-inch with spotted fronts and nose bands. Line 1-inch, 20-feet long. Flat leather back pads. Back straps 1-inch with brass buckle shields. Concord bolt harness with brass balls. Chain traces 1 1/2-inch. This harness can be made with buckle tugs or without back pads if wanted. Made from No. 1 guaranteed oak stock."

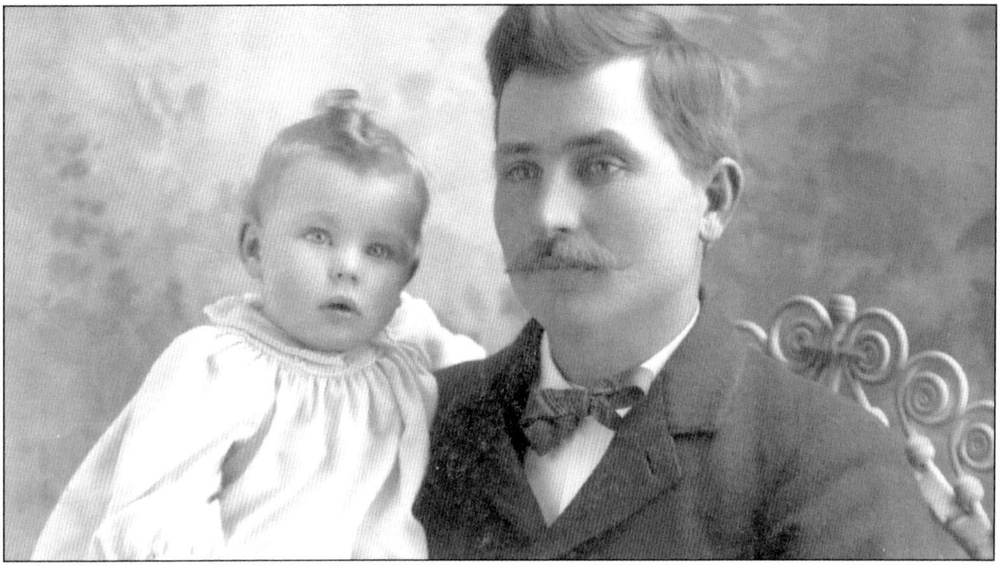

F.E. JOERG—PHOTOGRAPHER. Frank Joerg was one of Spring Grove's early photographers. He is shown here with his son Jerome, sitting on the wicker chair he used as his signature piece when photographing many residents. "Bring your babies to me and have their pictures taken," reads one of his advertisements. "All kind of photographing, copying and landscapes; also enlarging in crayon, India ink, water color, sepia and pastel at Joerg's gallery opposite the hotel." Joerg would have been in competition with Christian Engell, whose New Studio was just down the road.

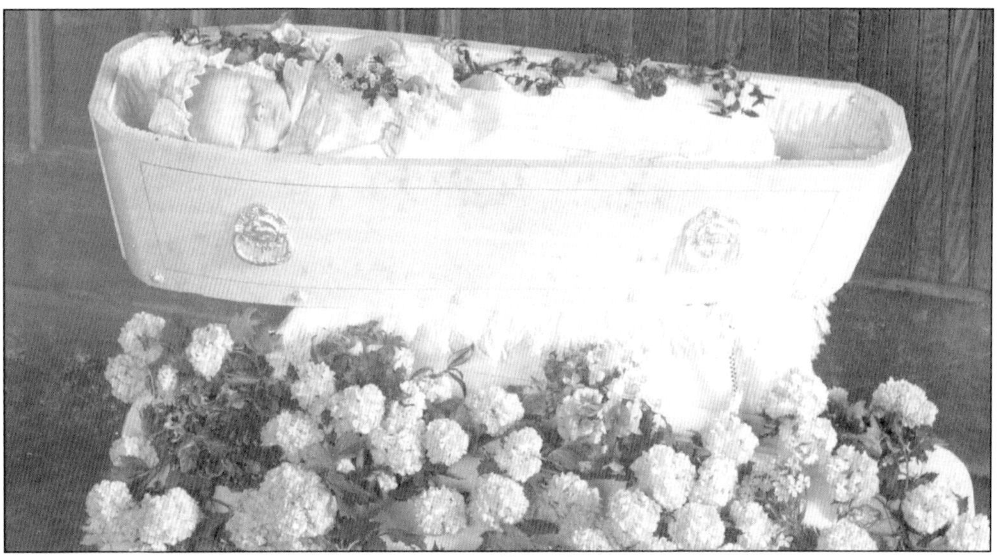

UNDERTAKING PHOTOGRAPHY. Christian Engell was born in Norway in 1841. He immigrated to America in 1870, and worked as a photographer in St. Paul before moving to Fillmore County, and finally to Spring Grove in 1872. In 1875, he built a studio, the first floor of which had a confectionary and tobacco stand, while the second was used for his art gallery. Later, he moved to a building closer to Main Street. In 1876, he was married to Anne Anderson. Besides photography, Engell was also the town undertaker. His son, James, worked with him and eventually took over the business. Their building was often cryptically referred to as "The Morgue." This photo of Oscar Quarve was taken by Engell.

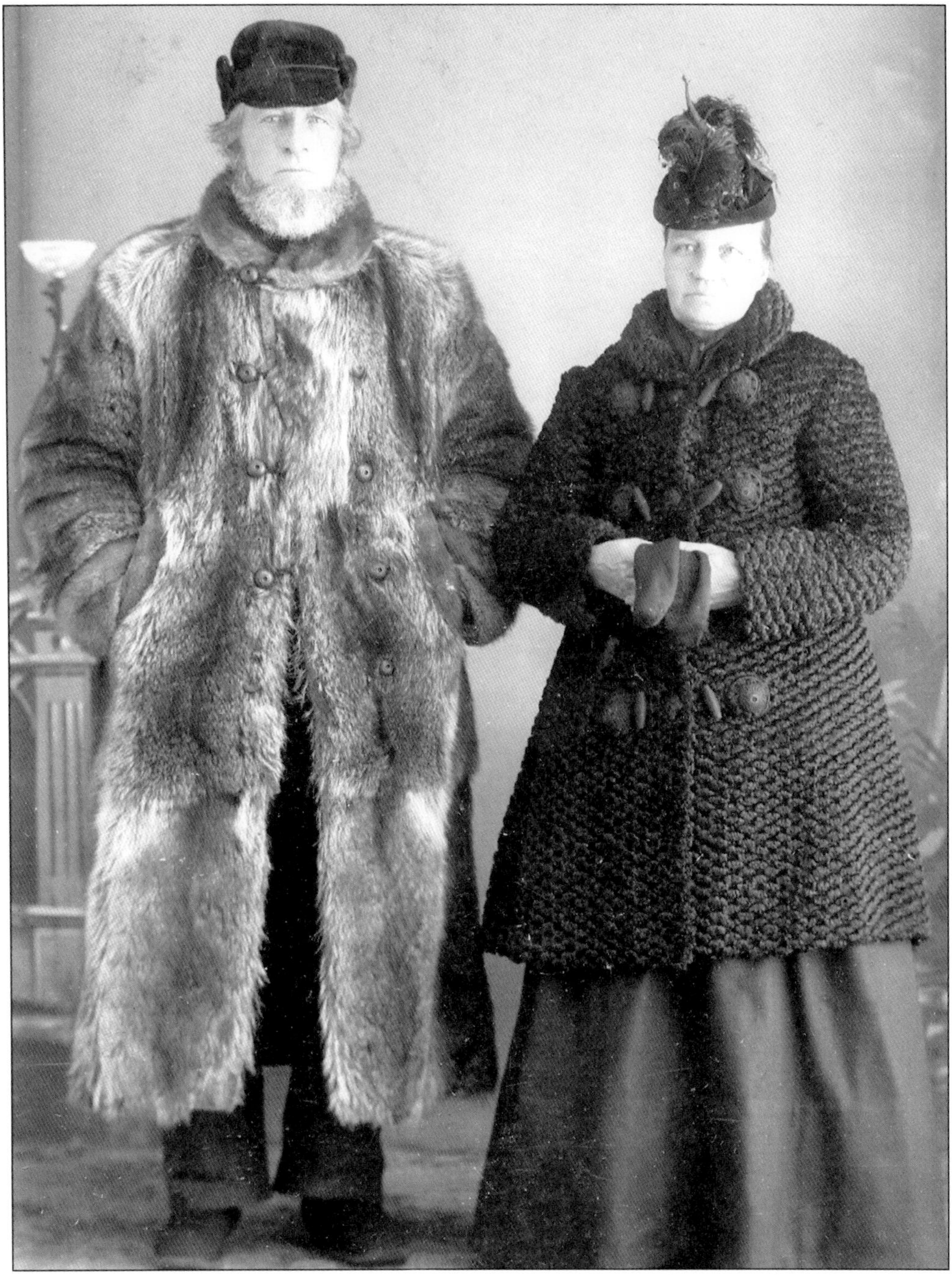

HOTEL OWNERS. Teman Gilbertson and his wife, Anne Kjos, owned a popular hostelry called the Gilbertson Hotel. Teman was born in Hallingdal, Norway, in 1837, and immigrated to America with his family when he was 10, settling in Dane County, Wisconsin. He attended school for only two years. In 1854, he moved to Spring Grove and through the years purchased large tracts of land in North Dakota and Washington, which proved to be financial goldmines. He and his wife were married in 1857, and they had 10 children. In 1871, Gilbertson represented Houston County in the Minnesota State Legislature during Governor Horace Austin's administration.

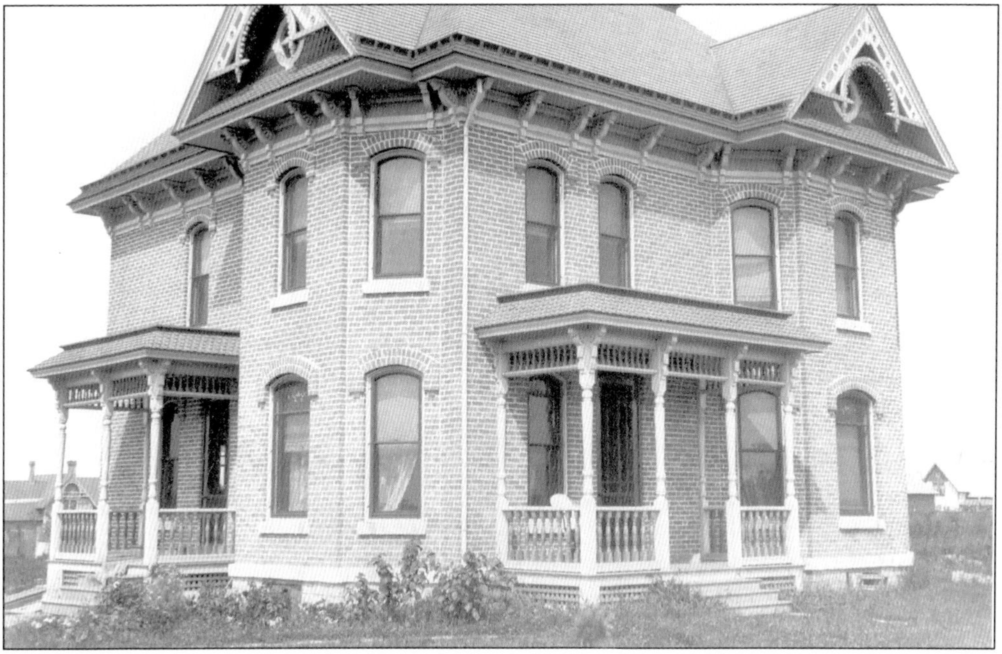

NELS HENDRIKSON HOUSE. This beautiful brick home was owned by Nels Hendrickson and built by Gilbert Askim. Hendrickson was a successful businessman who started a general merchandising business in 1865 with his cousin Nels Onsgard. Being that Onsgard was tall and stocky, and Hendrickson was rather diminutive, they were referred to as "Big" Nels and "Little" Nels. This partnership lasted for about four years. In 1864, Henrickson married Birget Sagdalen and they had 10 children.

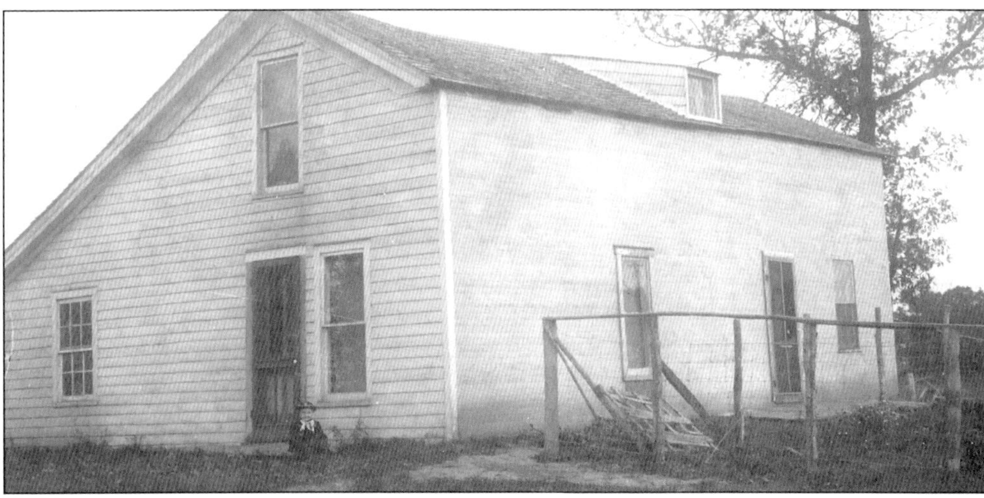

HINKLEY HOUSE. In 1855, James Smith left town and sold his stock of goods to William Hinkley, who erected the building shown here. As well as stocking groceries and general merchandise, Hinkley sold what was referred to as "whiskey straight." His supply room also served as his bedroom, and Hinkley did not hide the fact that late-night travelers were always welcome. They would simply need to tap on his window and pass their jug into his bedroom with "the equivalent" in compensation. Hinkley would fill the jug without rising from his bed and pass it to the grateful customer!

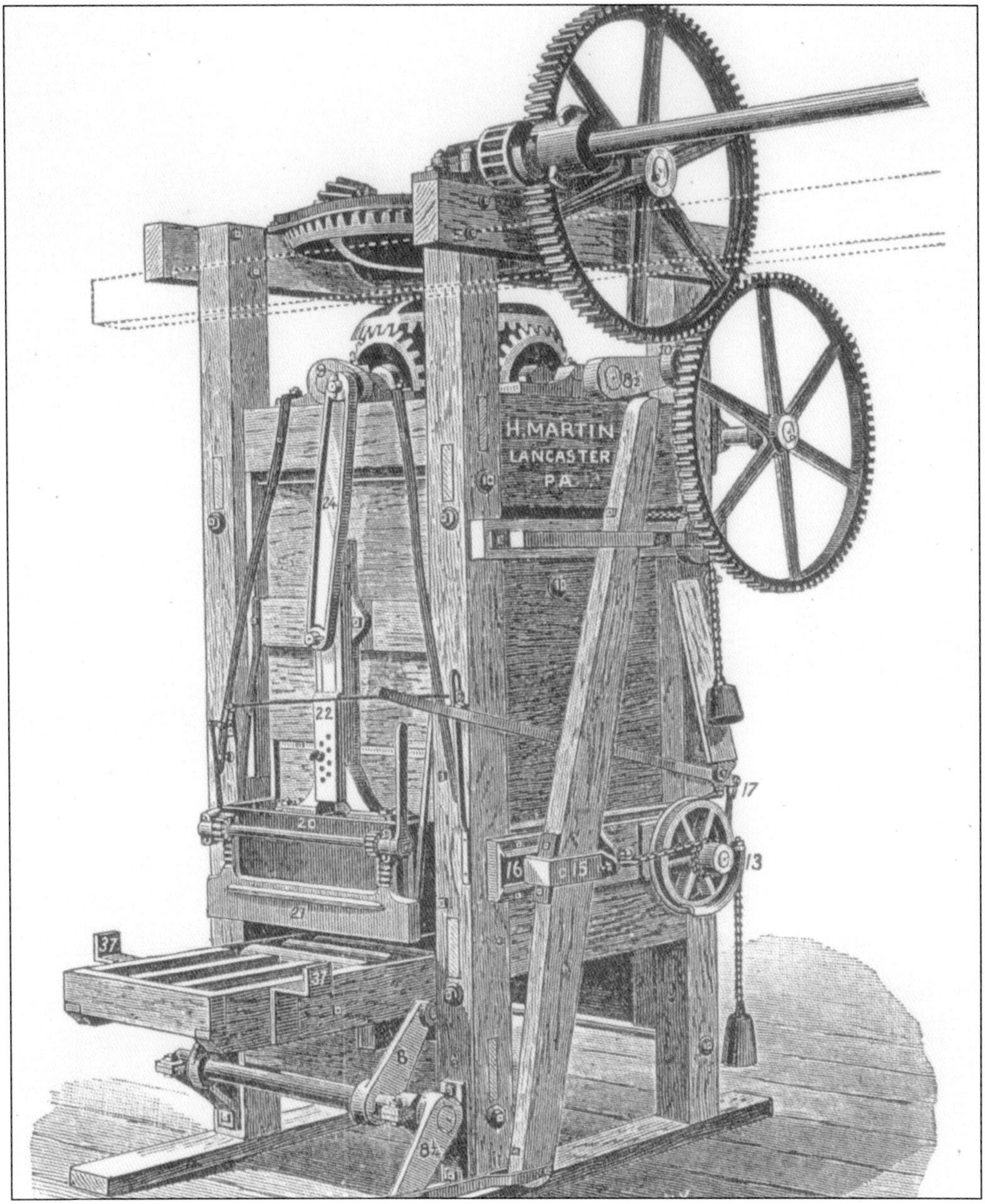

EARLY BRICK MAKER. This type of machine was used by the local Muller brickyard, which employed eight men. Ole Kjos was the foreman. Making bricks required a lot of fuel, and many new Norwegian emigrants were employed to chop wood for the kilns.From a Henry Martin Company brochure:

> *The cut on this page is a facsimile of the Henry Martin Steam Power Brick Machine, fit up with the large Crown Gear, the Top Plate, the 3-inch Shaft and Bevel Pinion, the Spur Gear, 10 feet Countershaft fit up with my Patent Clutch attached to Pinion, and is all ready for any size Pulley desired. When ordering a Steam Power Machine, it is necessary to give the speed of the Engine and the diameter of the Pulley on the same, also the exact inside measure of the moulds desired. The capacity of this machine is from 25,000 to 35,000 bricks per day. It weighs about 6,800 pounds.*

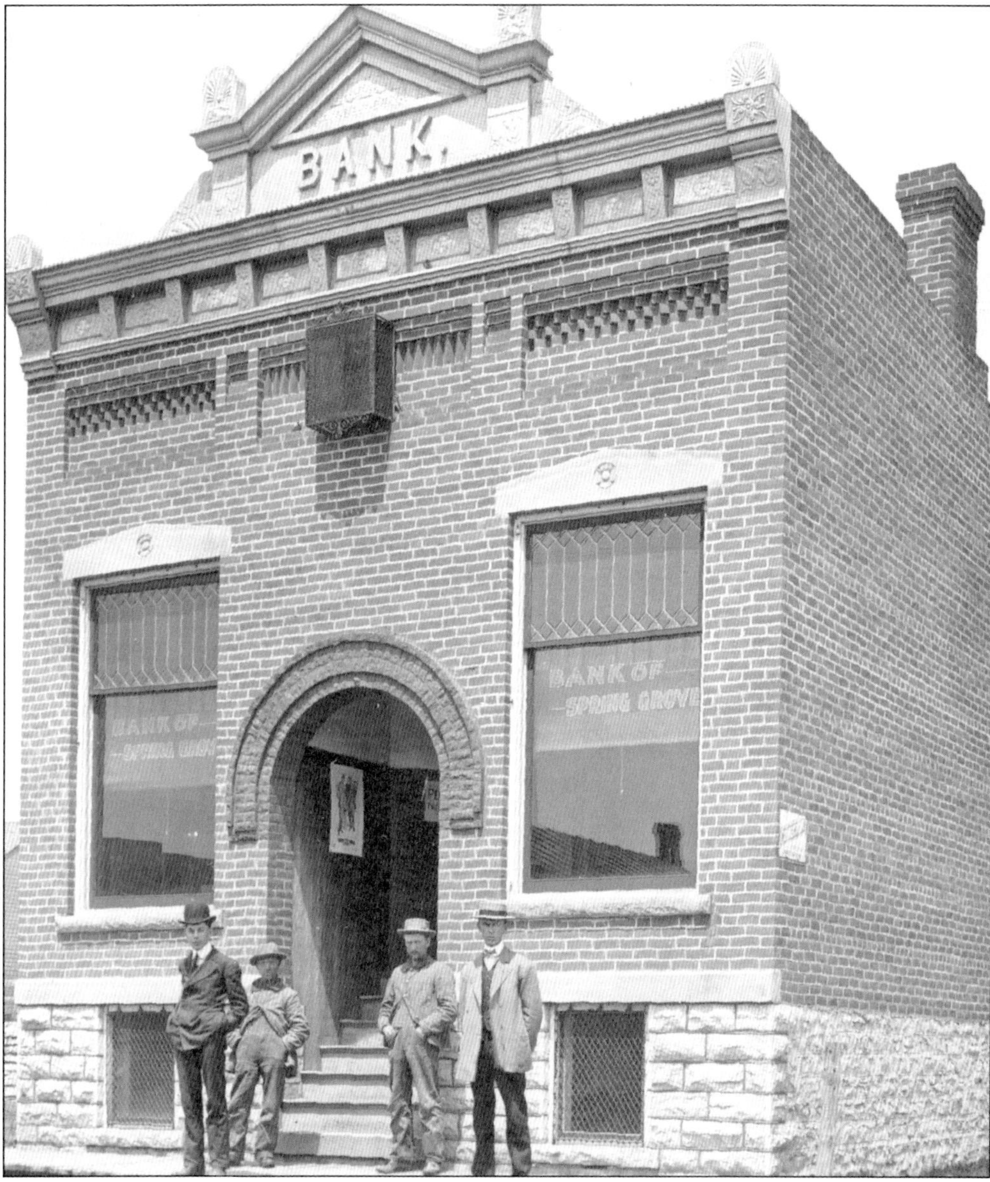

THE BANK OF SPRING GROVE. From a 1917 issue of the *Spring Grove Herald:*

> *Established 1890. Nels Onsgard, one of the sturdy pioneers of the community, was the founder of this institution and is still the sole owner. Like so many of the first settlers here, Mr. Onsgard came with practically no capital beyond that of a strong body, an upright character, and a serious purpose in life. The bank had its first home in the rear of the building formerly occupied by O.E. Kieland's general store. It is now in modern quarters fronting Wilmington Street [now Viking Memorial Park], equipped with burglar-proof screw-door safe, and a complete system of electrical burglar alarms. Ever jealous of the safety of funds and valuable papers entrusted to his care, the owner has spared neither pains nor expense to provide vault room and appliances of the best obtainable. The splendid patronage accorded this institution in the seventeen years of its existence speaks volumes for the ruling principles always employed in its management, namely scrupulous honesty and ceaseless thrift.*

BANK ROBBERY. Nels Onsgard is pictured here in the inset. From a 1903 issue of the *Spring Grove Herald*:

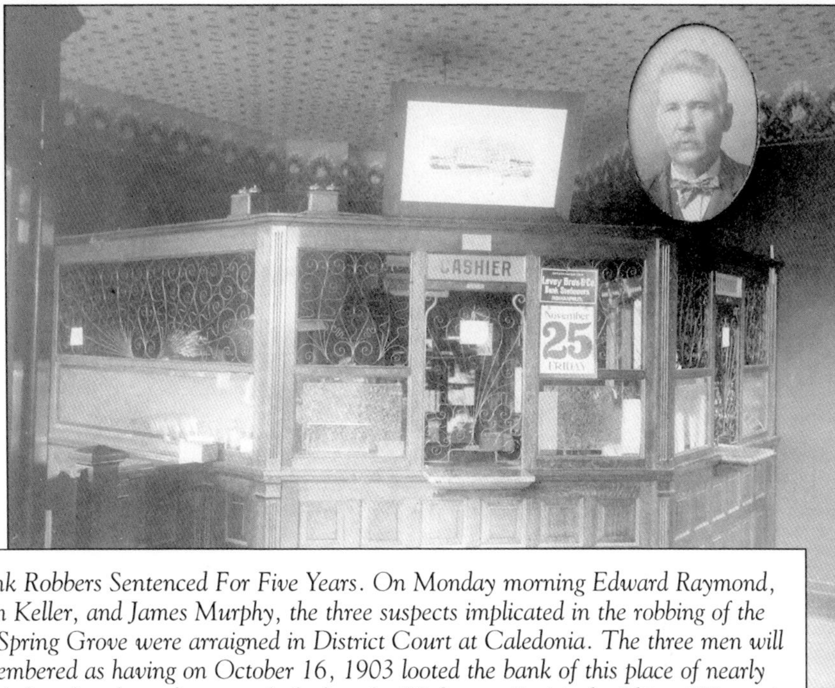

The Bank Robbers Sentenced For Five Years. On Monday morning Edward Raymond, William Keller, and James Murphy, the three suspects implicated in the robbing of the Bank of Spring Grove were arraigned in District Court at Caledonia. The three men will be remembered as having on October 16, 1903 looted the bank of this place of nearly $1,000. A few days later they were locked up for 30 days at Prairie du Chien, Wisconsin for carrying concealed weapons, besides which they also had on their person between $300 and $400, nitro-glycerine and burglar tools. The trial has been watched with great interest and large crowds from here were daily in attendance to listen to the proceedings.

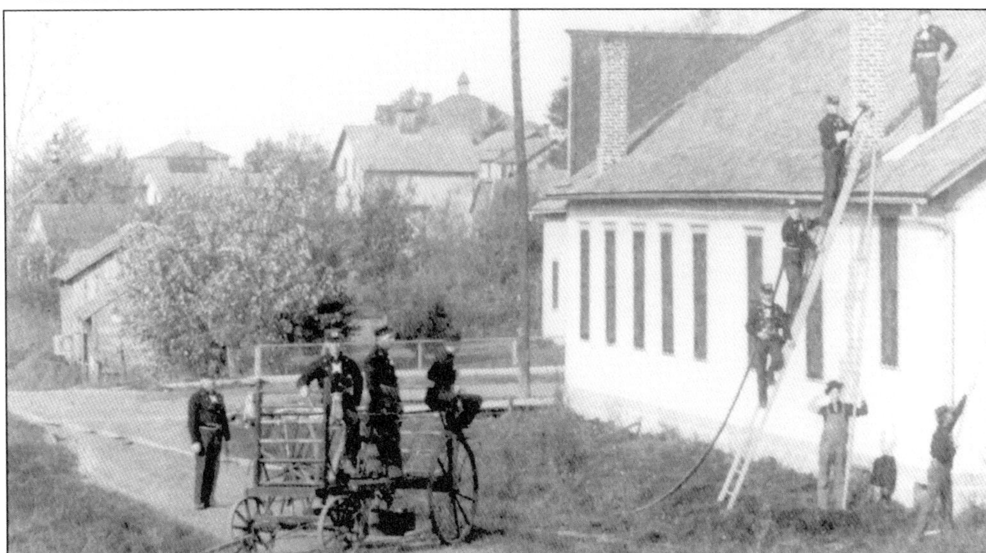

VOLUNTEER FIREMEN. Firemen are shown here practicing at the Spring Grove Opera House in 1915. In 1891, the state of Minnesota required all towns to organize a fire department. On land purchased by O.O. Roppe, an engine house was built and equipped with horse-carts, pails, and ladders. Early firemen were given $1.50 a year, as long as they attended practice 10 times. When it came to actually fighting fires, they were paid 50¢ an hour.

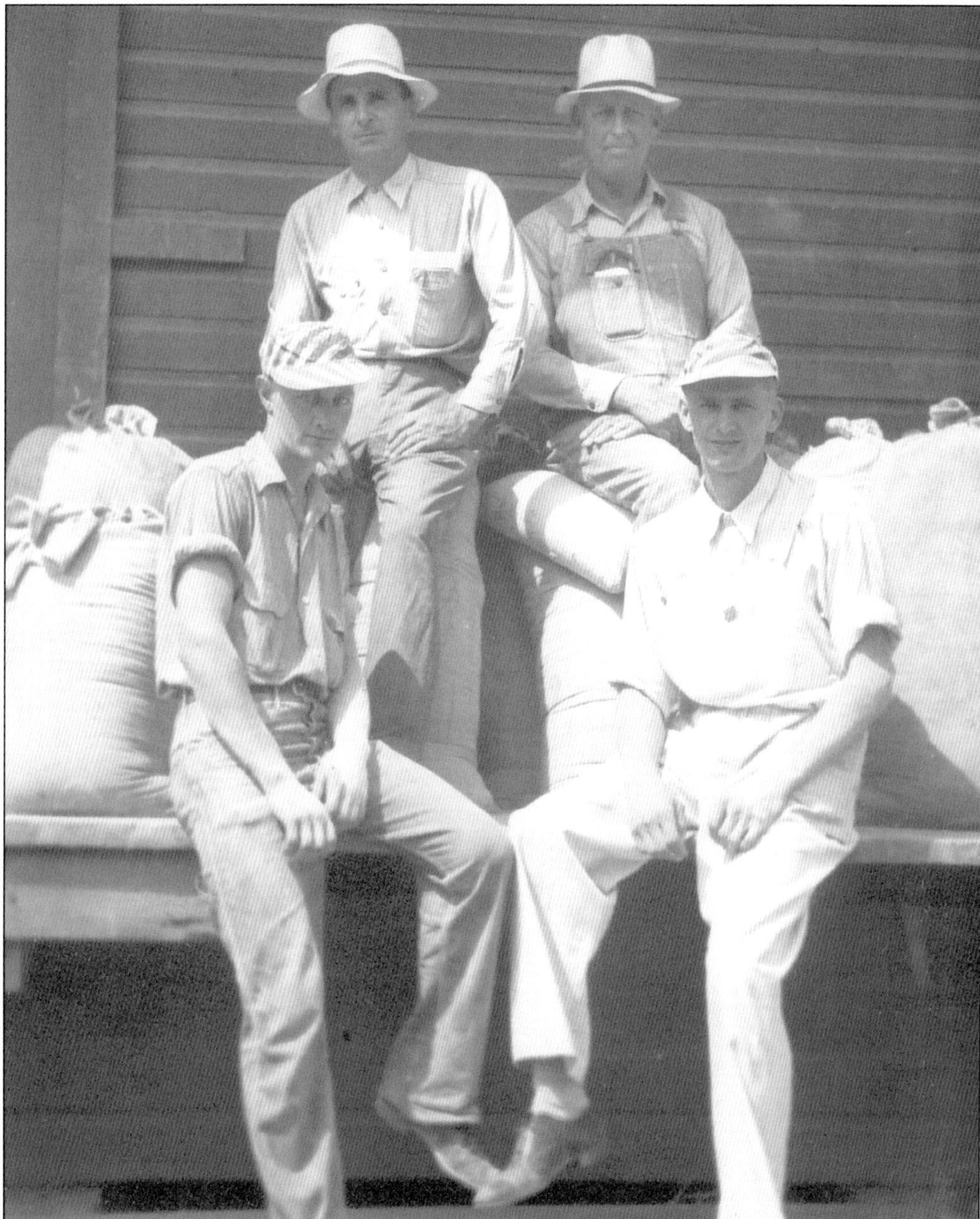

Grain Elevator. Shown here at the Ellingson grain elevator, clockwise from left, are Sivert Amunrud, Oliver Ellingson, Joseph Kroshus, and Oren Ellingson. Farmers would bring loads of wheat, oats, and barley to the mill where it was ground and then packed into grain sacks. These sacks were extremely heavy and would often leak as they were transported to the farm. The grain elevator was always located near railroad-track and financed by the railroad company. Large connecting silos held the grain for months on end, and when a boxcar pulled up next to the elevator, a swing-arm and spout would release enormous amounts of grain into the empty hulls. It would then be brought to markets around the Midwest. Elevators had to be constructed on a thick foundation and with strong walls to accommodate the tons of grain that could be stored. Besides the Ellingson elevator there were two others, the Danielson and the Sylling.

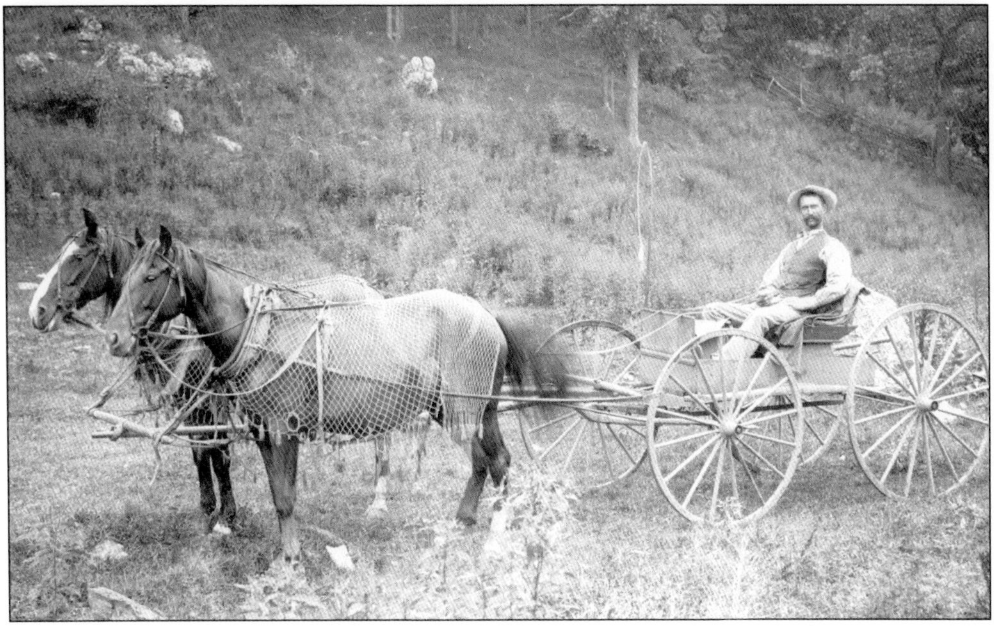

Mail Carrier and Mill Operator. Daniel E. Danielson (1890–1933) was one of the early rural mail carriers in Spring Grove. Even though postage stamps were in use by 1847, many residents still had the option of having the recipient pay postage. This, as can be expected, was rarely paid, and by 1855 it became mandatory to pre-pay postage. Danielson was also the owner of the Black Mill, which is pictured below. By 1917, this was the only mill of its kind to be run exclusively by steam-power.

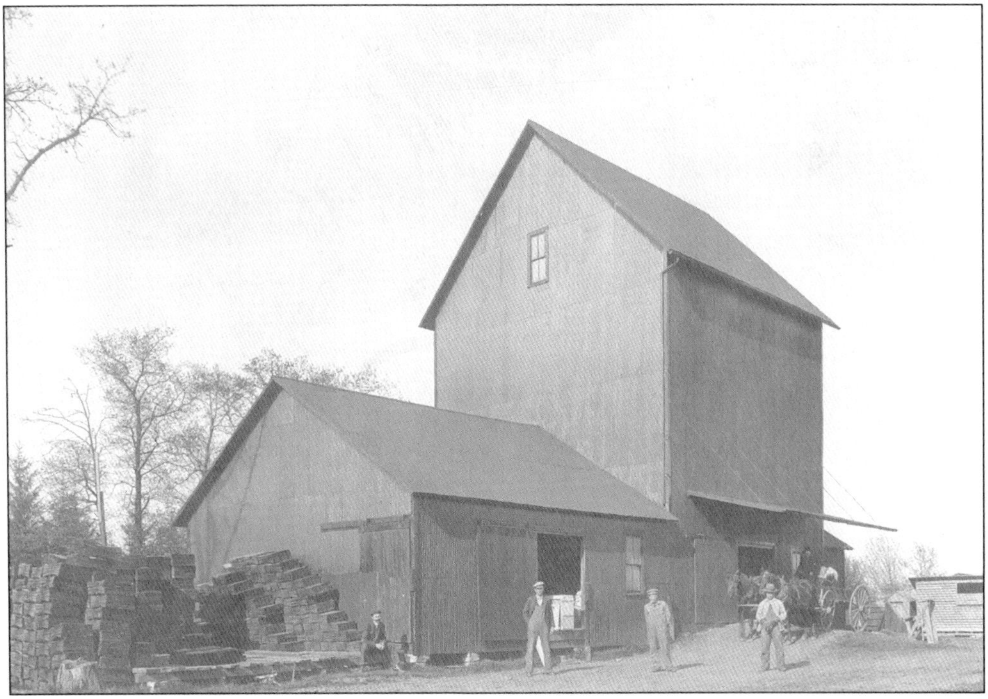

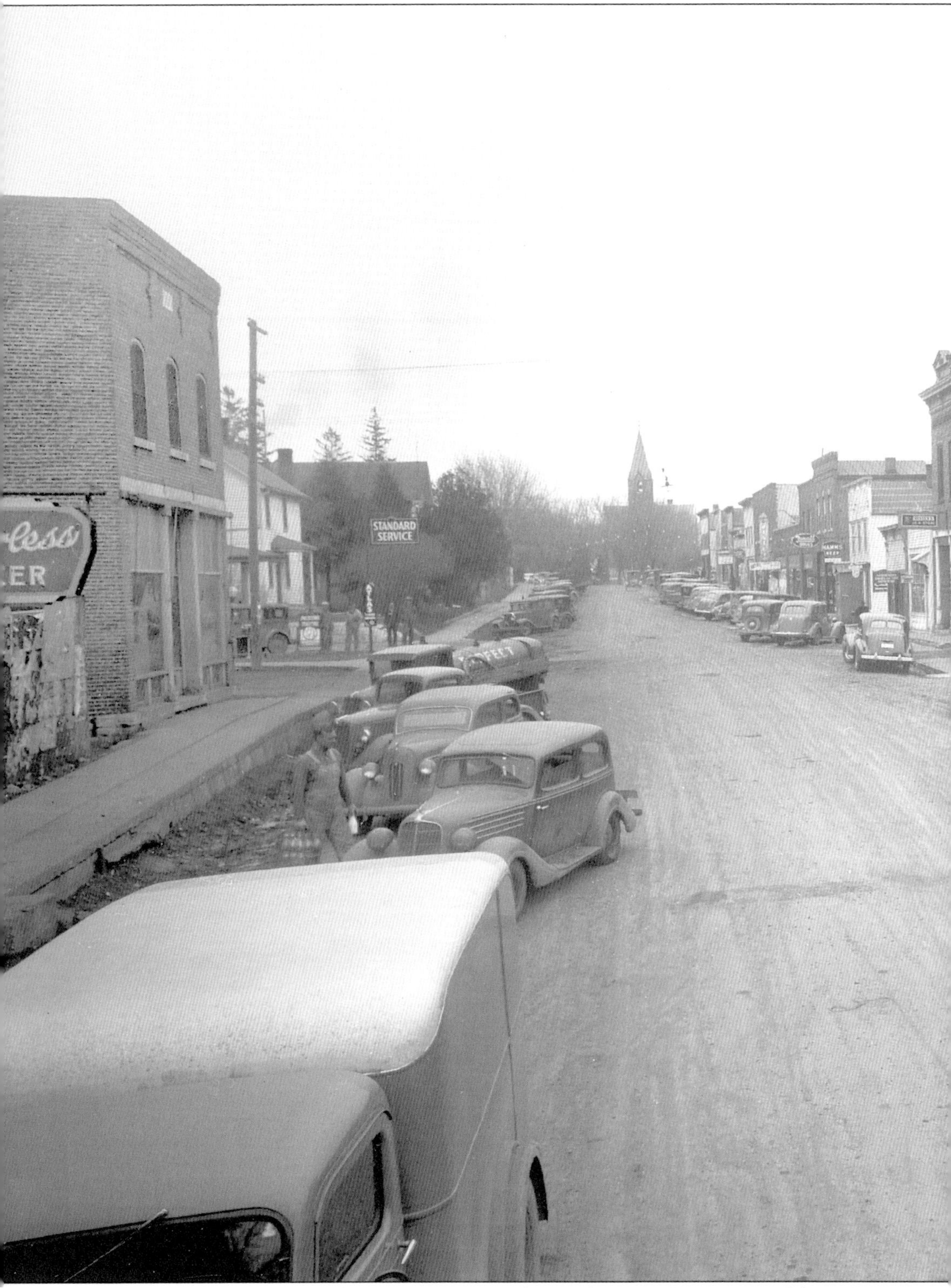

MAIN STREET. This picture shows Spring Grove during the Great Depression of the 1930s.

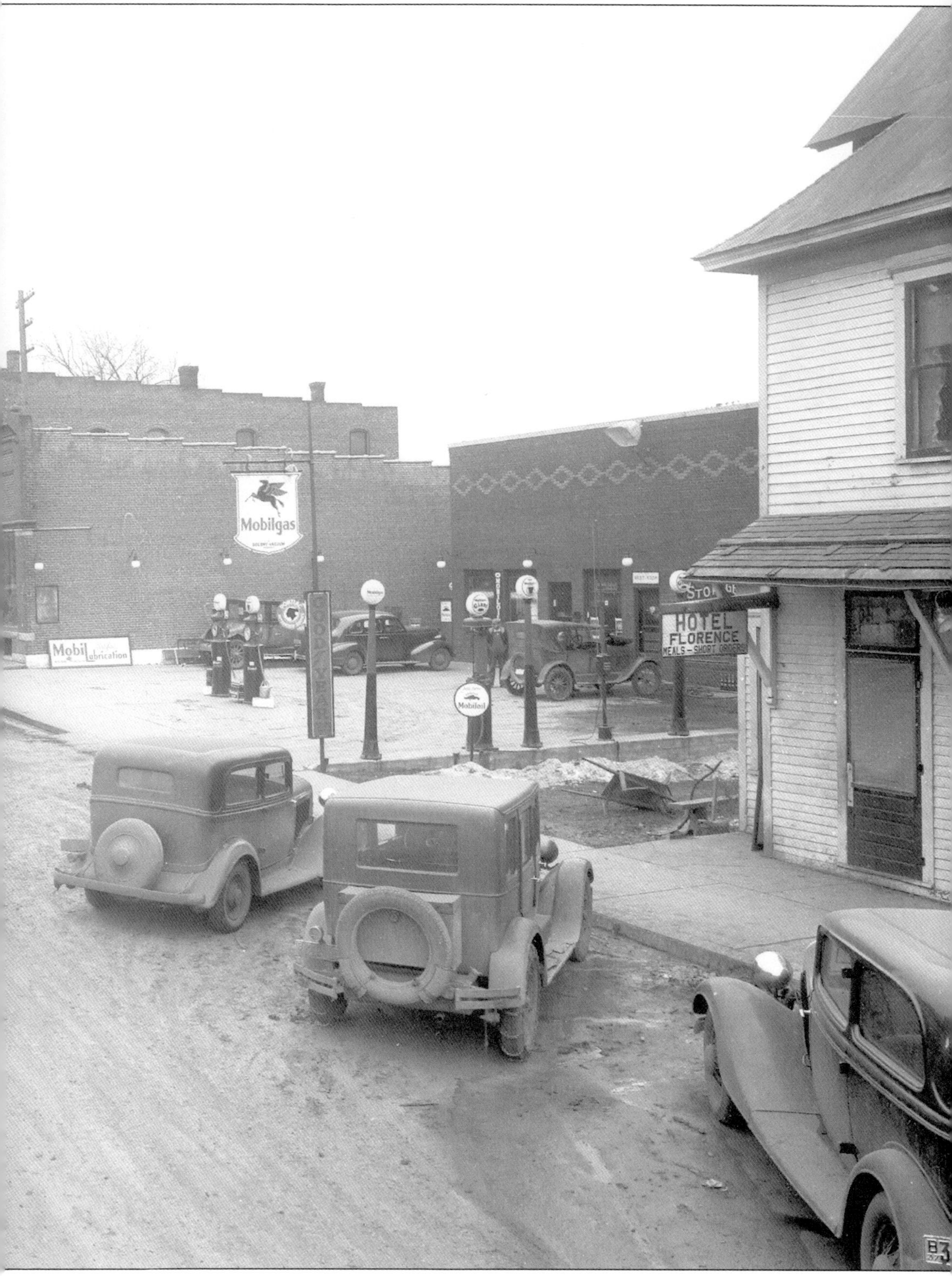
Mobilgas
Mobil Lubrication
HOTEL
FLORENCE
MEALS—SHORT ORDERS
Mobiloil

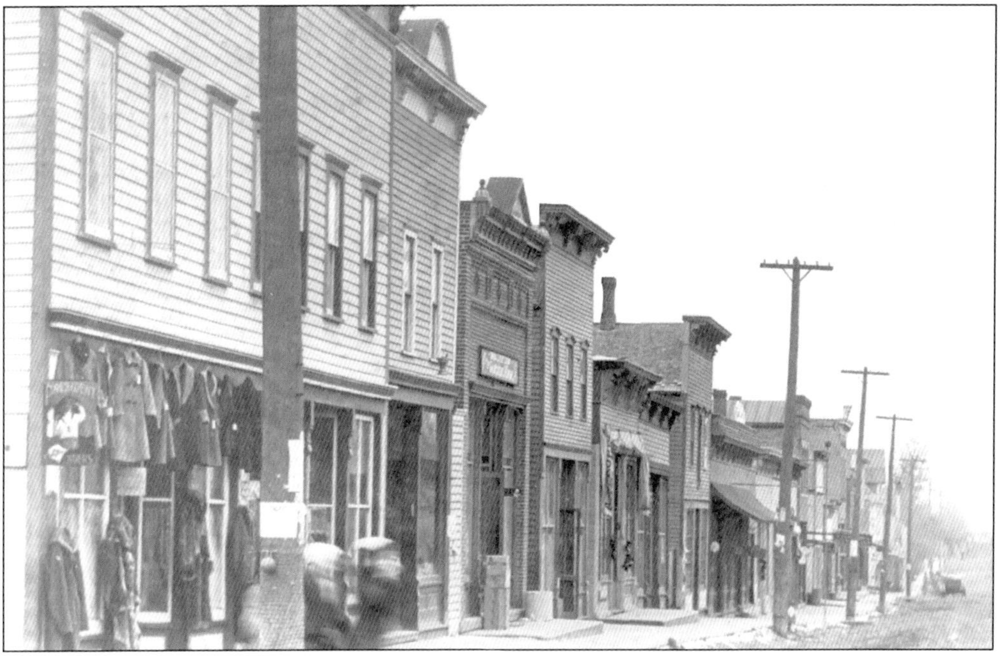

SIMILAR VIEWS. As late as the 1930s, it was common to see Winnebago Indian women and children selling hand-made baskets on the sidewalks of Spring Grove. These baskets were made from the white ash tree, and many of them have survived to this day. The second view of Main Street was drawn by Peter J. Rosendahl, the creator of the *Han Ola og Han Per* series, and is a good example of Spring Grove English.

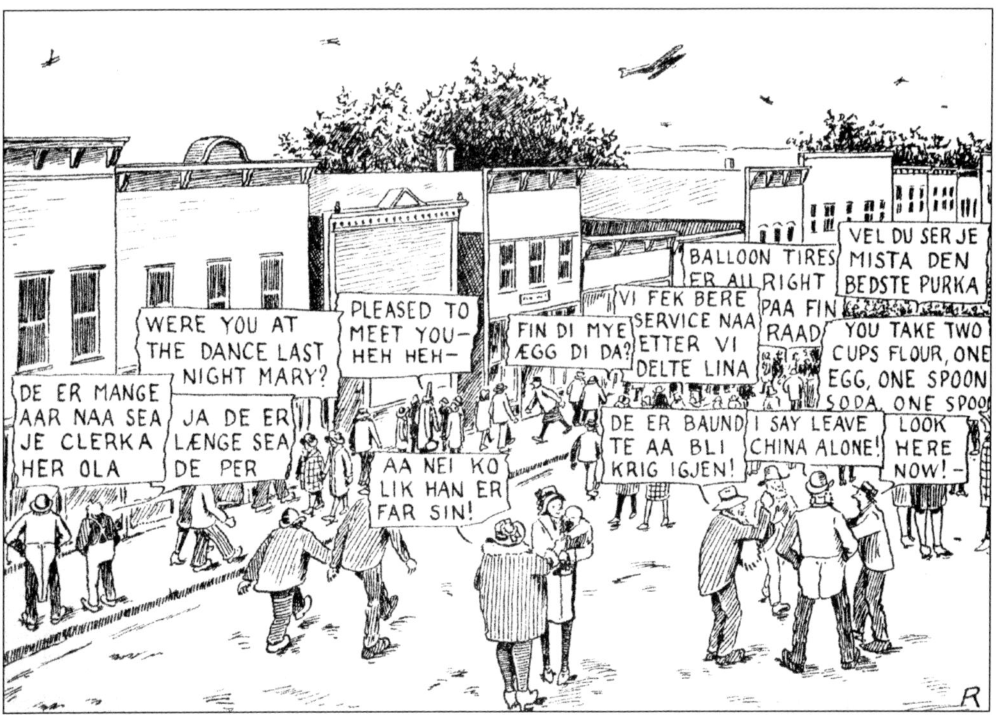

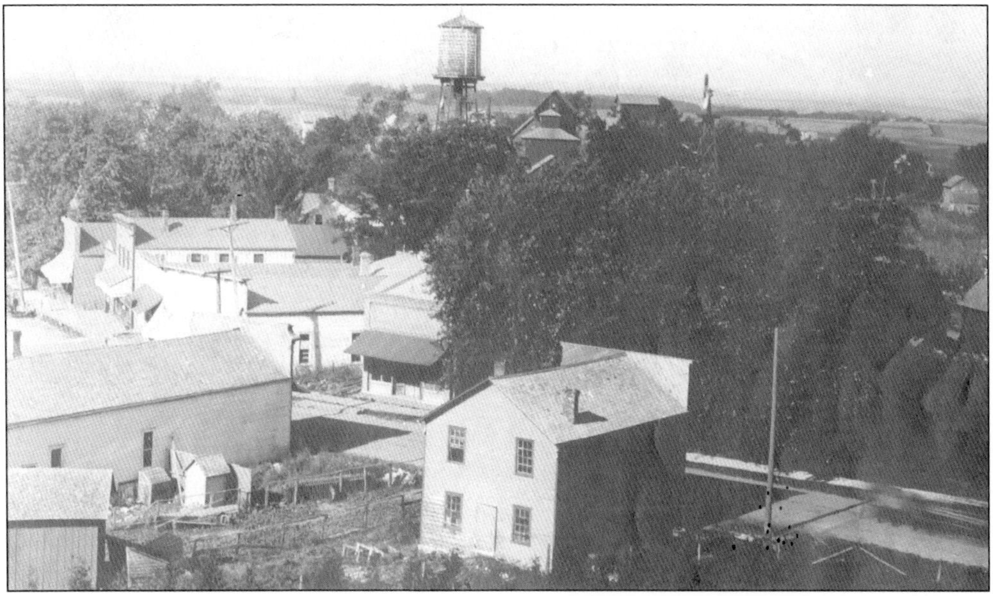

Wooden Water Tower. Mons Fladager commissioned Spring Grove's first water-well to be built. It went to a depth of 70 feet, was hand-dug, and lined with masonry. Water was raised in buckets using a windlass until a windmill was eventually erected over the well. As the windmill spun, water would be pumped from the well and sent down long troughs that extended to the street, providing water for horses. In 1894, a 400-foot well was dug and a gasoline engine was installed to pump water into a 75-foot wooden water tower that held 1,500 barrels of water.

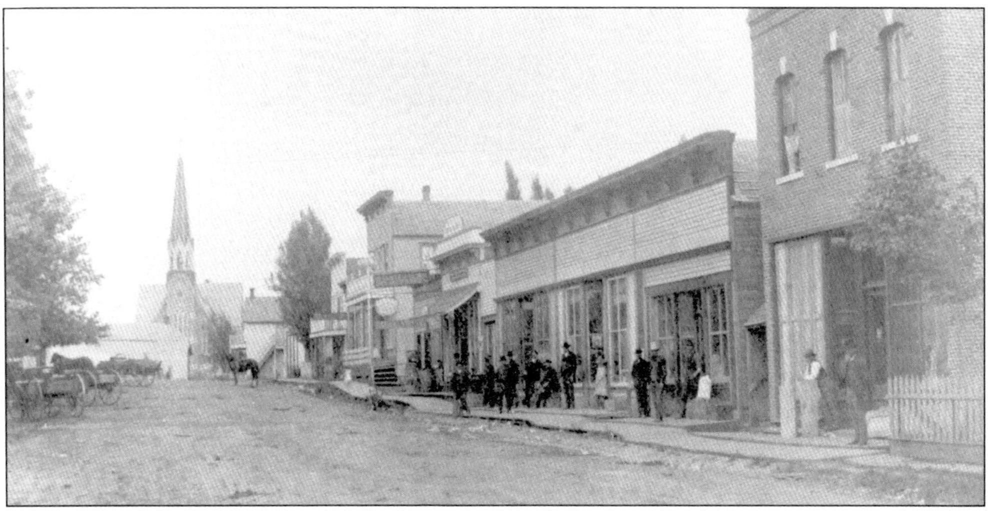

Wooden Sidewalks. Shown here is a view of Main Street before 1900. Notice the wooden sidewalks. Over time they would become extremely warped. From a 1904 issue of the *Spring Grove Herald*:

> *The Cement Side Walk Builders are Here. On Tuesday occurred the first move made by Spring Grove for the improvement of our sidewalks when a cement walk was placed around the dwelling of Banker Onsgard. A great many seem to be interested now since the improvement has commenced, and if present indications continue there will be a big supply of these walks in town before long. Let it boom.*

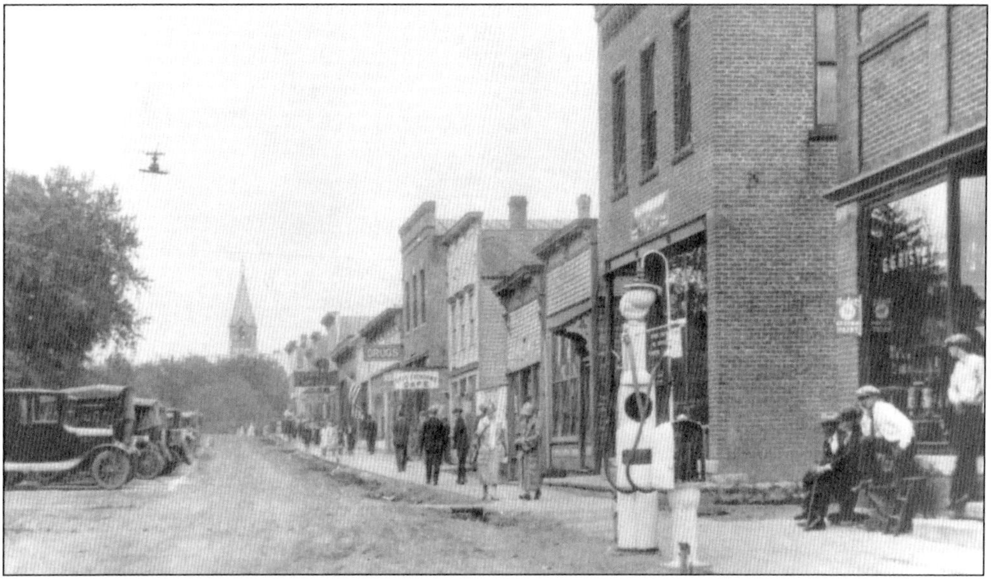

ILLUMINATING MAIN STREET. In 1889, the village council voted that kerosene lamps would be hung along Main Street, each of which had to be lit individually. In 1912, an electric light plant was built at City Hall, which also housed the jail, council chambers, and fire equipment. Three years later, electricity was supplied by the Root River Power and Light Company. Notice the single electric light hanging over the street in this photo. It is also interesting to note that cars at this time were parked in the middle of the street.

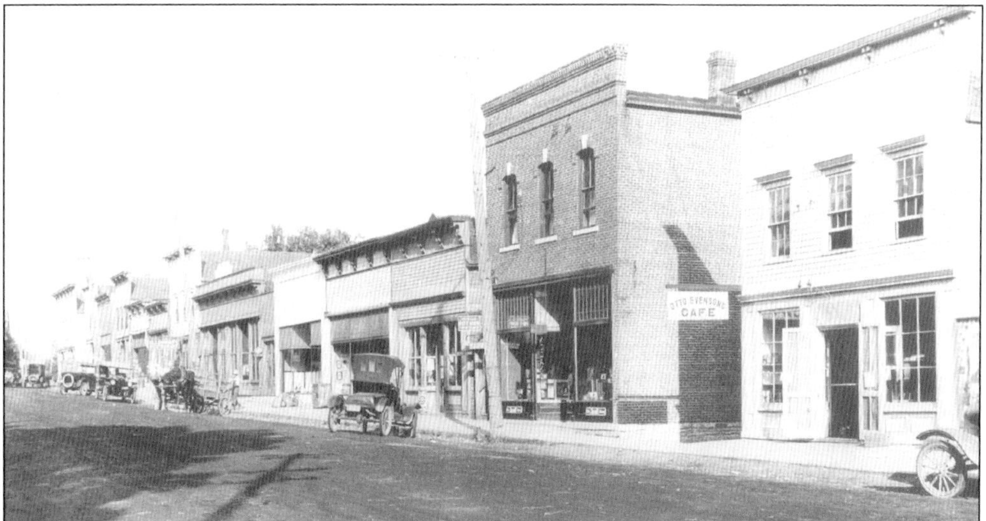

MAIN STREET CAFÉ. Driving down Main Street, in the early 1900s, one would have come upon the welcoming sign of Otto Evenson's café. From a 1917 issue of the *Spring Grove Herald*:

> *Good things to eat and a good place in which to eat them not only appeals to all the human race, but is one of the necessary business enterprises of every village and city. This place is situated in the heart of the business district and is liberally patronized from early morning until late at night seven days of every week. The popularity of this place is due to Mr. Evenson's natural genial manner, and his ability to produce good things to tickle the palate and satisfy the inner man.*

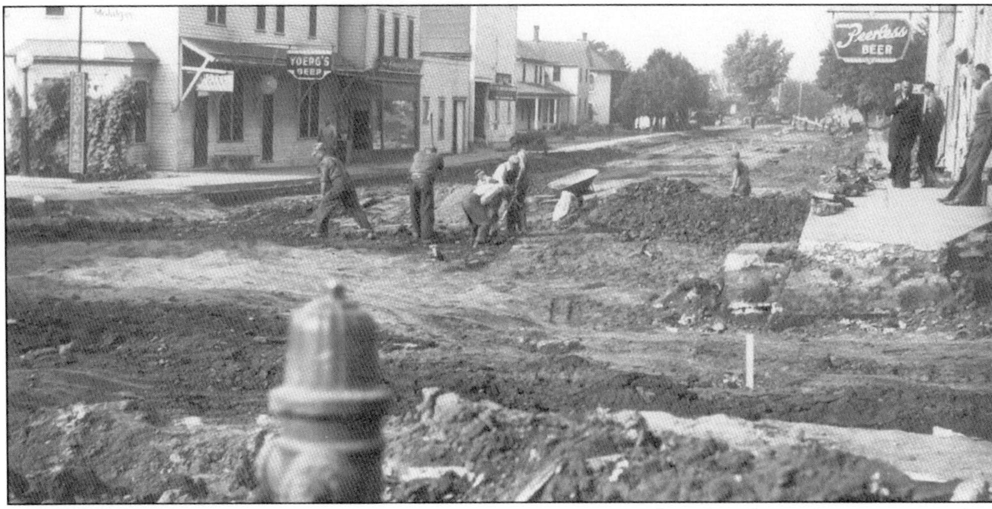

DIGGING UP MAIN STREET. In 1939, Main Street was paved and curbs and gutters were laid on all residential streets. Electricity, water, and sewer facilities were also installed. From the *Spring Grove Herald*:

> *Henry Fladager does not agree with those who claim good roads will work to the disadvantage of the country town merchant in carrying away local trade to the larger city. He says the home merchant need not lose his place in the sun if he will only wake up and go after business like the city stores and mail order houses do. The home merchant must buy right, advertise liberally, keep at it consistently, tell the public what he has and describe honestly and fully and adopt more modern methods of merchandising.*

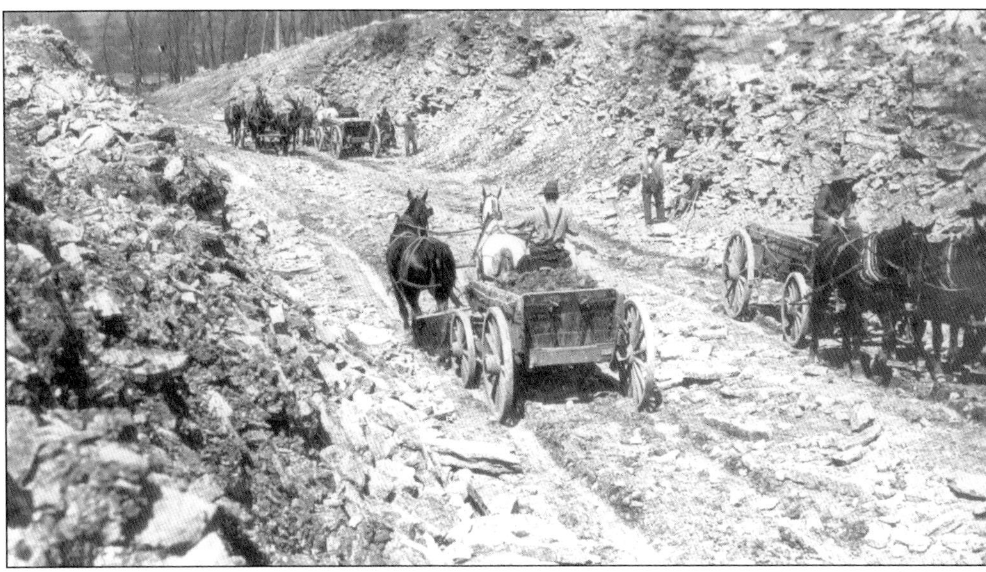

ROAD CONSTRUCTION. Shown here is a section of road being dug out at the east-end of town, which would eventually become Highway 44. This was extremely rough work, especially for the horses. Loads of rock were thrown into the wagons, and the men would push the animals to such an extent that they would literally die on the spot, either to be buried or left on the side of the road. A new horse would then be brought forward. This cycle continued until the Herculean task was done. The company hired to do this work was called Stark & Clark.

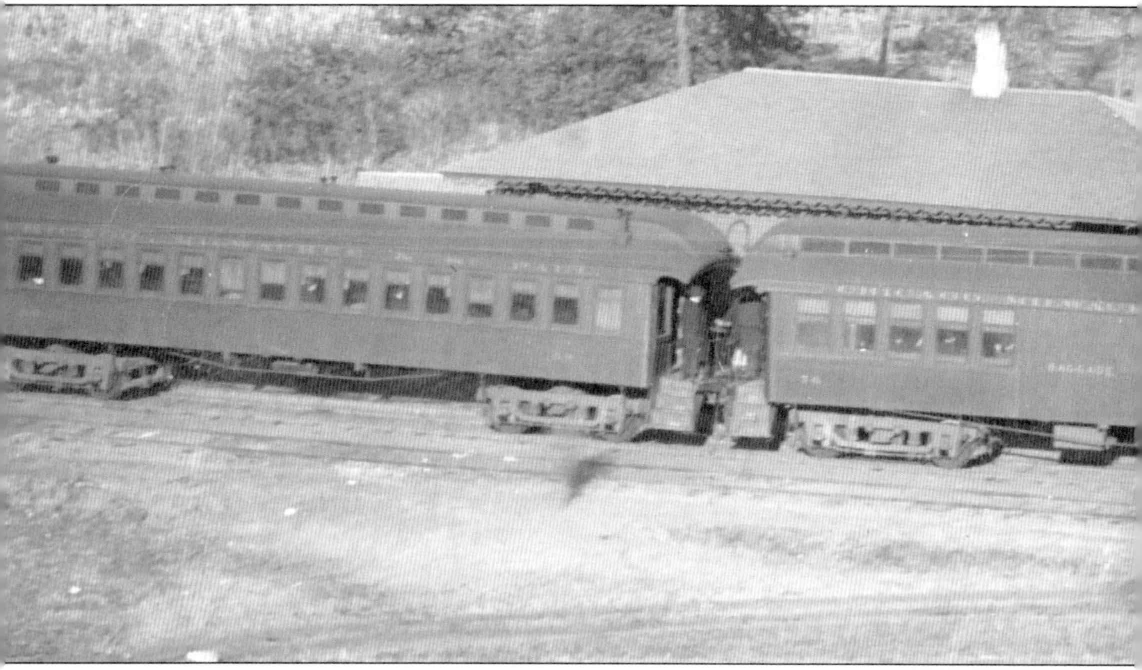

THE RAILROAD. The coming of the railroad dramatically changed Spring Grove's economy. Farmers no longer had to travel great distances to river towns such as Winona, Minnesota. They had to travel 35–50 miles, which by wagon could take up to two weeks. Materials arriving by rail caused a building boom. Lumberyards came into existence as well as grain elevators.

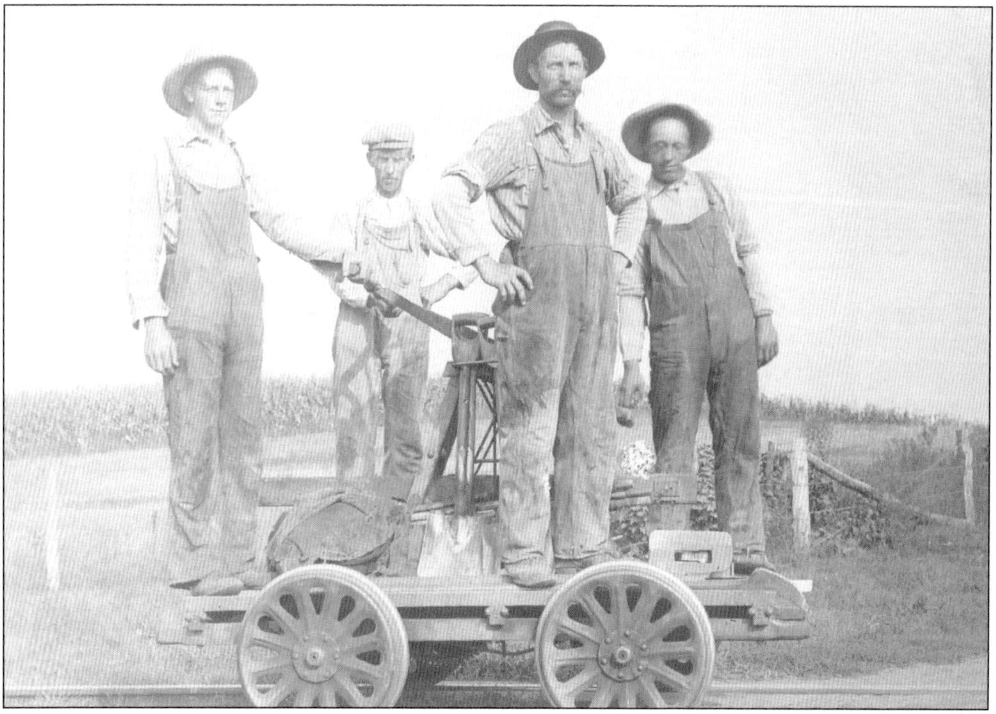

FIXING TRACK. Four unidentified railroad workers.

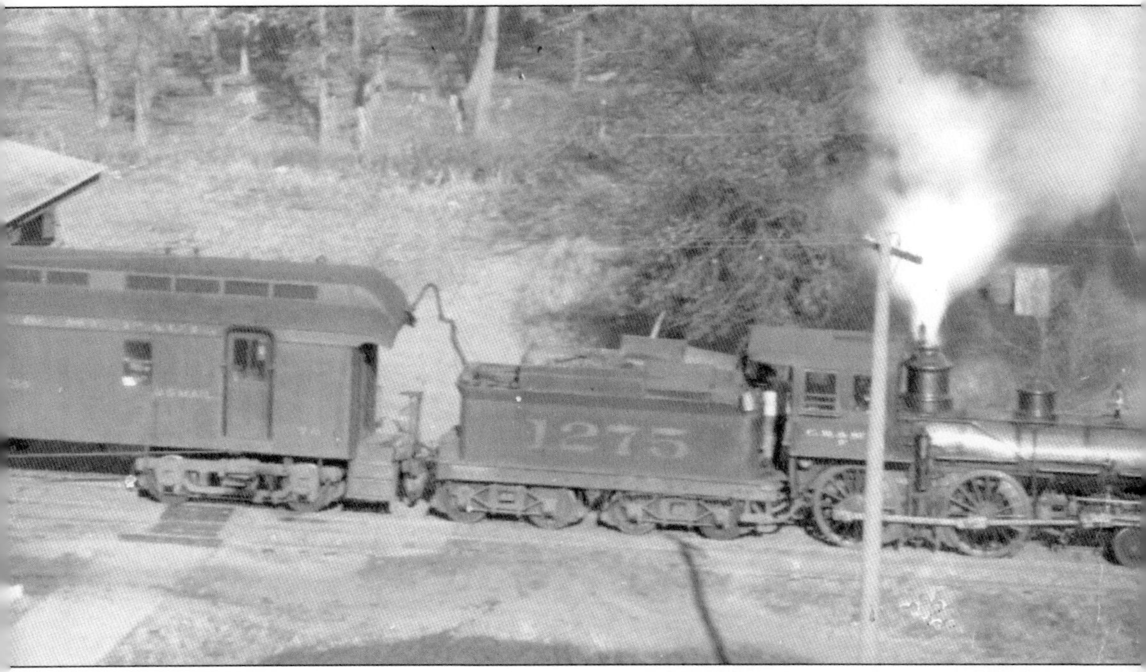

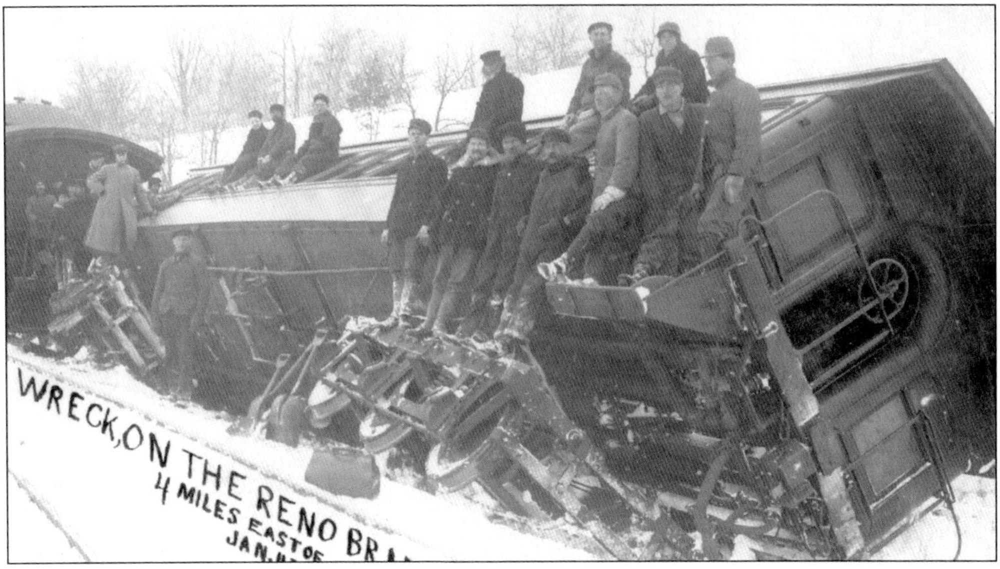

TRAIN WRECK. From a 1910 issue of the *Spring Grove Herald*:

> *Our station agent was somewhat surprised last evening when No. 425 pulled in. Conductor Merwin quickly informed him that his passengers and both cars were left about four miles east of here alongside the track. They left some 30 minutes late and going rather slow up grade, some fifty rods north east of the trestle bridge, when the engineer noticed the jerking of the train and quickly discovered that both the passenger and mail coach were off the track. When the crew became satisfied that the mail car would not tip over, the engine was uncoupled and came up here where two box cars were quickly coupled onto a crew of men all made haste back after the passengers, some forty-five in number, who were found hovering about a fire that they had started on the track at the rear of the wreck.*

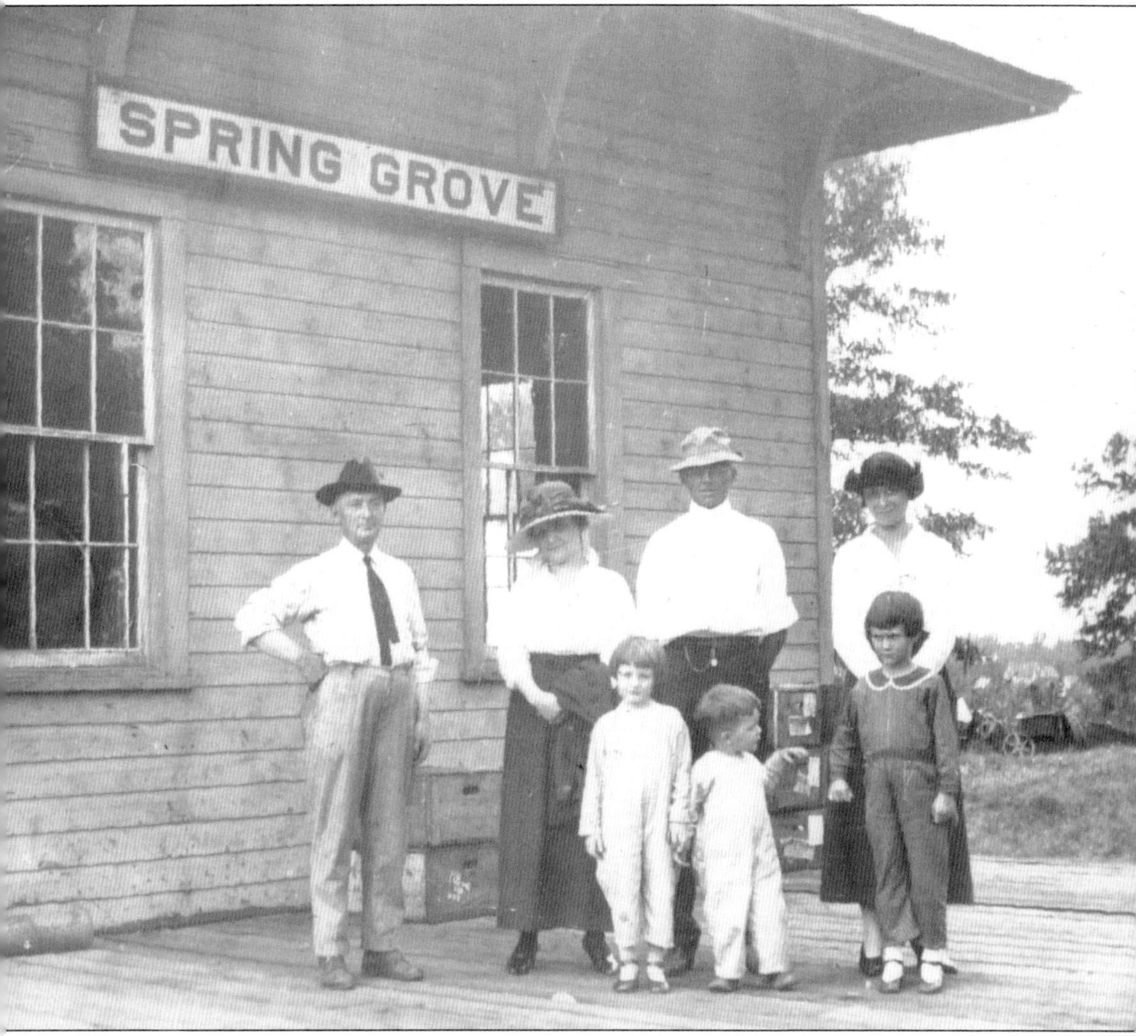

SPRING GROVE DEPOT. A group of unidentified residents wait for the train to arrive. In 1879, a narrow-gauge track was laid through Spring Grove. By 1900, it was replaced with a standard gauge track. Frank Bartholomew was the first station agent.

Five

Tradition and Celebration

Norwegian immigrants in Spring Grove celebrated many old and new traditions when they came to America. One of the most important new traditions was Homecoming. The first celebration was held in 1907, and continues to this day. Every ten years, thousands of past and present residents meet in Spring Grove to reminisce and celebrate their history.

A similar tradition is the *lag* (gathering), which brings together immigrants from the same region or *bygd* (township), and gives them the opportunity to celebrate their common heritage and local traditions. Hallingdal and Toten *lags* are featured this chapter. *Syttende Mai* (May 17th) is celebrated annually in Spring Grove. Ever since 1814, Norwegians have come together on this date to celebrate their independence from Danish rule. Traditional costumes, dances and songs are always part of these gatherings.

In 1880, the literary society *Fremad* (to move forward) was founded. Its members met weekly in the church basement and hosted lectures, readings, music and "whatever of an entertaining character may be suitable for healthy presentation to the public." Another organization, active since 1928, is a chapter of the Sons of Norway known as the Valheim Lodge #364, which was organized by Eyvind Ager.

Many old country traditions carried over to Spring Grove, but none stranger than *julebukk* (Christmas goat). During *julebukk*, participants disguise themselves and roam from house to house trying to conceal their identities from their hosts. Regardless of his or her success, the *julebukker* stays to visit and to dance. Old world tradition is also preserved in immigrant furniture and textiles, which had symbolic as well as practical utility. Two examples of important traditional objects, a *hengeskap* (hanging cupboard) and a *Kristen teppe* (christening blanket), close this chapter.

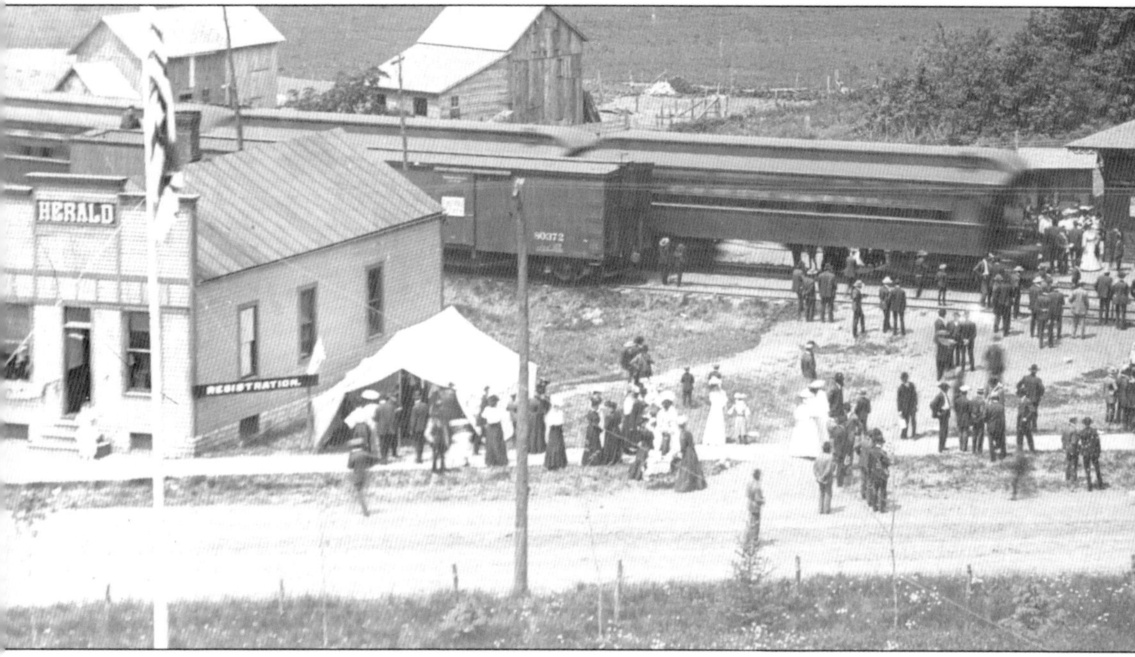

1907 HOMECOMING. From a 1907 issue of the *Spring Grove Herald*:

> *Tuesday evening marked the beginning of Homecoming Week, when the evening train brought in from the east about 200 Homecomers, all from the Dakotas. It required four coaches to bring them here and the passengers cheered loudly when they made their final stop at their dear old home, Spring Grove. The band and hundreds of citizens were at the depot to meet and welcome*

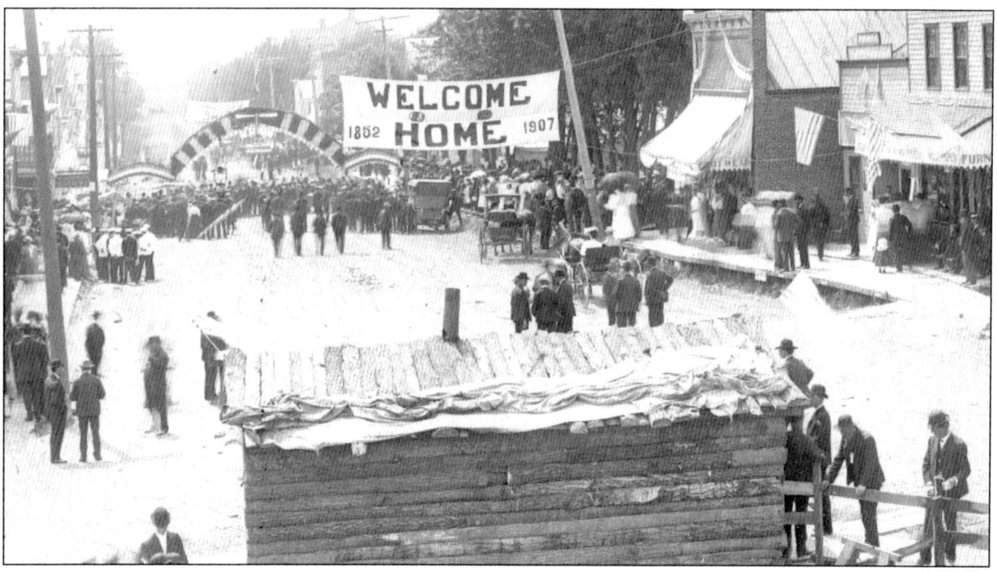

HOMECOMING MUSEUM. The first Homecoming featured a historical museum. The log cabin seen in the foreground was constructed especially for the occasion. Inside, many pioneer objects were displayed, one of which was a saddle owned by the Civil War colonel Hans Christian Heg. Admission was 10¢ for adults, 5¢ for children. The museum was located in what is now Viking Memorial Park.

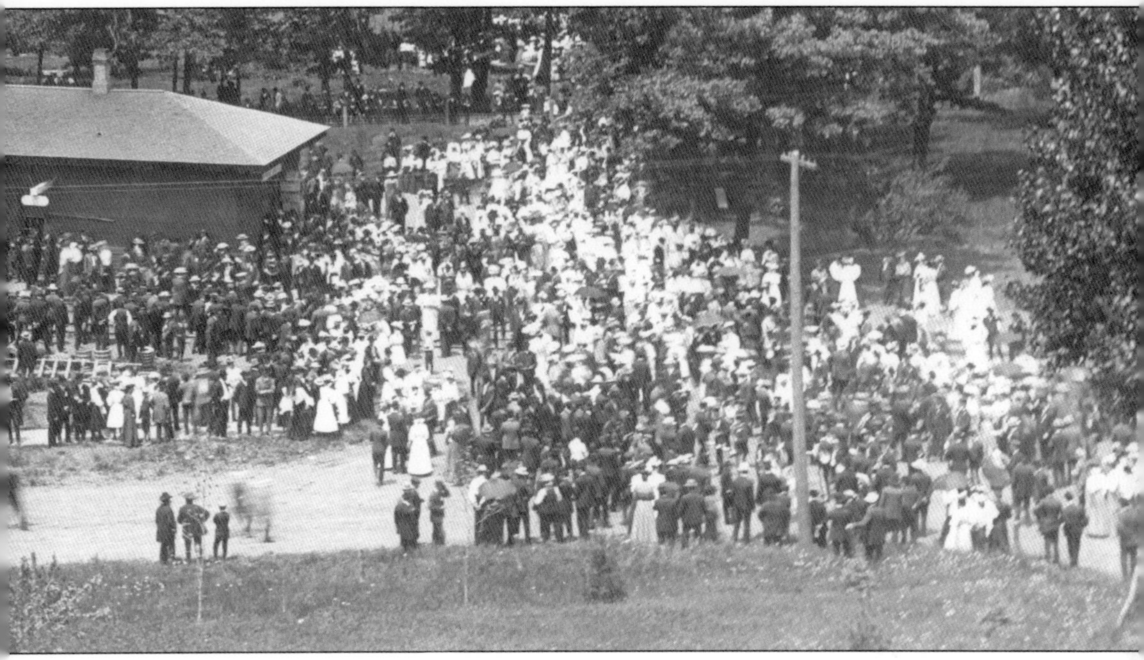

them home. . . thousands of people flocked to eagerly put down their name so they might be among the ones who displayed a Homecoming badge. Nearly 1,500 people registered and as many more would have, had there been more badges to distribute.

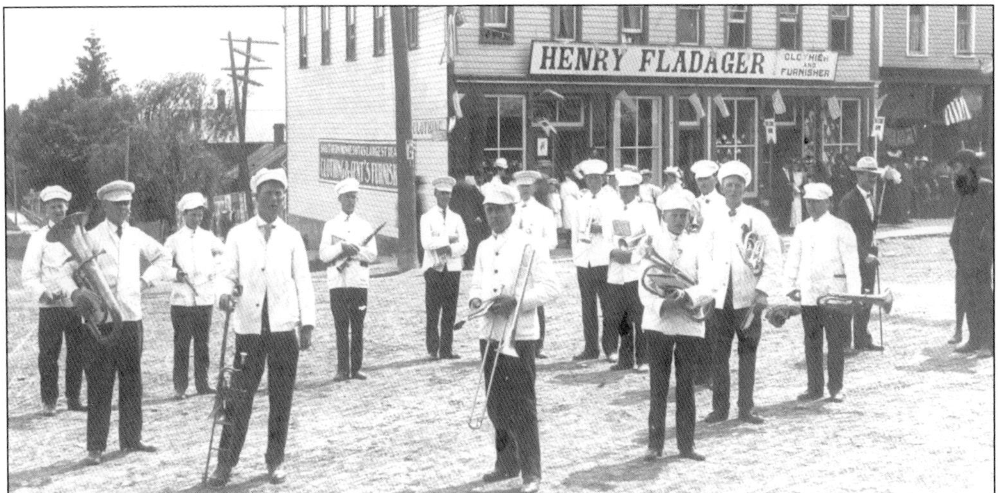

1917 HOMECOMING. From a 1917 issue of the *Spring Grove Herald:*

> *Wednesday's program was a success from the time of starting until the Home Sweet Home was played by Carpenter's Orchestra at the Opera House. Each speaker held the crowd at attention and by recalling many little incidents of the past made them eager for more. Thursday proved to be the banner day. Auto after auto rolled in filled to their capacity. Promptly at 2:45 roasted steer was served and, although it weighed about 1,300 pounds, was quickly devoured and proved from the people in line that it was the drawing card of the day. The music in the afternoon by the three bands was very pleasing and enjoyed by all*

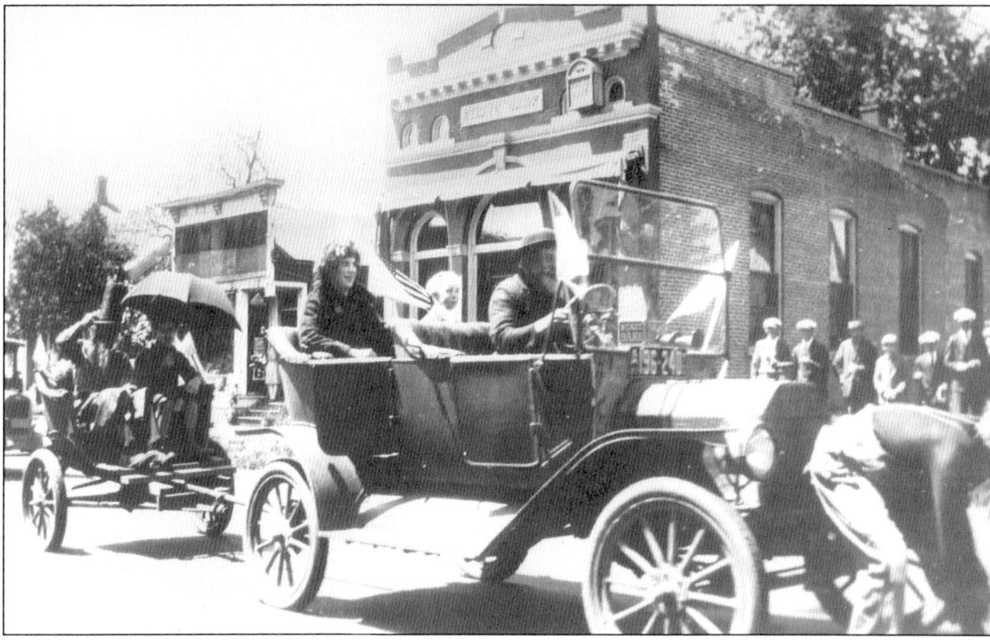

1937 Homecoming Parade. During the 1937 parade, residents would have seen their favorite cartoon-strip, *Han Ola og Han Per*, come to life. Driving the 1917 Ford, and dressed as Per, is Arnold Peterson. His companion Ola, played by Leonard Tollefsrud, is shown here squatting in front of the car. Other characters featured in the strip also made their way down Main Street: Lars (Rinaldo Ellestad), Værmor (Clarence Husmoen), Polla (Andrew Miner), and Dada (Harold Olsgard). Below is a cartoon by Peter J. Rosendahl, drawn especially for Homecoming, and featuring said characters.

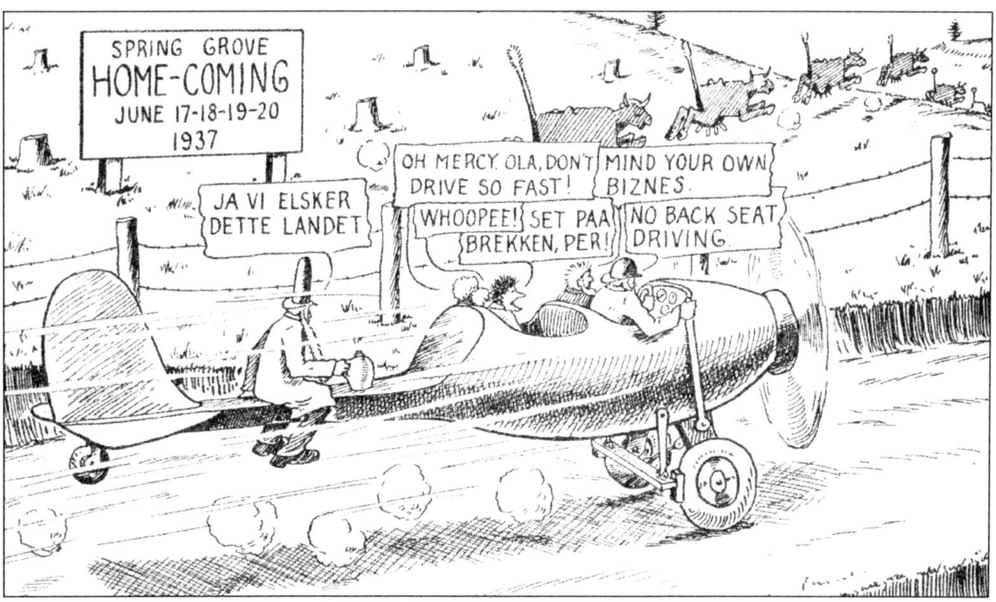

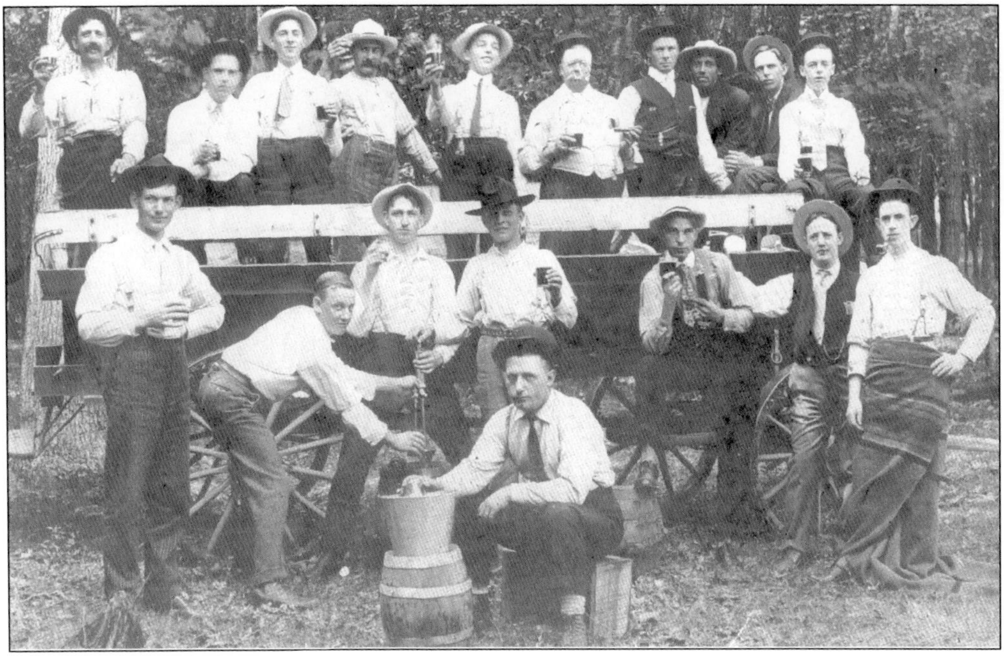

MYHRE BREWERY. For a short time there was a brewery in Spring Grove. Although long defunct by the time this photo was taken, it started in 1866, after Johan Myhre built a stone cellar in the side of a small hill on his land. The cellar was used for cold storage until 1870, when Reverend Reque came to town and forced the brewery to be closed. Pictured here, from left to right, are the following: (front row) Ted Hendrickson, Albert Rauk, Albert Anderson, Thomas Goldberg, Earl Humphrey, Martin Fladager, Helmer Ostlie, and Oscar Muller; (back row) Olaf Narveson, Albert Solberg, Edwin Newhouse, Ole Harstad, Baldwin Onsgard, Mr. Liudahl, John Schansberg, Herman Jenson, Oliver Onsgard, and Emil Engell. Even though Spring Grove was a "dry" town, kegs of beer, or "blind pigs," were still secretively slipped from the train and set-up in the nearby woods. Moonshining was also quite prevalent in Spring Grove, especially during Prohibition.

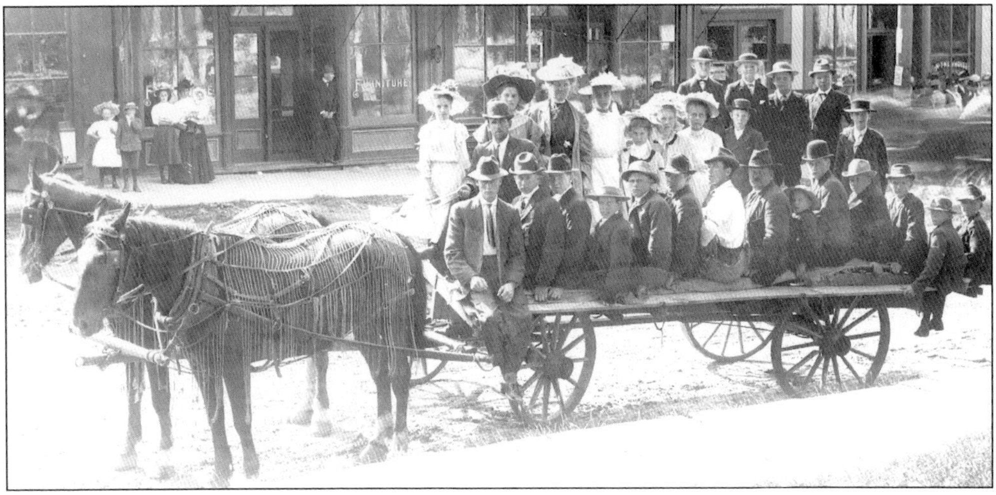

SPRING OUTING. A group of unidentified young people ride in a wagon around town. It is interesting to note that the buildings in the background, along Main Street, no longer exist—they were destroyed by a devastating fire.

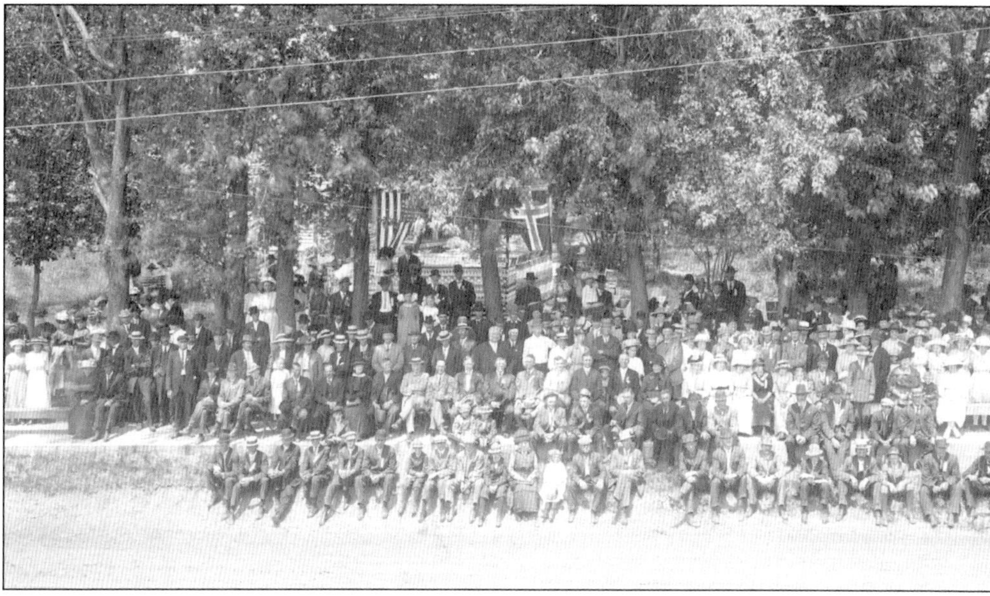

Totning-Lag. A 1913 issue of the *Spring Grove Herald* declared, "The Totning festival was a success from start to finish. The weather was ideal and nature wore her prettiest dress. The Totning were numerous and in a peaceful mood." These immigrants came from Toten, Norway. The cartoon below was drawn by Peter J. Rosendahl, who caricatured many residents in his drawings. The figure on the podium is Johan Gran, who was the Totning president. Otto Evenson, a café owner, is shown selling "flatbrod" and "sur melk." The constable on the far left is E.J. Myrah, carrying two drunks to jail.

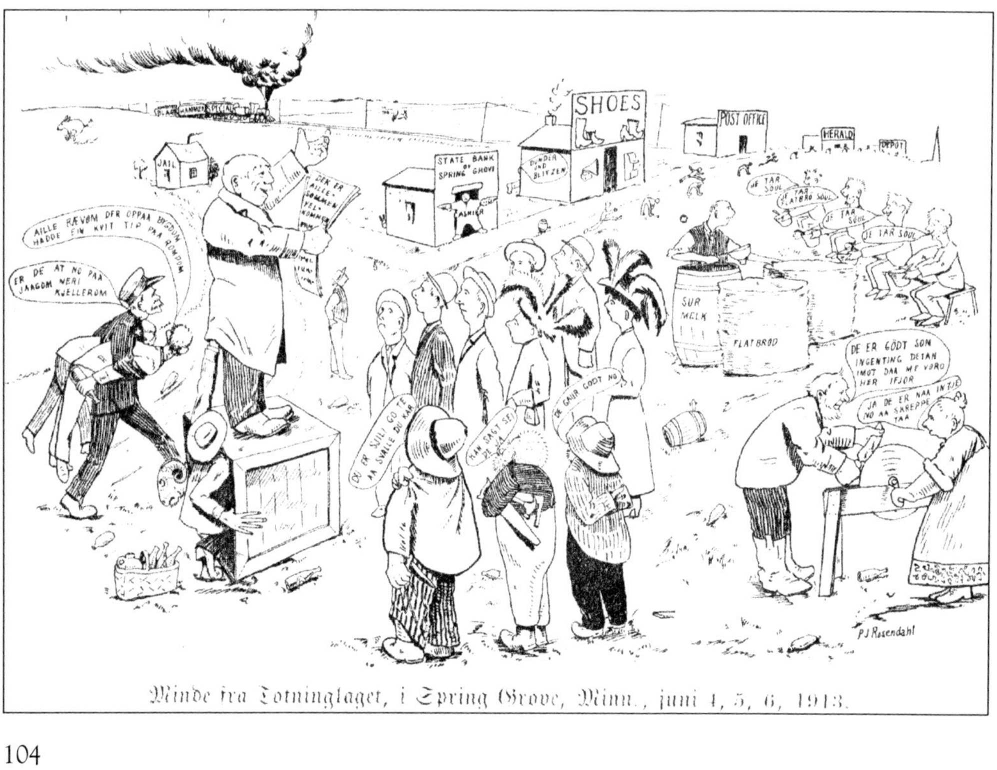

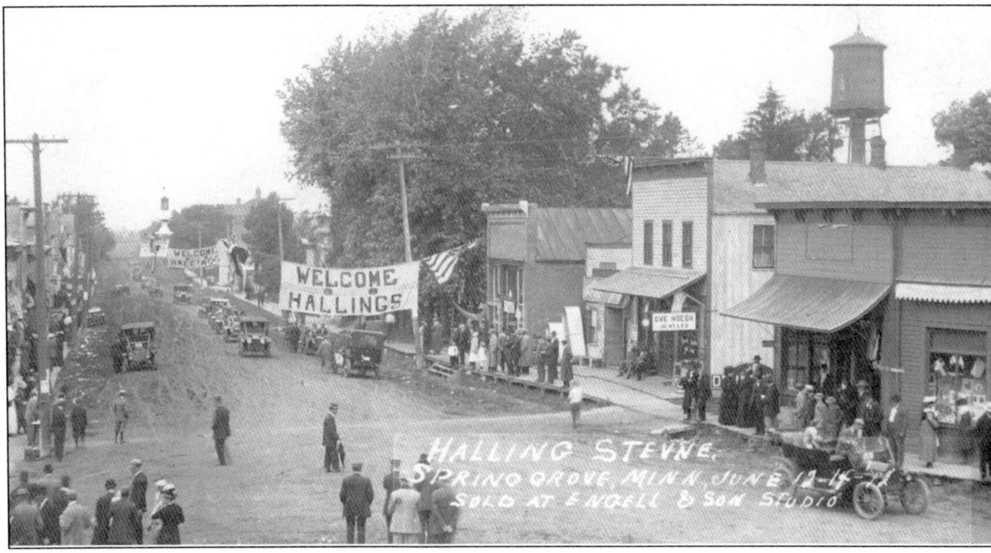

HALLING-LAG. A 1912 issue of the *Spring Grove Herald* observed, "Hallings and their descendants by the thousands are invading Spring Grove this week and are having one of the greatest reunions in the history of this particular clan. Special trains and automobiles are bringing crowds of these energetic Vikings to our little city." *Lag* is the Norwegian word for gathering. In this case, the immigrants from Hallingdal celebrate and reminisce. One of their acrobatic dances involved a wheeling leap called the *Halling kast*, which is shown in the cartoon below by the artist Peter J. Rosendahl, who hardly exaggerates this fast-paced dance.

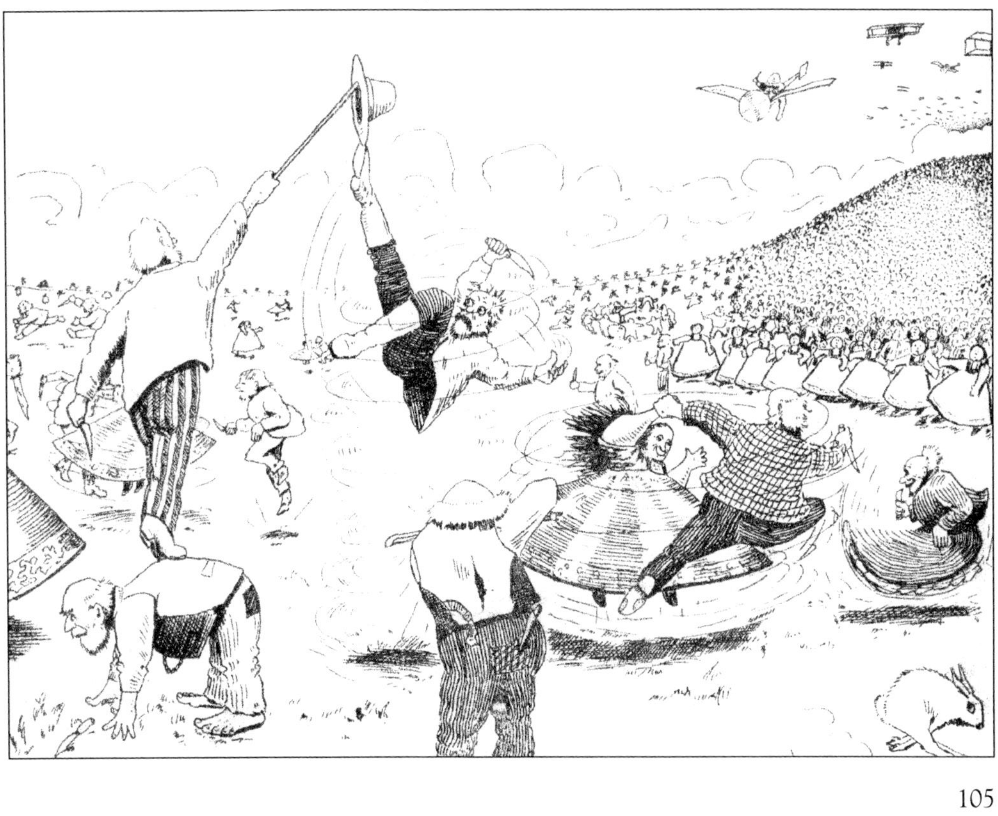

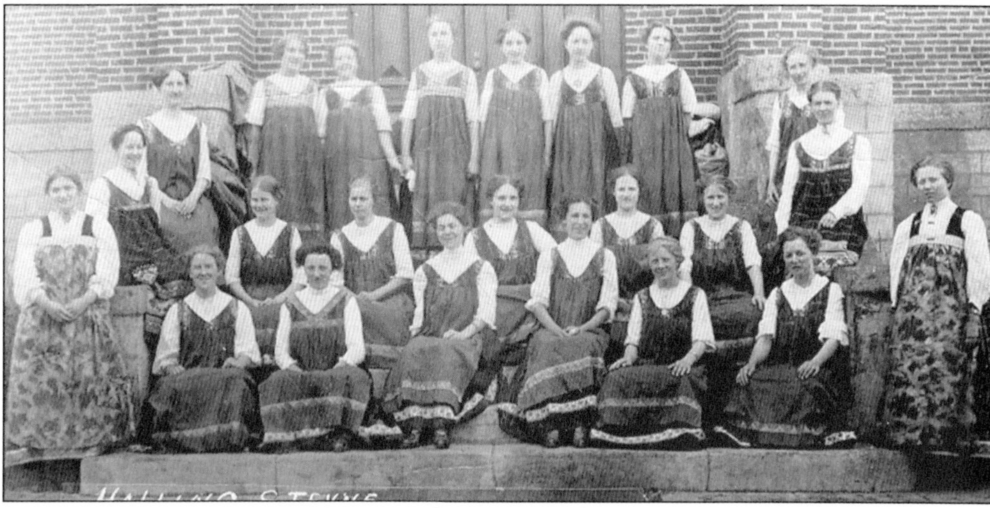

HALLING-LAG WAITRESSES. A group of waitresses who served in the church basement for the 1912 Halling-Lag, shown here from left to right, are as follows: (front row) Edith Quarve, Theoline Kolsrud, Alma Qualey, Nettie Bakke, Inga Solberg, Emma Johnsrud, Cora Kroshus, and Clarissa Storlie; (middle row) Lena Reierson, Minnie Quanrud, Olga Myrah, Mabel Torkelson, Idella Johnson, Rose Vaaler, and Inga Tweeten; (back row) Clara Johnsrud, Clarissa Hallan, Mandy Tone, Ella Stenehjem, Bertha Fladager, Nettie Fladager, Palma Goldberg, and Agnes Blexrud. Their dresses were patterned after authentic Hallingdal *bunads*, which were costumes typically reserved for special occasions.

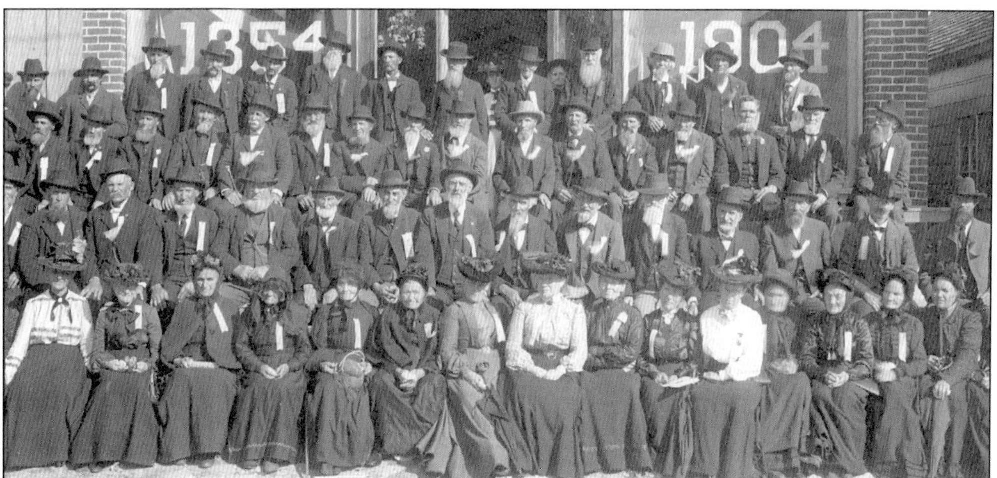

OLD SETTLER'S REUNION 1904. From a report of the Territorial Pioneer and Veterans Banquet, written by O.K. Dahle:

> *Based upon the report of the registration committee, persons who were present and registered at Caledonia on the day of the celebration (September 28th), have been awarded prizes as follows: Most aged Veteran who enlisted in either war, O.P. Wolden, Spring Grove Township, 80 years. The person who made the earliest entry of land (still holding), Embrick Opheim, Spring Grove; squatted May 1853; official entry, September 11, 1854.*

These were only two of the awards presented to attendees from Houston County. Other contests included Ladies Nail-Driving, Ball-Throwing by Women, and The Heaviest Old Settler.

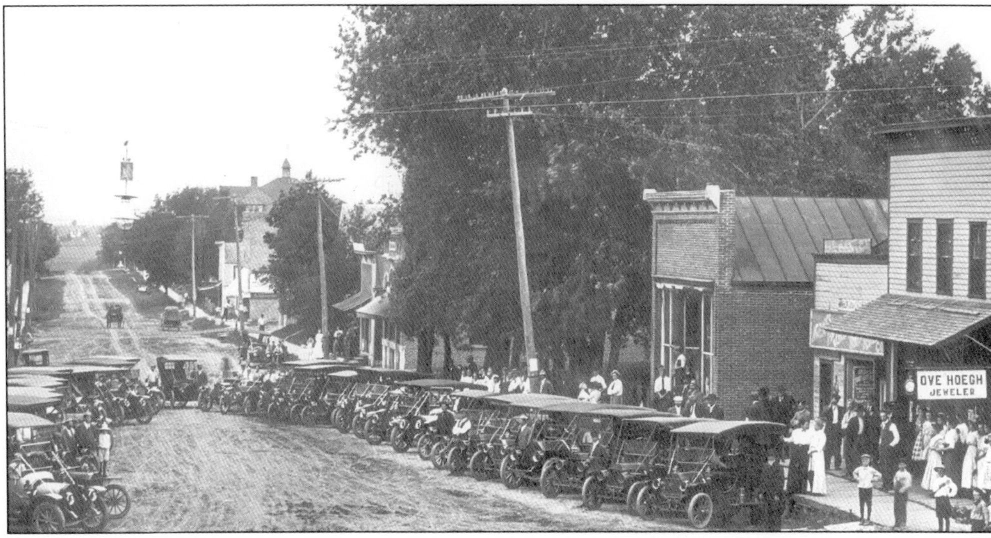

AUTOMOBILE CLUB. In 1911, Spring Grove hosted the First Annual Houston County Auto Association. The rise of these new horseless carriages was a passion for some, but a never-ending nuisance for others, who said that nothing could replace the horse.

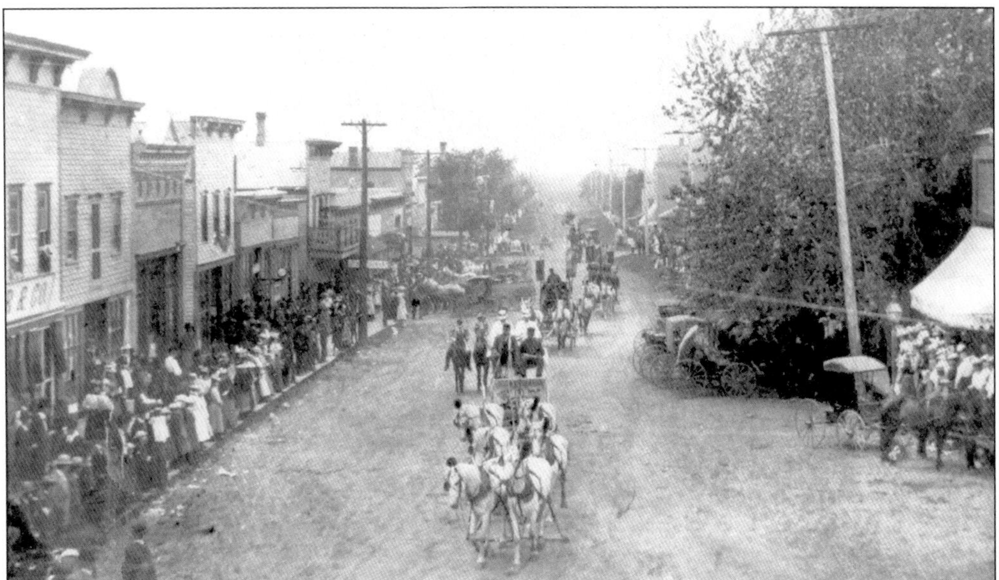

TRAVELING CIRCUS. From an advertisement in a 1900 issue of the *Spring Grove Herald*:

> *Coming Soon! Gollmar Brothers Leading Shows of the World, Two Ring Circus, Monster, Menagerie, and Museum will exhibit at Spring Grove, Tuesday, May 22. Seen now for the first time in America, John Rooney, Champion Summersault Rider of the World. Troups of Athletes, Gymnasts, Acrobats, Jugglers, Contortionists, Aerialists, Tumblers, Leapers, Riders, Japanese and Arab Horsemen. The finest in African Lions in America, Giant Kangaroos, Black and Spotted Leopards, Nero, the summersault riding dog, the equestrian Goat, Golmar Brothers drove of Educated Boars, Minnie, the smallest pony on earth, Performing Bears, Acting Dogs, Trained Horses and Ponies, seven Funny Clowns, three Brass and Reed Bands, and a host of other attractions too numerous to mention. Remember the Grand Free Street Parade at 12:30.*

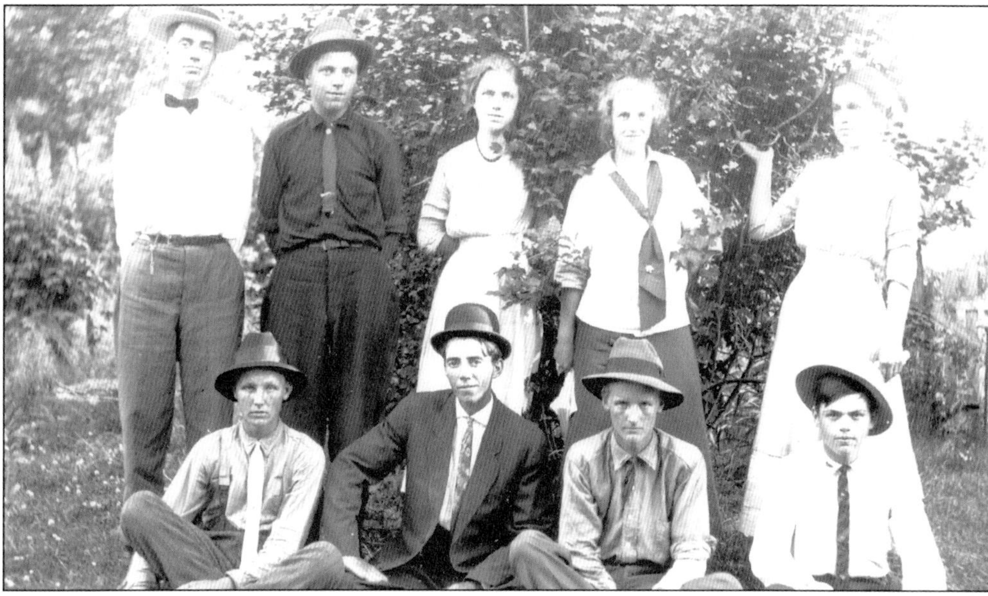

Weekend Gathering. Shown here, from left to right, are Melvin Ovestrud, Arnt Dyrdal, Geneva Ovestrud, Mabel Kroshus, Millie Ovestrud, Oscar Kroshus, Andrew Kroshus, Edwin Kroshus, and Ernest Ovestrud. Arnt Dyrdal (second from left) was the town's first casualty in World War One. The American Legion Post 249 in Spring Grove was first named after him, receiving its charter in October 1919.

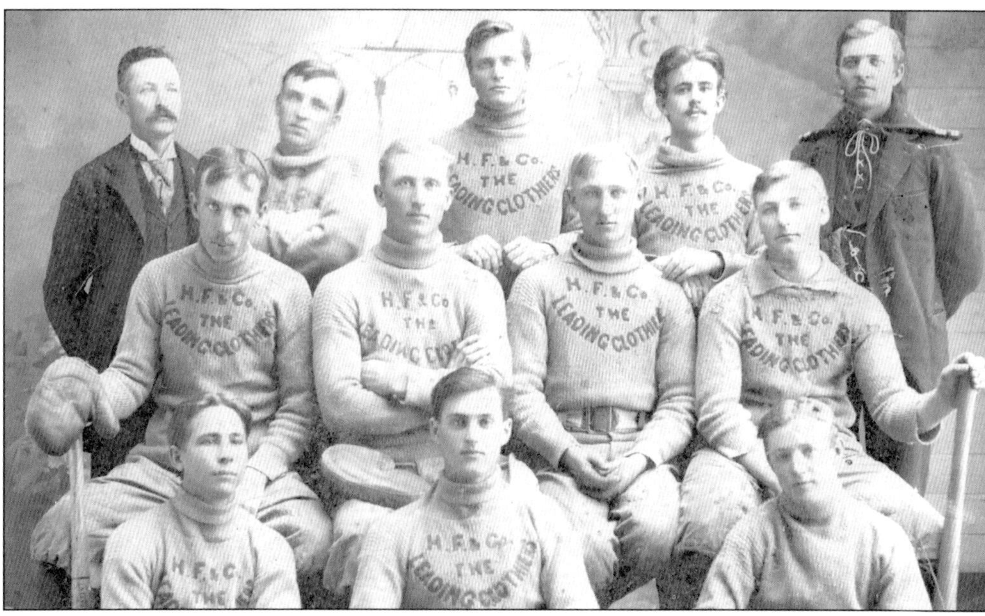

Champions of Houston and Fillmore Counties. Members of the1897 Clothiers baseball team, shown here from left to right, are as follows: (front row) E. Foss, first base; J. Kern, pitcher; and M. Fladager, shortstop; (middle row) O. Quandahl, center field; P. Ruffridge, catcher; H. Ruffridge, second base; and O. Roppe, substitute; (back row) Henry Fladager, secretary; P. Budahl, right field; E. Muller, left field; H. Ostlie, third base; and J. Kjomme, assistant manager. (Courtesy of Patricia Ashman Foss.)

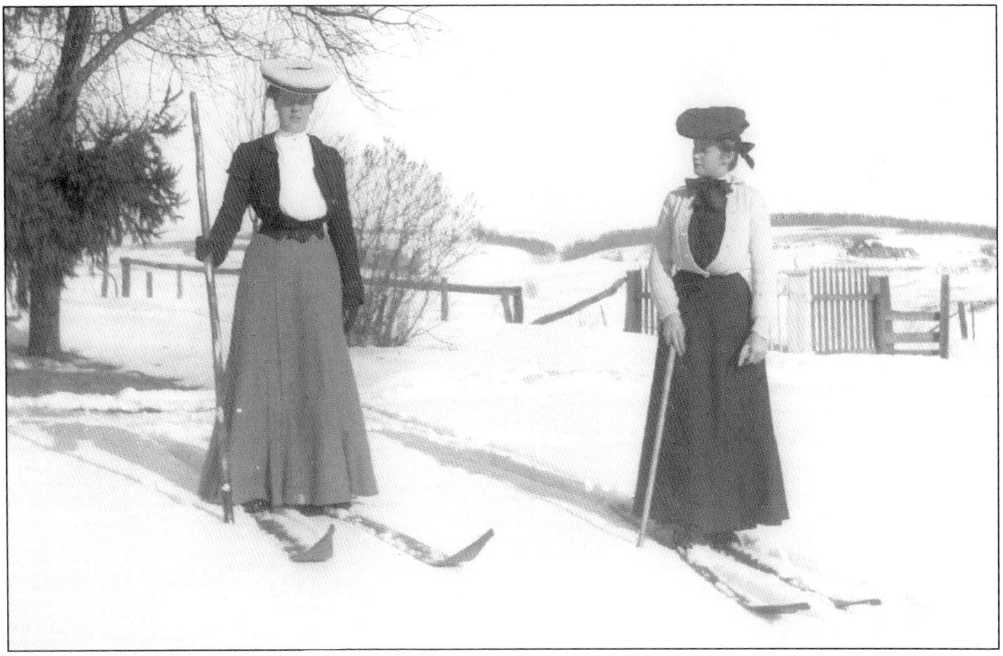

CROSS-COUNTRY SKIING. Othellia Melbraaten Rosendahl and Anna Sylling Bekkemoe take a leisurely ski through the countryside. This Norwegian winter tradition started as a sport in the early 1700s in Telemark, Norway. A copy of this print belongs to the Vesterheim Norwegian-American Museum in Decorah, Iowa, and was on exhibit for a short time at Union Station in Washington D.C.

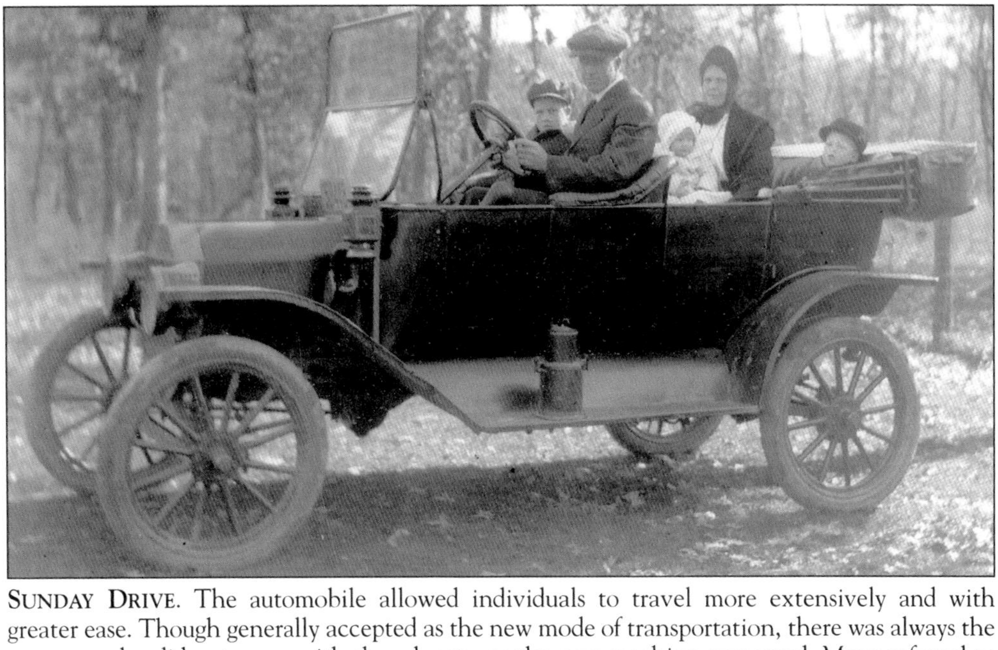

SUNDAY DRIVE. The automobile allowed individuals to travel more extensively and with greater ease. Though generally accepted as the new mode of transportation, there was always the naysayer who did not agree with the advantages the new machine purported. Many referred to these horseless carriages as "devil wagons." Shown here is the Rosendahl family preparing to set out for a Sunday drive. Paul and Peter are in front. Othelia, Gladys, and Harold are in back.

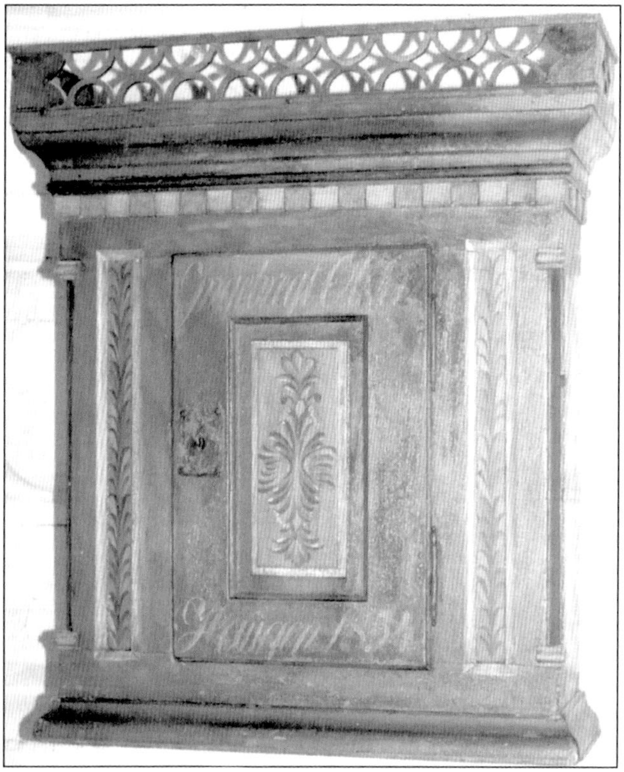

HANGING CUPBOARD. Tradition was extremely important to Norwegian immigrants. Both husband and wife had a separate *hengeskap* (hanging cupboard) where they stored meaningful things. For the husband it was his Bible and liquor; while the wife kept her current handwork, as well as important documention such as a land-deed. This *hengeskap* was brought to America from Valdres, Norway. The inscription reads: "Ingebret Oleson Haugen 1854." It was acquired from Spring Grove by the Vesterheim Norwegian-American Museum in Decorah, Iowa.

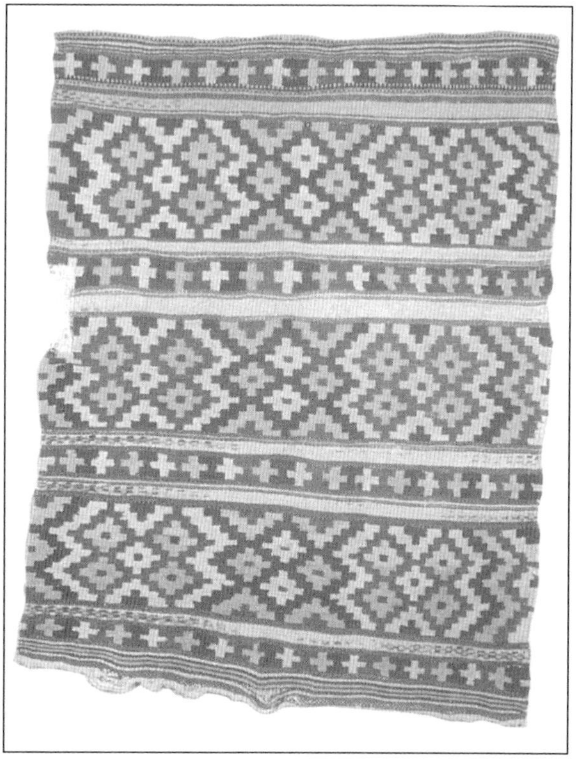

CHRISTENING BLANKET. Textiles such as this *Kristen teppe* (christening blanket) were an important part of rituals such as baptism, confirmation, marriage, and death. This particular *åklæ* (coverlet) was used as a baptismal blanket. According to Norwegian folklore, the time between birth and baptism could be very dangerous for a child. The *huldrefolk* (mountain people) could steal your child if it was not wrapped in an *åklæ* such as this. It was acquired from Spring Grove by the Vesterheim Norwegian-American Museum in Decorah, Iowa.

Six

Ola, Per, and Other Famous Norwegians

Many famous Norwegians had connections to Spring Grove. Bjørnstjerne Bjørnson, the national poet of Norway, lectured here in 1881. His tour through the Midwest was organized by Rasmus B. Anderson, a professor and promoter of Norwegian cultural life. Two of Anderson's siblings lived in Spring Grove. O.E. Rolvaag, the Norwegian-American novelist, based the fictional pioneers of his novel *Giants in the Earth* on his wife's family, who lived in Spring Grove for many years. Waldemar Ager, the great Norwegian-American idealist, lectured here at least twice. His topics included temperance and cultural assimilation. L.A. Stenholt, a Norwegian-American pulp writer, lived in Spring Grove long enough to gather information for a section in his *Minnesota Bibelen*. Elias Molee, a linguist and early resident of Spring Grove, wrote a translation of Henrik Ibsen's play *A Doll's House*. Herbjørn Gausta, a Norwegian-American painter, was commissioned by the Norwegian Evangelical Lutheran church of Spring Grove to paint their altarpiece. Hans Engan, an accomplished Norwegian-American wood-carver, lived and worked in Spring Grove.

Peter J. Rosendahl, who lived a quiet life on his Spring Grove farm, sketched the popular cartoon strip *Han Ola og Han Per*. His characters gave voice to many emigrants who felt the pressures of cultural assimilation, often to comic effect. Rosendahl once said, "Life becomes easier when mingled with a little foolishness and nonsense." This chapter also highlights three residents who have documented Spring Grove history: O.S. Johnson, Percival Narveson, and Sigmund Bergrud.

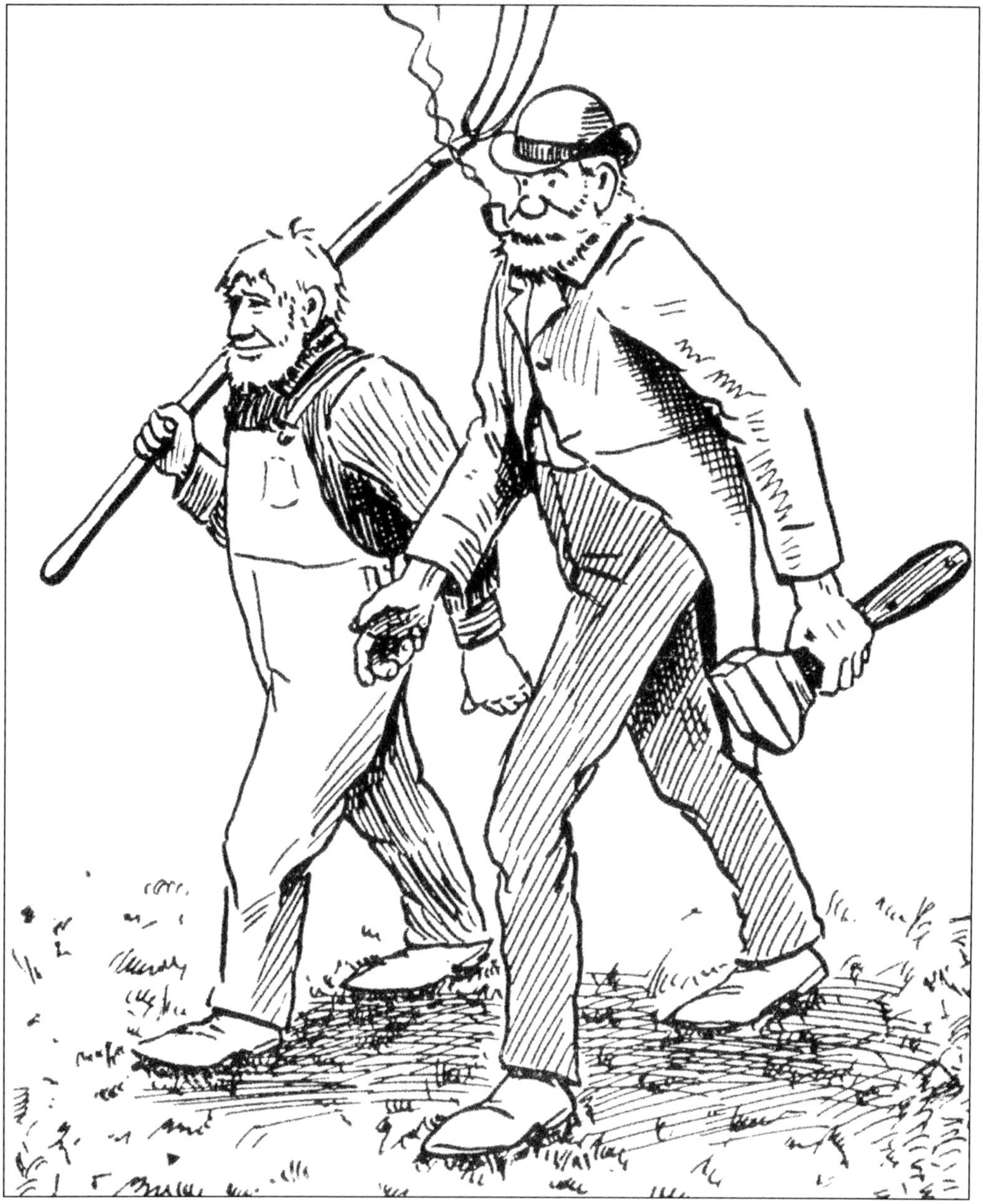

MR. OLA AND MR. PER. Early Spring Grove residents spoke a language that combined a variety of Norse dialects and English. This hybridizing of words and phrases is best exemplified in Peter J. Rosendahl's cartoon-strip *Han Ola og Han Per*, which features six characters. Per, who is tall and wears a tail-coat and derby hat, tends to overreact in nearly every situation. His neighbor Ola dresses and behaves like a typical farmer and is Per's foil, easy-going and even-tempered. He relies on Per for advice, especially around new farm implements. Polla is Per's wife. She is a city girl from Fargo, North Dakota. Dada is Per and Polla's little girl. Værmor is Polla's mother and represents the hardy pioneer women of the day. Finally there is Lars, who is Per's older brother, newly arrived from Norway. He is well-educated but has not adjusted to American ways. These characters, in essence, capture the mixed feelings many new emigrants were experiencing in their new world.

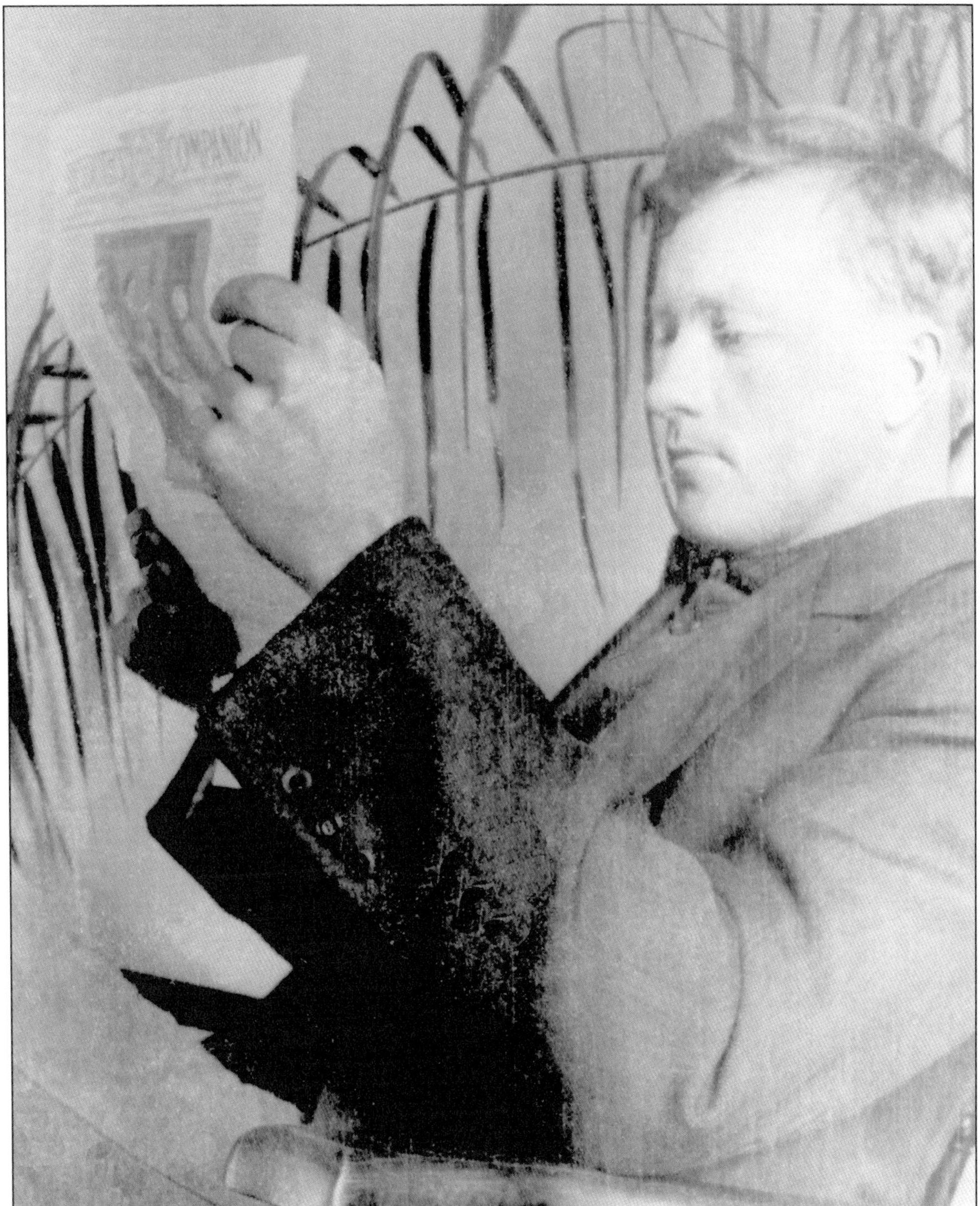

NORWEGIAN-AMERICAN CARTOONIST. Peter J. Rosendahl was born in 1878, and lived a quiet life on his farm with his wife, Othellia, and their four children, Gladys, Paul, Harold, and Donald. Rosendahl never completed high school, but read widely and took correspondence courses in engineering and art. When he was 41 he enrolled in the Federal School of Applied Cartooning, and in 1918 submitted his first cartoon strip, *Han Ola og Han Per*. Little did he know at the time that it would continue for 24 years and he would produce over 700 strips. It was printed in the *Decorah Posten*, and became the most popular Norwegian-American cartoon. It still continues to be reprinted in Norwegian-American publications such as the *Western Viking*. In this cartoon, Rosendahl left an important document for understanding the way life was lived and the way in which language was spoken in early Spring Grove.

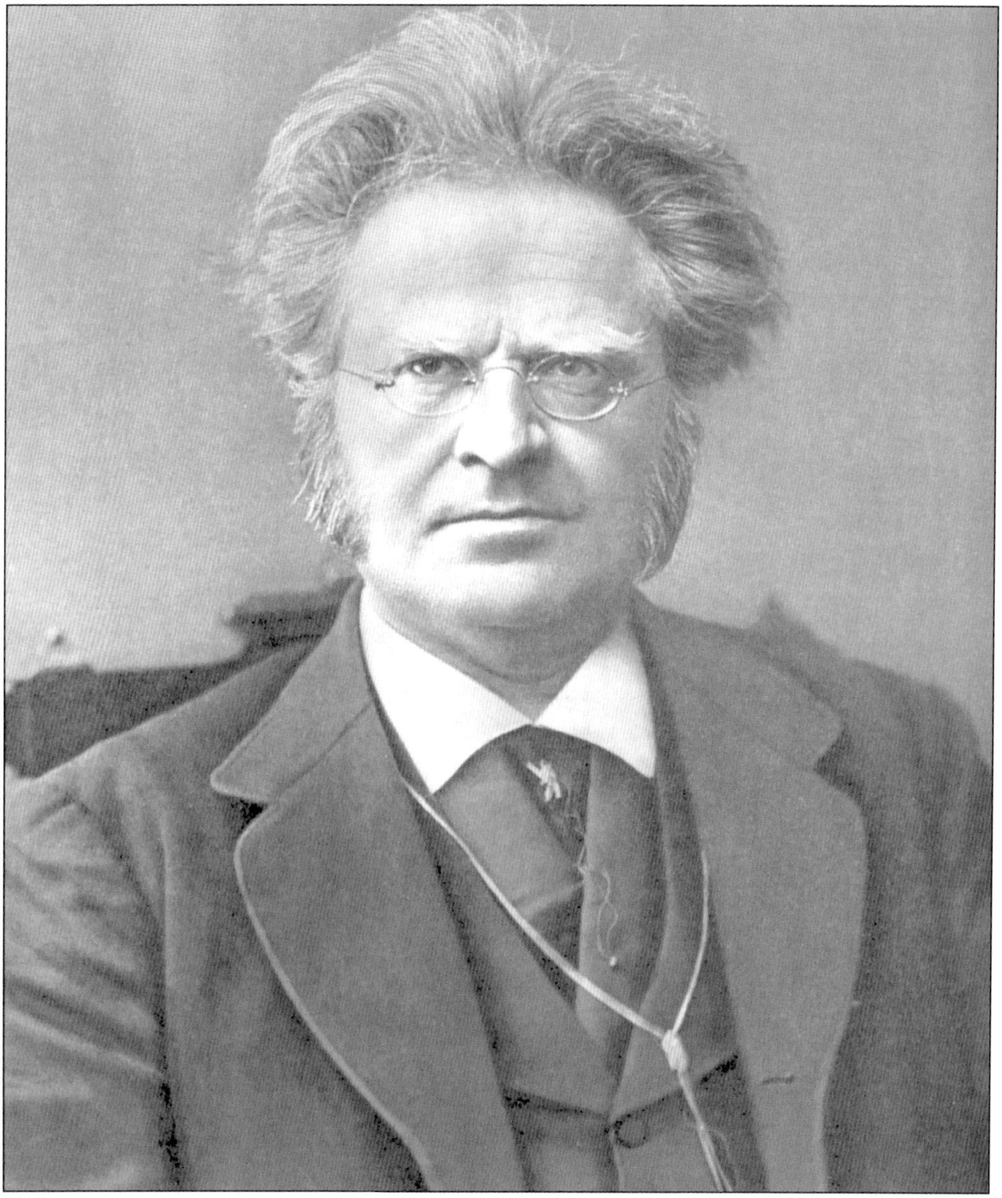

NORWAY'S POET. Bjørnstjerne Bjørnson gave an extensive lecture tour through America in 1880 and 1881. To his promoter, Rasmus B. Anderson, he wrote, "Dear Anderson, they didn't get the letter soon enough here, so the lecture has been poorly advertised. You should have telegraphed, you rascal! Then the morning after the lecture I have to get up before the devil gets his shoes on and speak in Spring Grove at two o'clock." And, upon arriving in town on March 11, 1881, Bjørnson adds, "By team from La Crosse to Spring Grove, where I spoke about the prophets gratis on the evening I arrived, and the day after about Norway for pay. Great enthusiasm. They drove me—three of their best men—to Decorah." The men in question were the sons of Mons Fladager, who let Bjørnson lodge in his home. Preferring the railroad for transport, he was unhappily taken by horse and sleigh. At some point during their journey, so the story goes, Bjørnson ordered the sleigh to stop. There was a strange creature skittering in front of them that he had never seen before. It was a skunk, or, in Spring Grove English, a *piss-kat*. (Courtesy of Paul Wiste.)

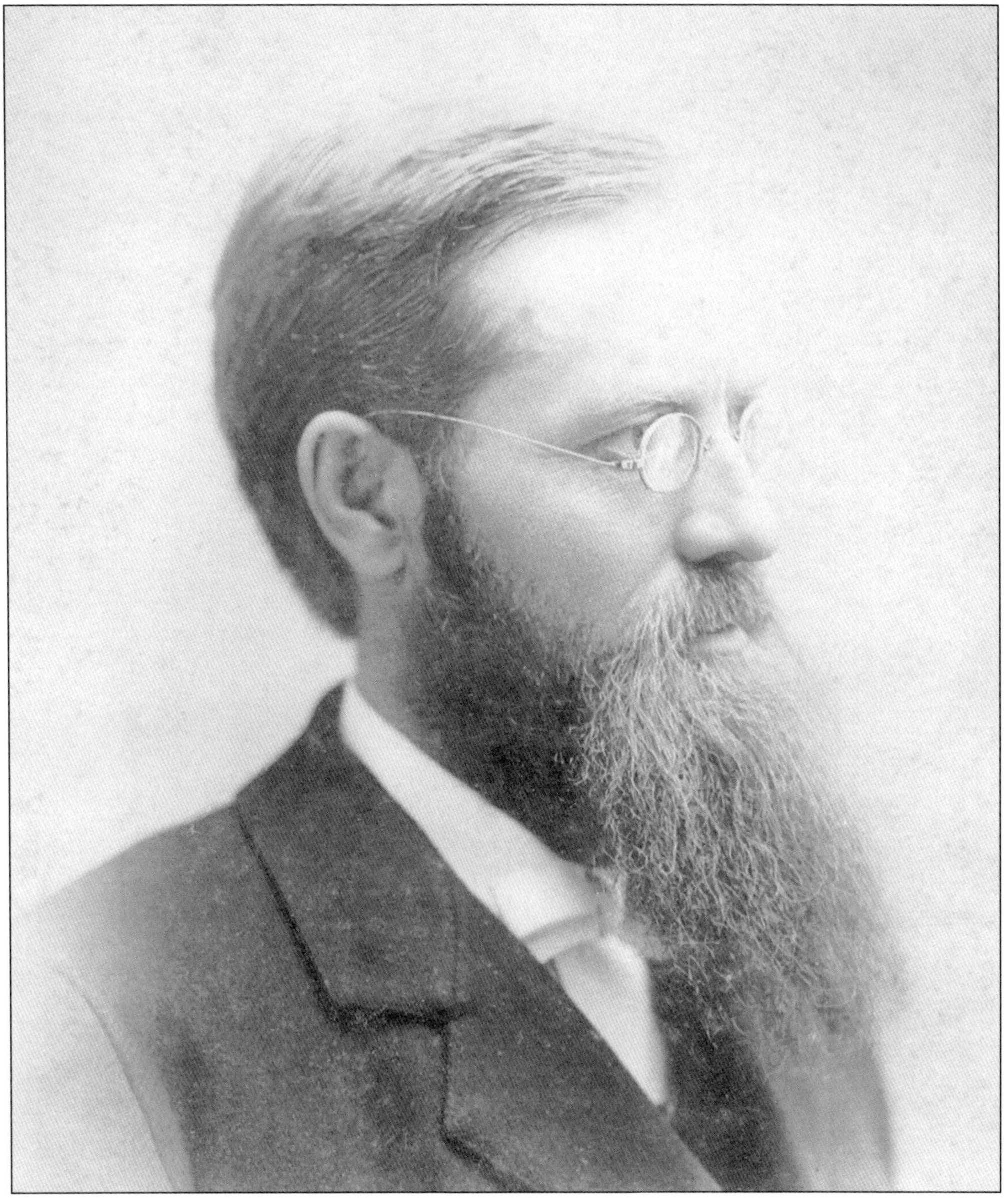

LITERARY REBEL. Rasmus B. Anderson attended and was later expelled from Luther College in Decorah, Iowa. Amongst other things, he did not agree with the college's policy of making students chop wood for professors. Anderson eventually founded the Scandinavian Studies department at the University of Wisconsin at Madison, as well as a literary group called *Ygdrasil* (in Norwegian mythology, it is the "World Tree"). He wrote over 60 books and was considered an authority on Scandinavian history. In 1874, he published a book called *America Not Discovered by Columbus*, in which he claimed that Leif Erickson was the true discoverer of America. Anderson also organized Bjørnstjerne Bjørnson's lecture tour in America. His connection to Spring Grove was through his sister Cecelia, who was married to Reverend Styrk Reque. Anderson and Reque got along well to begin with, but later clashed on a number of topics such as slavery. Anderson's brother, Bruun (later changed to Brown) Anderson, was a long-time businessman in Spring Grove.

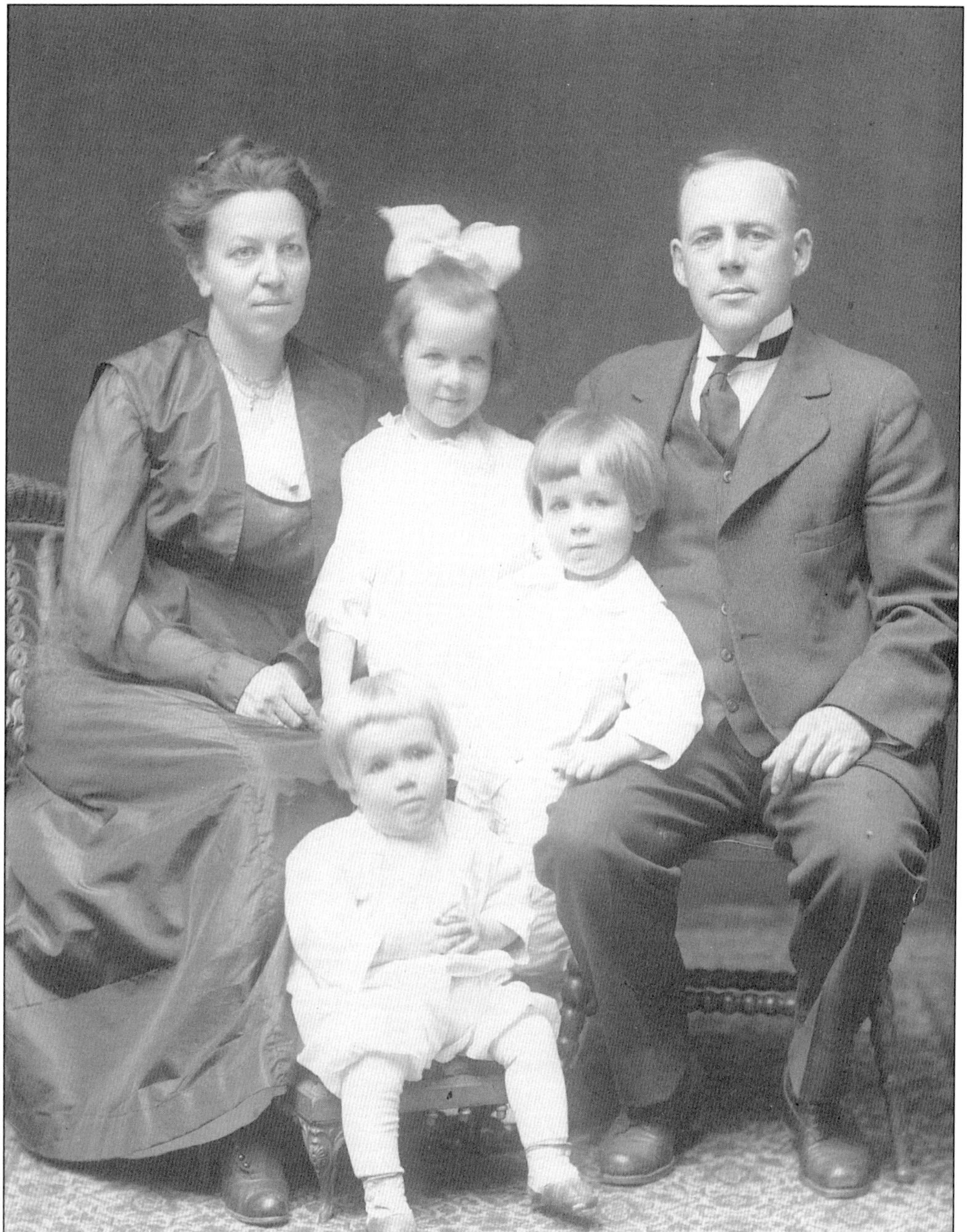

LITERARY GIANT. Best known for his novel of immigrant life, *Giants in the Earth*, O.E. Rolvaag came to America in 1896, and married Jennie Berdahl in 1908. Before moving to the Dakota prairies, the Berdahl family lived in Spring Grove from 1860 to 1866. Through Rolvaag's close relationship with his father-in-law and uncle, he drew directly from their life stories. He used the Berdahls as a basis for the family in *Giants*. As Rolvaag said, "All of the characters in my novels are of their own making; yet not entirely. I spun their psychology, then wove it into human forms after patterns that I knew well." The name of the fictional community Rolvaag created was Spring Creek. (Courtesy of the Norwegian-American Historical Association.)

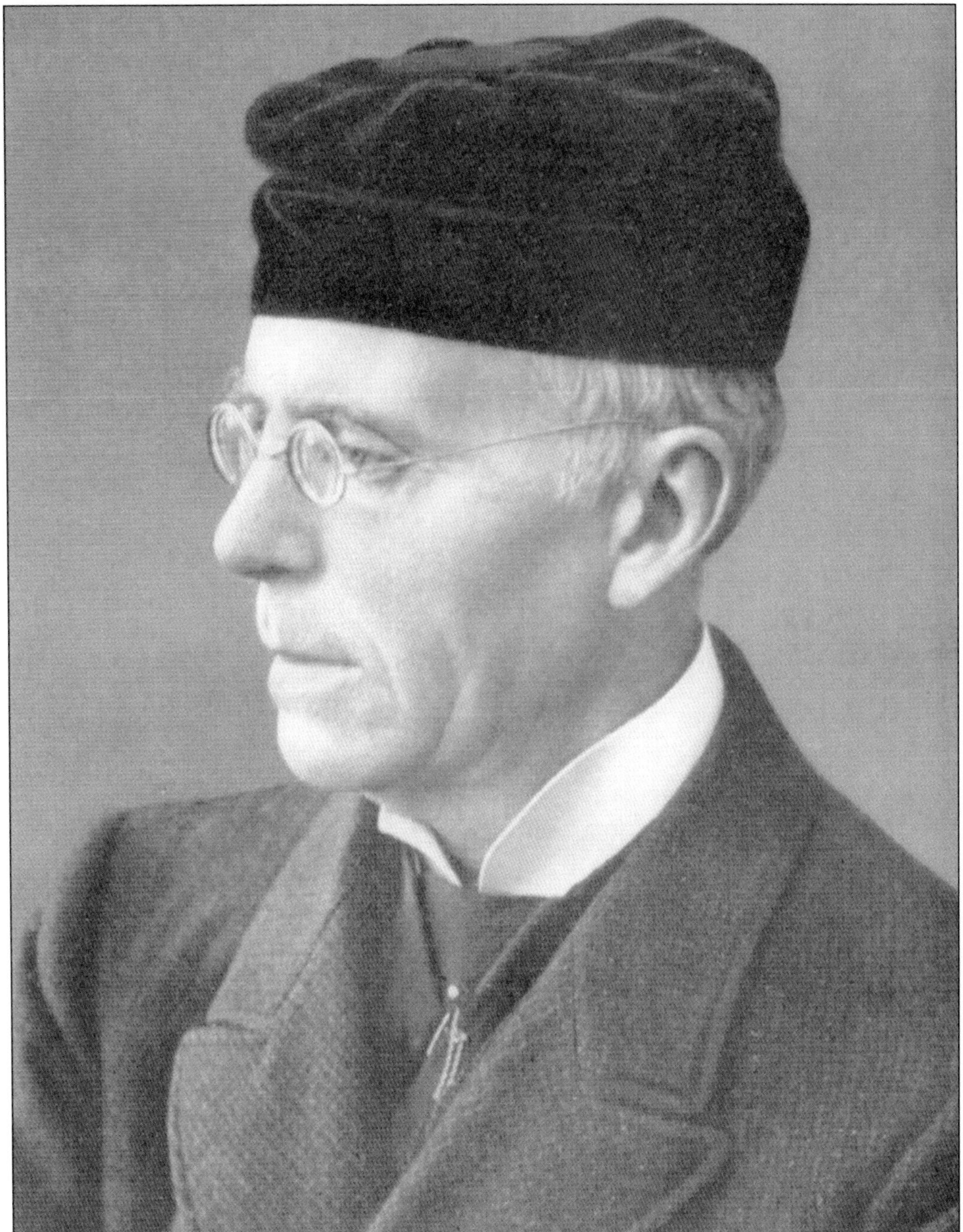

POPULAR NORWEGIAN AUTHOR. Jonas Lie was one of the most popular Norwegian authors in the mid-1800s. He was a contemporary and friend of Henrik Ibsen, Bjørnstjerne Bjørnson, and Alexander Kieland. Together they are commonly referred to as the *Store Fire* (Big Four) of classic Norwegian writers. Though he lived in Paris for much of his writing life, his fiction was set in Norway. All of his books were written in collaboration with his wife and first cousin, Thomasine Lie. Three of their most popular works are *Den Fremsynte* (The Visionary), *Familie pa Gilje* (The Family of Gilje), and *Trold* (Trolls). Lie's connection to Spring Grove is through Ingvald Muller, whose mother Rebekka Lie was a cousin to Jonas.

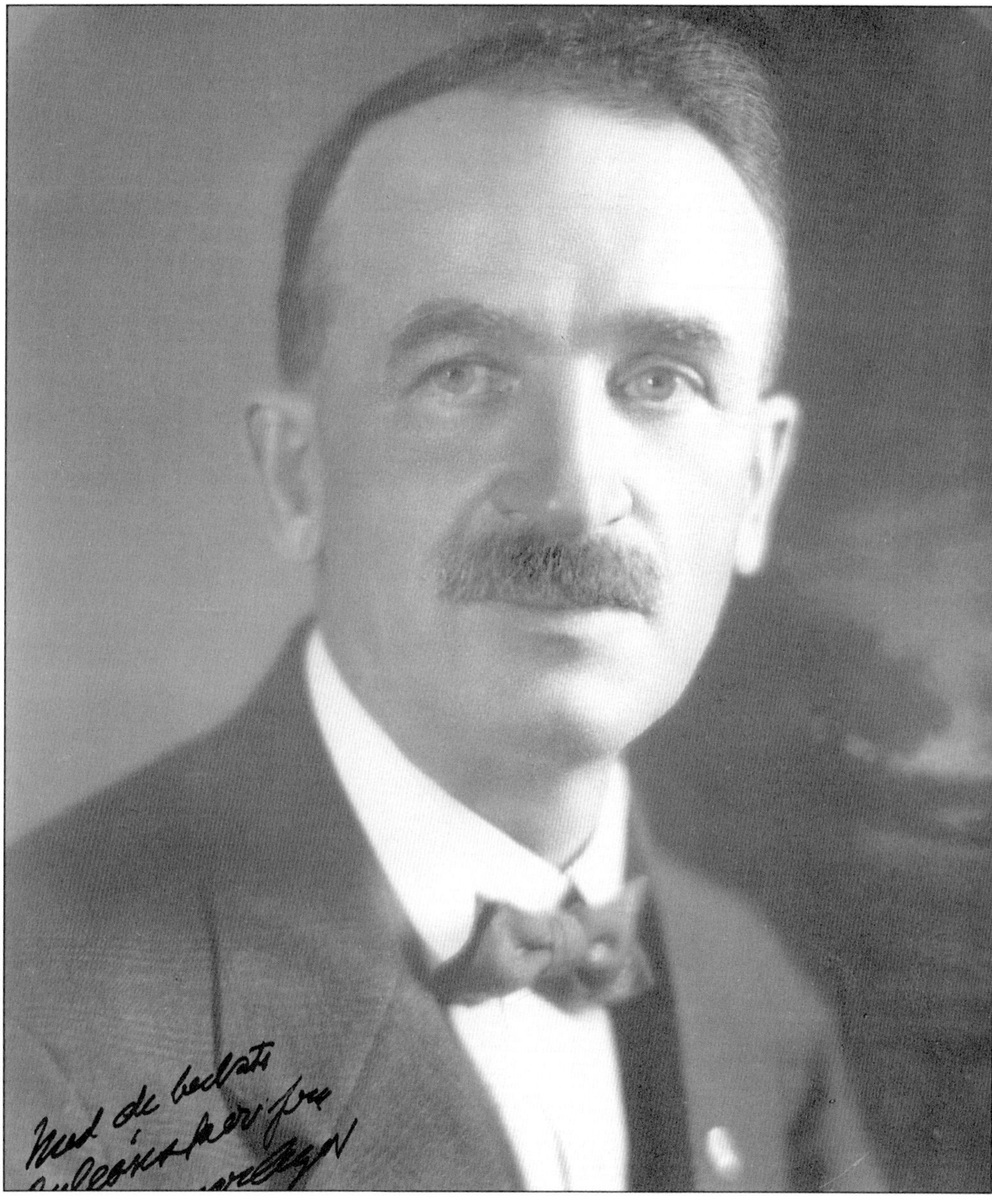

TEMPERANCE MAN. From a 1915 issue of the *Spring Grove Herald*:

> *The lecture and entertainment given by Waldemar Ager at the Woodmen Hall was well attended and everyone present reported a very enjoyable evening. He told of his trip made to Norway and compared that country with this. His talk was made in a humorous vein. Eilert Eilertson was also present and rendered several selections on the violin. Norsk lunch was served to all present and several were called upon to give impromptu speeches.*

Ager was an idealist and tireless lecturer known for his adherence to the temperance movement. He wrote many short stories and novels, two of which are *Paa veien til smeltepotten* (On the Way to the Melting Pot) and *Gamlelandets sønner* (Sons of the Old Country). He was also the editor of *Reform*, one of the most controversial Norwegian-language newspapers in America. (Courtesy of the Nordmanns-Forbundet archives.)

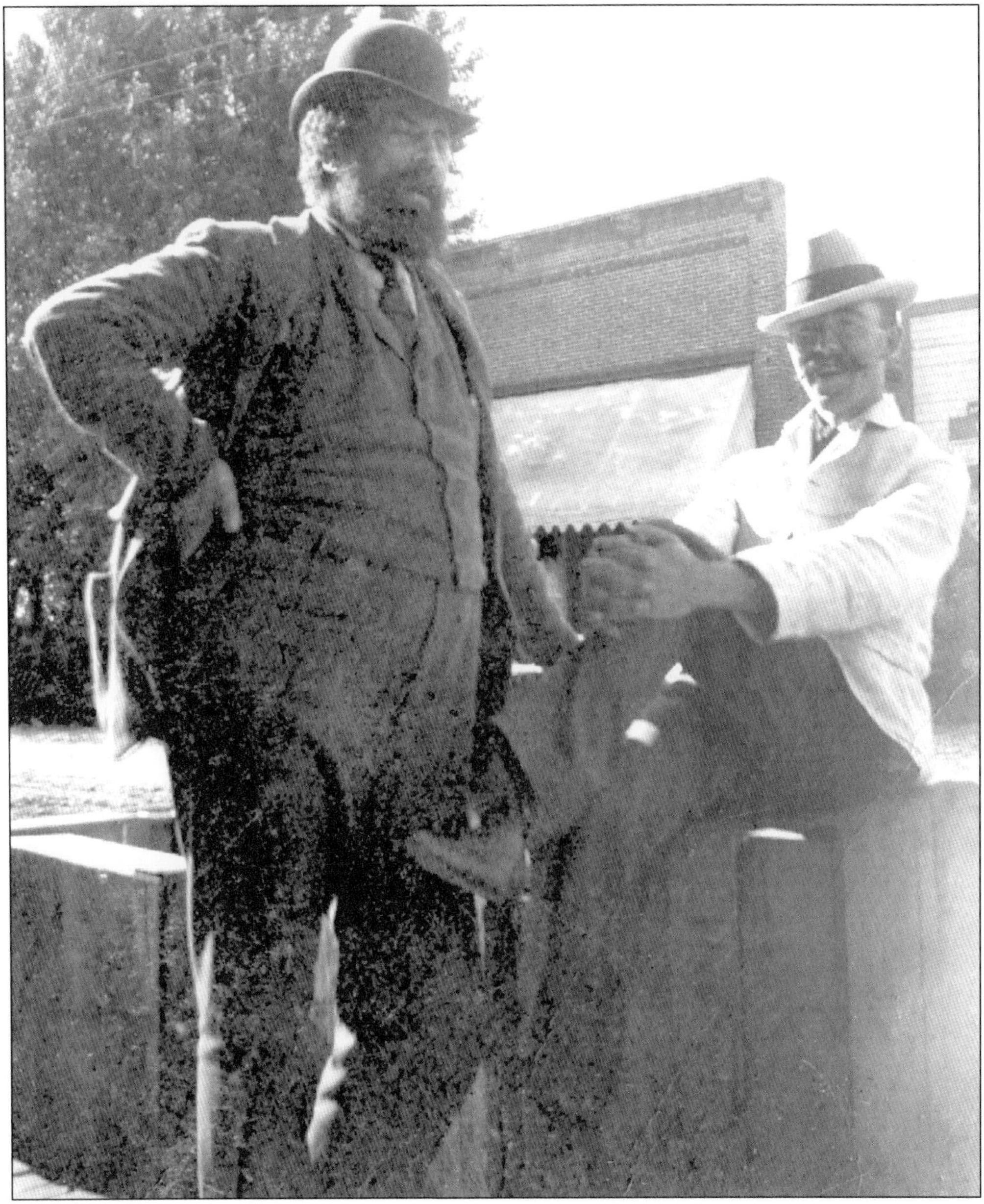

PULP WRITER. In this photograph, L.A. Stenholt (left) and Henry Narveson (right) talk on Main Street. Stenholt was the only Norwegian-American author to make a living exclusively from his writing. From 1887 to his death in 1911, he wrote 43 books on a variety of topics. In 1901, the *Minnesota Bibelen* (The Minnesota Bible) was published. It imitated the archaic, lofty language of the Norwegian Bible, and reported humorous stories involving priests and vagrants from small Minnesota towns. Stenholt gave the reading public exactly what they wanted, churning out cheap paperbacks that were sold at newsstands and on trains. The *Bibelen* featured a section on Spring Grove in which Stenholt attacks the church for not allowing a vagrant named Ole Krogstad to be buried in the cemetery. When a resident named Teman Gilbertson, whose property was right next to the cemetery, threatened to bury Krogstad on the edge of his land, the clergy changed its mind. This is the fodder Stenholt sought, and he blasted the clergy accordingly.

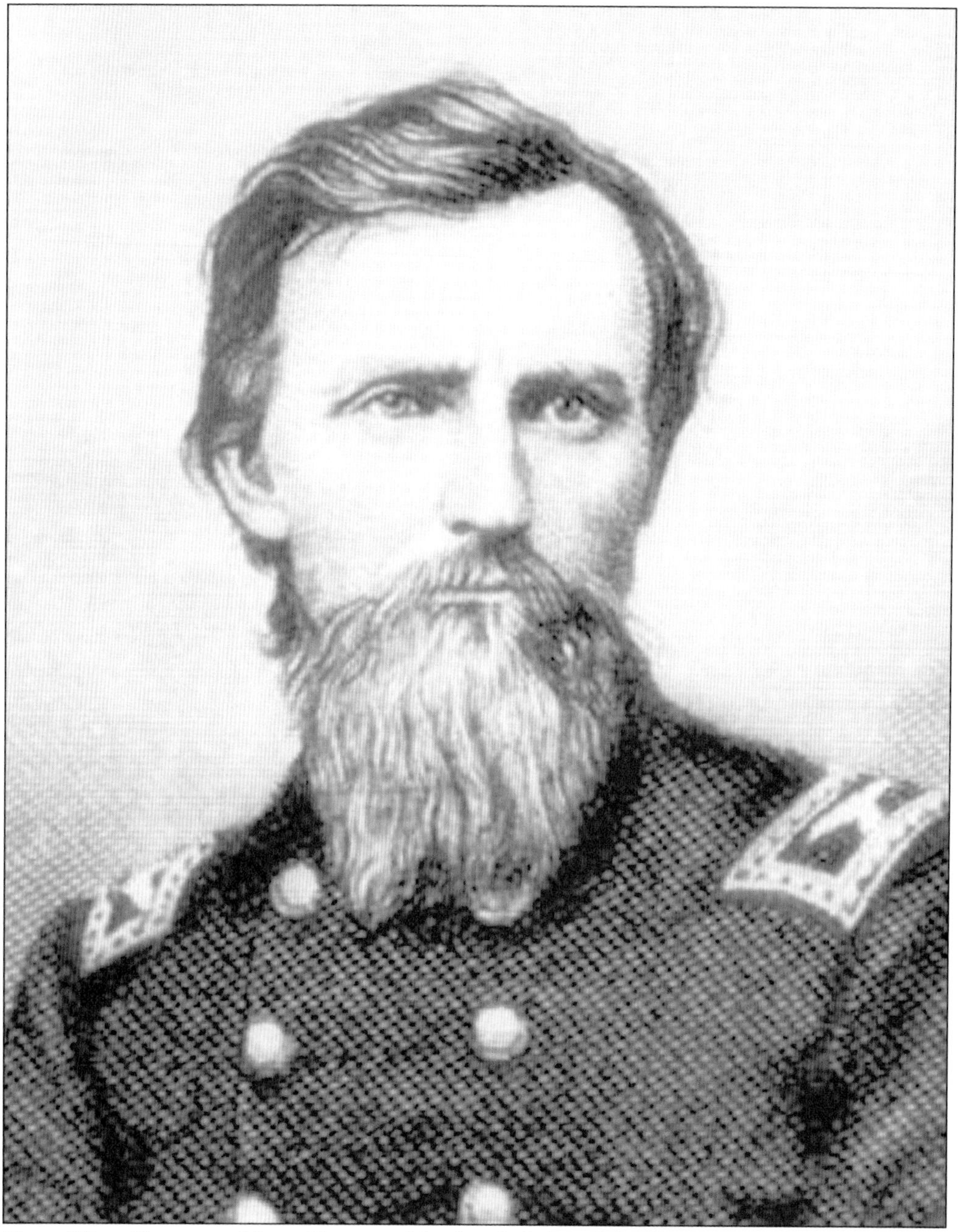

CIVIL WAR COLONEL. Hans Christian Heg headed the 15th Wisconsin Volunteer Infantry, known as the Scandinavian Regiment, and died in the Battle of Chickamauga. One man who enlisted into Company H, known as "Heg's Rifles," was the 21-year-old Christian Storlie of Spring Grove. Storlie mustered in as a private at Camp Randall, Wisconsin. After a month of training, he participated in campaigns through Tennessee, Mississippi, and Alabama. He was honorably discharged after suffering illness. After the war he worked on a farm in nearby Fillmore County, receiving a veteran's pension. Colonel Heg also had ties to Spring Grove through a sister-in-law who lived here. Her name was Aslaug Einong. (Courtesy of the Norwegian-American Historical Association.)

Wood Carver. Hans Engan (1833–1917) was 36 years old when this tintype was taken. He was one of the earliest well-known carvers in southern Minnesota. The carved American draft horse, below, Engan's specialty features real horse-mane, and was on tour from 1995 to 1997 at New York's Museum of American Folk Art, at Oslo's Norwegian Folk Museum, and finally in St. Paul, Minnesota. (Courtesy of Roger and Shirley Johnson.)

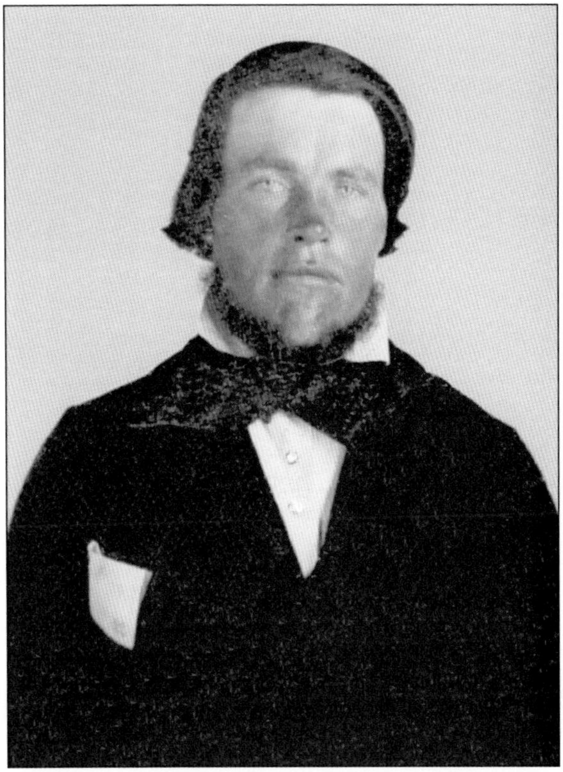

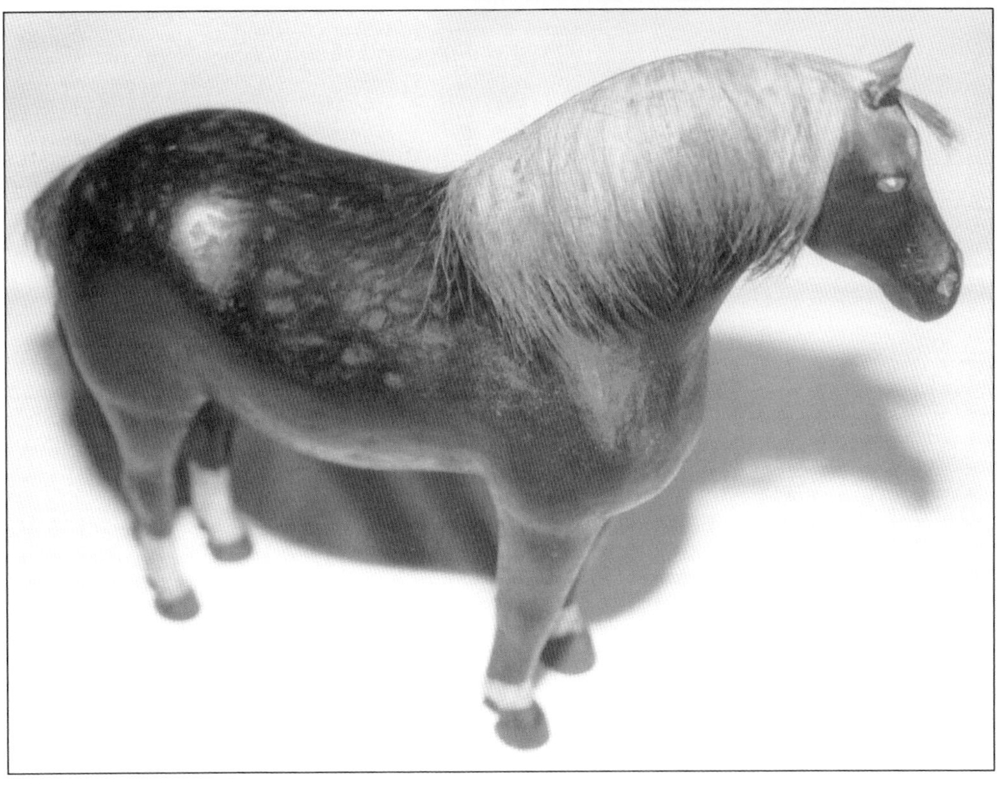

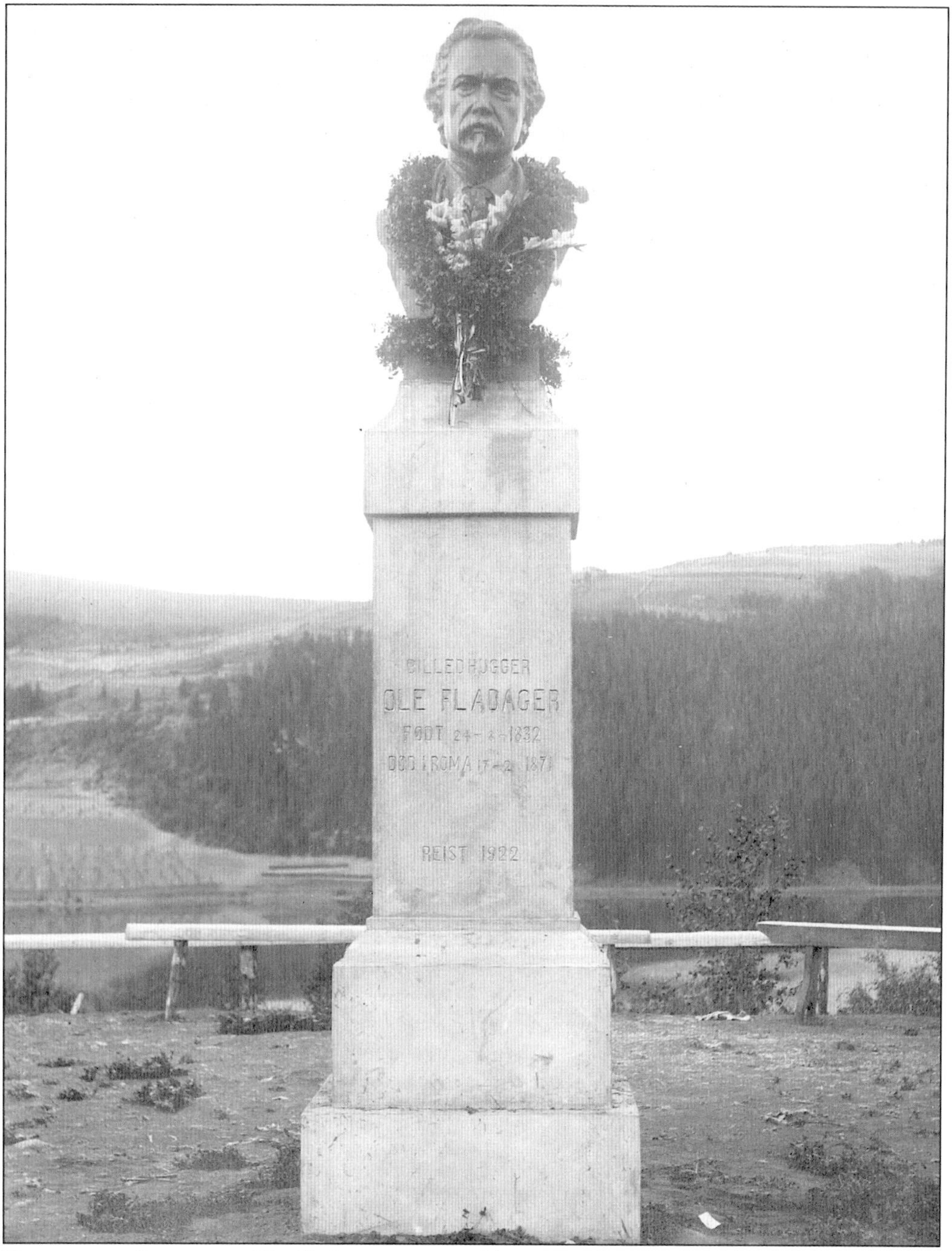

NORWEGIAN SCULPTOR. Ole Fladager was a world-renowned sculptor. He was also the brother of Spring Grove's successful merchant, Mons Fladager. He was born in 1832, and when he was 17 ventured off to become an artist. He was apprenticed at the woodcarving shop of Edmund de Conich in Kristiania. This monument is not his tombstone, but a meeting place where an annual celebration honors his memory. The location is on Ivarshaug Hill, not far from the Fladager farm in the Valdres Valley where he grew up. He is actually buried in Rome, where he lived most of his life. Many of his sculptures are preserved in the Norwegian National Art Gallery in Oslo, Norway.

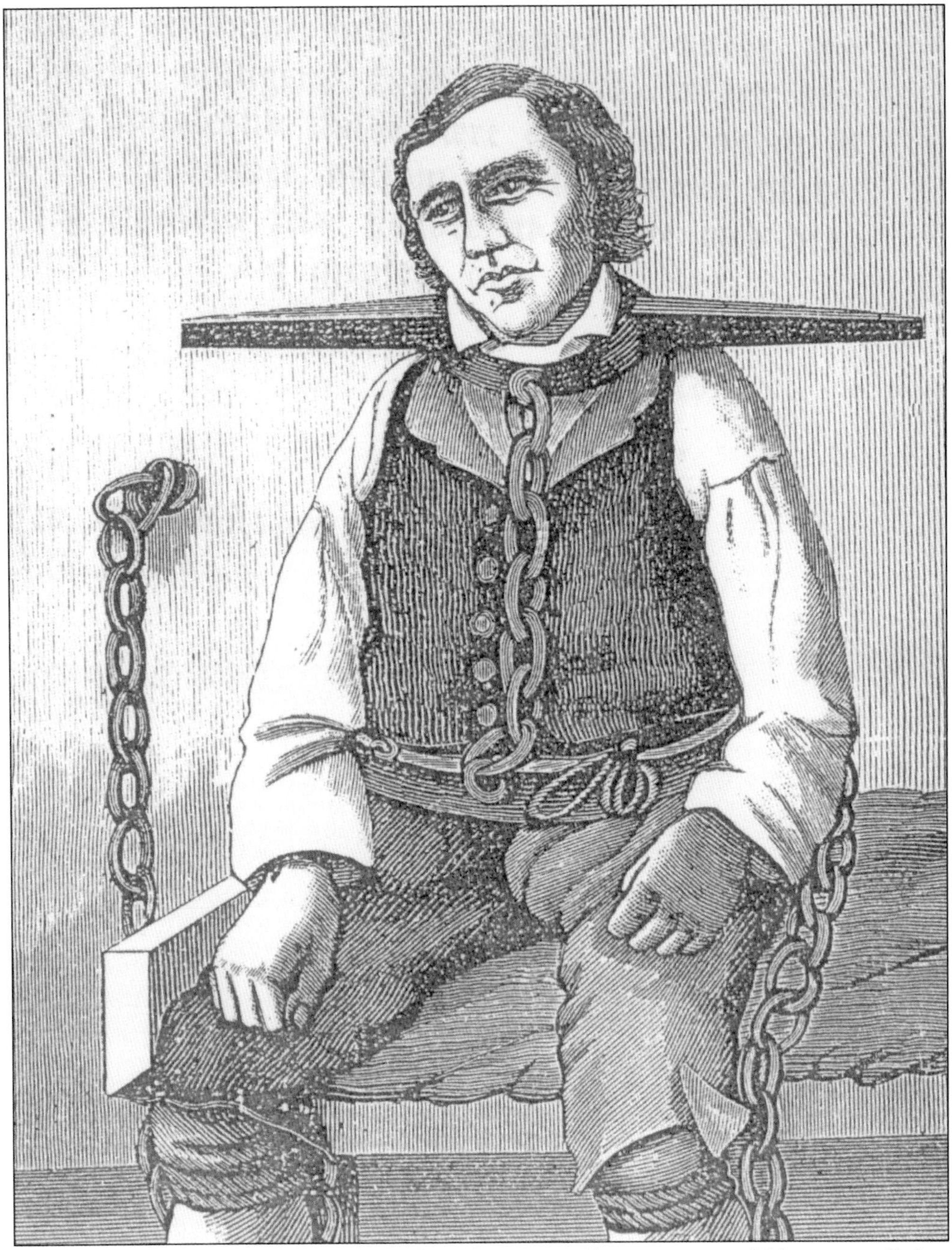

NORWEGIAN FOLK HERO. Gjest Baardsen (1791–1849) was a sort of Norwegian Robin Hood, a master-thief who stole from the rich and gave to the poor. Gjermund Lommen, the brother of Peter and John Lommen of Spring Grove, came to America in 1848, and settled in nearby Wilmington. Lommen lived in Sogndal, Norway, for a number of years before coming to America, and had on several occasions seen and talked with Gjest Baardsen. According to family history, Lommen met up one day with Baardsen's wife, who asked if he would like to visit Gjest at their home. Lommen said that he would be unable to attend, for he was about to board a ship bound for America.

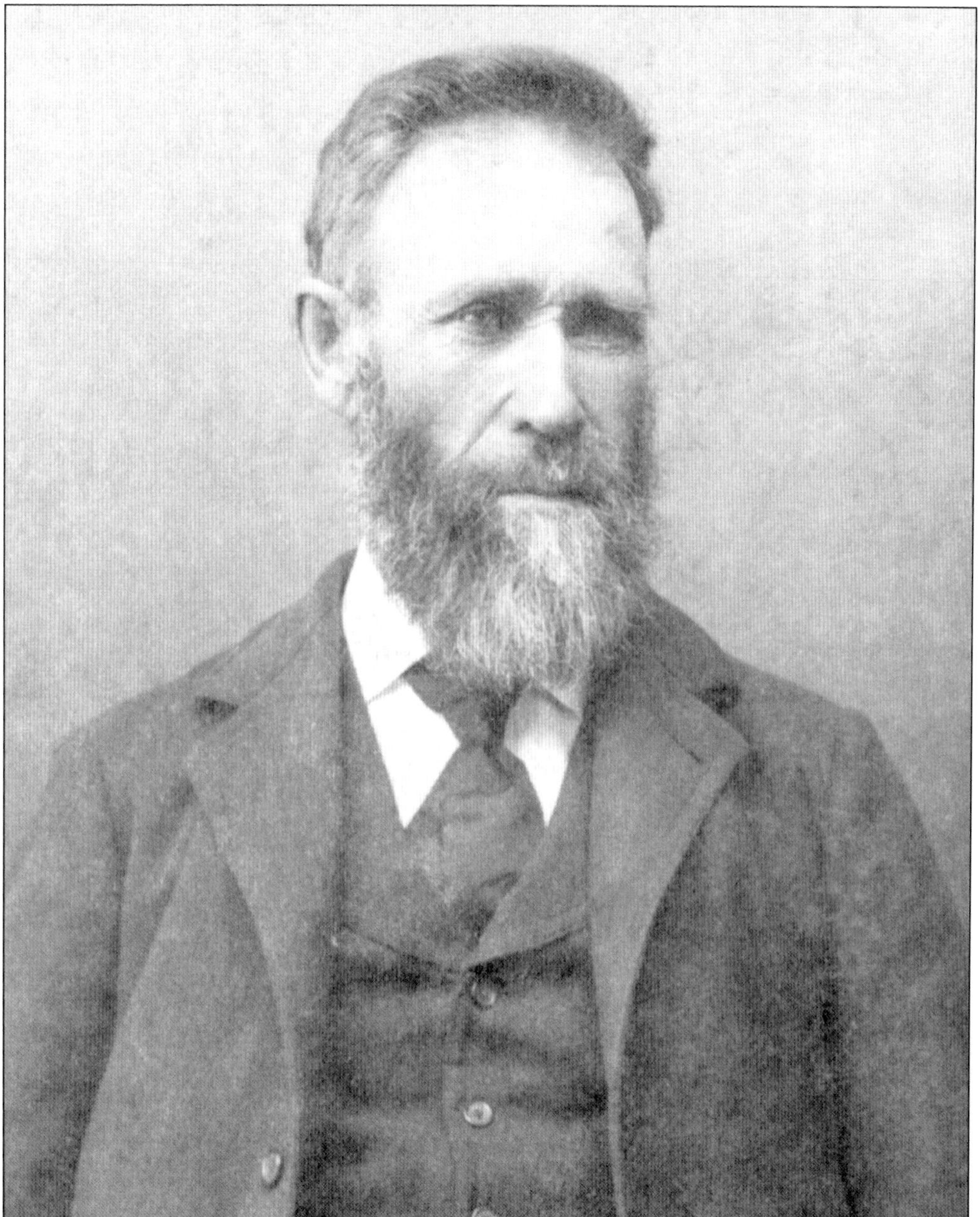

SPRING GROVE HISTORIAN. In 1870, O.S. Johnson emigrated from Ringerike, Norway, with his wife, Marie Ringerud. During his first two years in America, he farmed in the summer and logged in the winter. He and his wife had four children: Johan, Mathilde, Olava, and Bolethe. Though he was primarily a farmer, he also wrote a number of books. His *Nybyggerhistorie fra Spring Grove og omegn* (The Pioneer History of Spring Grove and Vicinity) was published in Minneapolis in 1920. It profiled many citizens living at the time, as well as some of the earliest settlers. He was encouraged to write articles about Spring Grove for the Norwegian journal *Samband*, and eventually expanded these sketches into the above-mentioned history. Driving around on his horse and buggy, Johnson would often stop in unannounced and talk to residents about their lives.

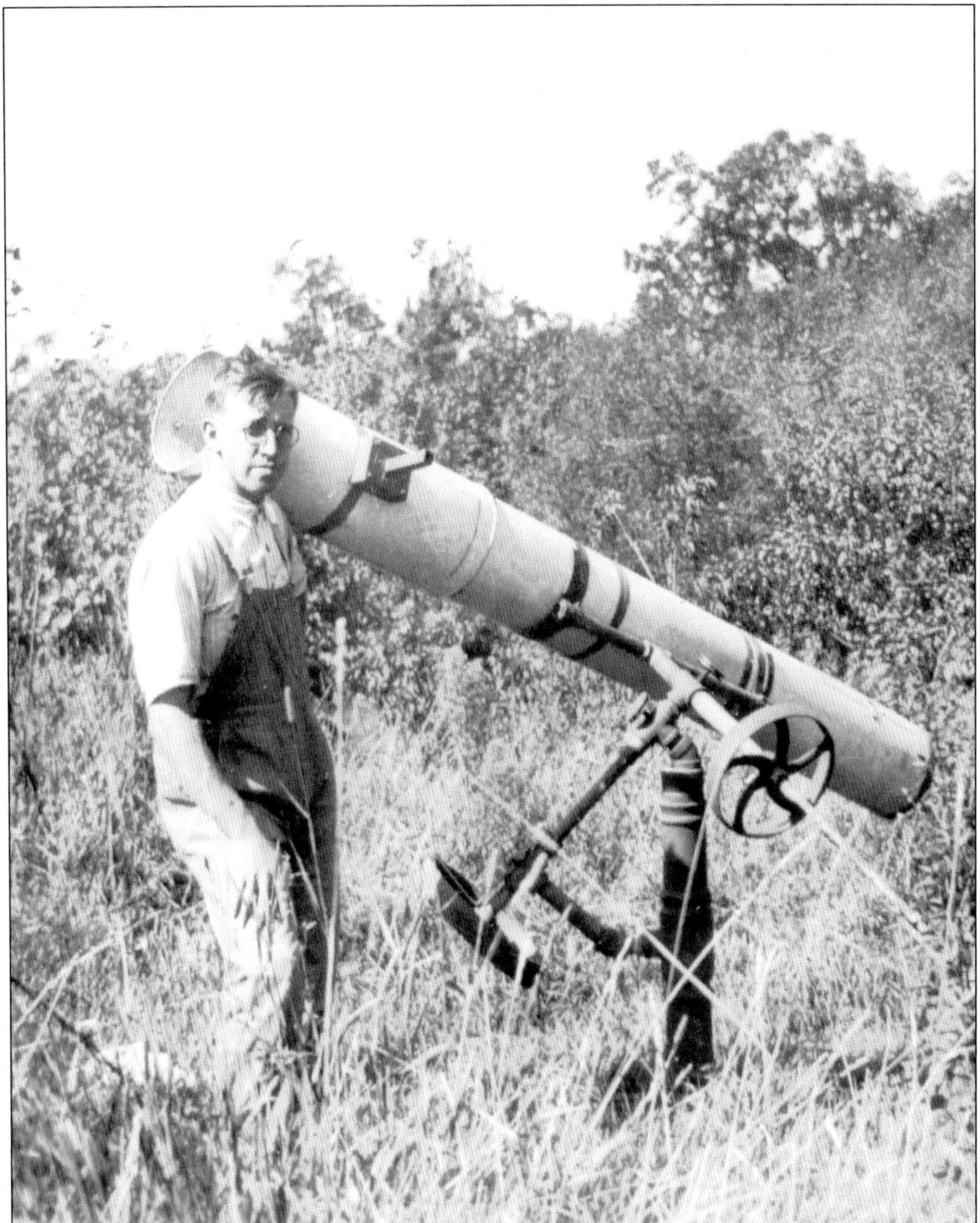

TOWN HISTORIAN. Percival Narveson was born in Spring Grove in 1899, the son of Narve and Hannah Narveson. His grandfather was Haaken Narveson, one of the first Norwegians to settle in the area. He attended both Luther College in Decorah, Iowa, and the Dunwoody Institute in Minneapolis, Minnesota, where he taught masonry from 1935 to 1940. A stonemason by trade, he was also a self-educated historian who wrote many articles about Spring Grove and Houston County. These historical sketches were published both in the *Winona Daily News* and the *Spring Grove Herald*. In 1952, he married Inga Hendrickson from Spring Grove. Much of his retirement was spent at his books and manual typewriter. Narveson is shown here standing next to his "reflector," which he made from a stove-pipe and threshing-wheel.

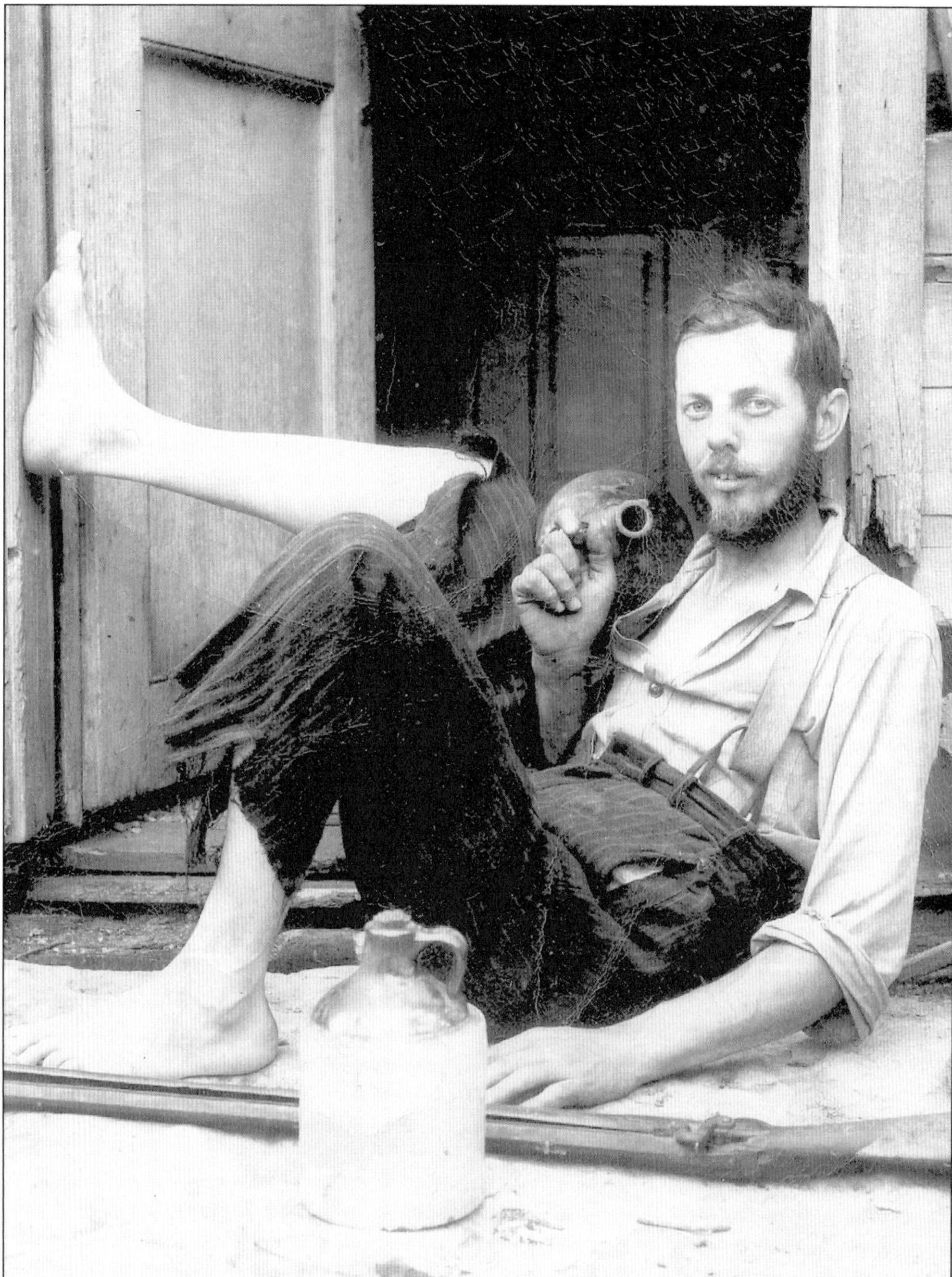

ORAL HISTORIAN. Farmer, oral historian, and Spring Grove resident Sigmund Bergrud (1911–1998) is show here dressed as a "hillbilly" for the Centennial Celebration in 1952. Sigmund, a descendant of Stengrim Bergrud, was known for his interest in theater and in flight. He could quote passages from Shakespeare, and had a private pilot license. His favorite poem was Emerson's *The Rhodora.* This photo was taken on the threshold of his father Peter's original homestead. In 1983, the Bergrud farm was given special recognition as a Minnesota Century Farm, being that it had remained in the family for over 100 years.

References

Andreassen, Odd Gunnar. *Lars Andreas Stenholt: Norwegian-American Author*. Oslo, Norway: University of Oslo. 1977.

Blegen, Theodore. *Norwegian Migration to America: 1825-1860*. Northfield, Minnesota: Norwegian-American Historical Association. 1931.

Blegen, Theodore. *Norwegian Migration to America: The American Transition*. Northfield, Minnesota: Norwegian-American Historical Association. 1940.

Curtiss-Wedge, Franklyn. *History of Houston County*. Winona, Minnesota: H.C. Cooper, Jr. Company. 1919.

Johnson, O.S. *Nybyggerhistorie fra Spring Grove og omegn*. Minneapolis, Minnesota: Forfatterens forlag. 1920.

Gabler, William. *Death of the Dream: Farmhouses of the Heartland*. Afton, Minnesota: Afton Historical Society Press. 1997.

Guthrie, Nora. "Notes on the History of Medicine in Houston County Prior to 1900." Rochester, Minnesota: Mayo Clinic Press. 1946.

Haugen, Einar and Eva. *Land of the Free: Bjornstjerne Bjornson's American Letters, 1880-81*. Northfield, Minnesota: Norwegian-American Historical Association. 1978.

Lovoll, Odd. *The Promise of America*. Minneapolis, Minnesota: University of Minnesota Press. 1999.

Nelson, David. *The Diary of Elisabeth Koren*. Northfield, Minnesota: Norwegian-American Historical Association. 1955

O'Neill, Edward & Bryant, Charles. *History of Houston County*. Minneapolis, Minnesota: Minnesota Historical Company. 1882.

Onsgard, Blaine & Roppe, Sydney. *History of Spring Grove*. Spring Grove, Minnesota: Onsgard Publishing Company. 1952.

Palen, Jane Briggs. *Soil, Timber, and a Spring: The Story of Spring Grove, Minnesota*. Spring Grove Area: Past, Present and Future Publications. 1991.

Qualey, Carlton. "A Typical Norwegian Settlement: Spring Grove, Minnesota." Northfield, Minnesota: Norwegian-American Historical Association.

Qualey, Carlton and Gjerde, John. *They Chose Minnesota: "The Norwegians."* St. Paul, Minnesota: Minnesota Historical Society Press. 1981.

Semmingsen, Ingrid. *Norway to America* (translated by Einar Haugen). Minneapolis, Minnesota: University of Minnesota Press. 1978.

Wiste, Paul and Joan. "The Prehistory of Houston County." Caledonia, Minnesota: Caledonia Pride, an Historic Journal.